# Books That Teach Kids to Write

Marianne Saccardi

 LIBRARIES UNLIMITED

AN IMPRINT OF ABC-CLIO, LLC
Santa Barbara, California • Denver, Colorado • Oxford, England

**Library of Congress Cataloging-in-Publication Data**

Saccardi, Marianne.
   Books that teach kids to write / Marianne C. Saccardi.
      p. cm.
   Includes bibliographical references and index.
      ISBN 978–1–59884–451–1 (pbk. : acid-free paper) — ISBN 978–1–59884–452–8 (ebook)
1. English language—Composition and exercises—Study and teaching (Elementary)—United States.
2. English language—Composition and exercises—Study and teaching (Secondary)—United States.
3. Creative writing (Elementary education)—United States. 4. Creative writing (Secondary education)—United States. 5. Literature—Study and teaching (Elementary)—United States. 6. Literature—Study and teaching (Secondary)—United States. 7. Children—Books and reading—United States. 8. Children's literature—Bibliography.  I. Title.
LB1576.S2227   2011
028.5—dc22              2011001866

ISBN: 978–1–59884–451–1
EISBN: 978–1–59884–452–8

15  14  13  12  11      1  2  3  4  5

This book is also available on the World Wide Web as an eBook.
Visit www.abc-clio.com for details.

Libraries Unlimited
An Imprint of ABC-CLIO, LLC

ABC-CLIO, LLC
130 Cremona Drive, P.O. Box 1911
Santa Barbara, California 93116-1911

This book is printed on acid-free paper ∞

Manufactured in the United States of America

To my husband, Thomas, my first reader and computer mentor, who encouraged me to write this book and supported me through its completion. I love you!

# Contents

# Acknowledgments

Many thanks to:

My sons, Christopher and Daniel, who helped their technology-challenged mother navigate the computer glitches with patience and grace.

My editor, Sharon Coatney, for her insight and her gracious willingness to keep track of all the cover images.

The many publishers who allow me the privilege of reviewing their books and the dedicated children's book authors and illustrators who continue to delight and inform us through their wonderful work.

And always, my husband, Thomas, whose constant love and support brightens my days.

# Introduction

*Writing today is not a frill for the few, but an essential skill for the many.*

— The National Commission on Writing in America's Schools and Colleges

"Writing is more integral to our lives in the 21st century than ever before," Dr. Barbara Cambridge stated in a keynote address at Wabash College on March 9, 2009. Educators and employers agree that good writing is a necessary tool for success in the global environment in which our students will live and work when they leave school. We want our students to write well, and to be able to express themselves in several different genres from reports, to essays, to poetry. We want them to score well on the many standardized writing tests they will take as they progress through the grades. Most importantly, we want them to achieve all the writing skills they will need to live enriched and successful lives as literate, productive citizens. This means that they will have to achieve greater writing competency than previous generations as manufacturing jobs shrink and positions requiring higher literacy levels replace them. "Although only a few hundred thousand adults earn their living as full-time writers," states the National Commission on Writing in America's Schools and Colleges (2003, 10), "many Americans would not be able to hold their positions if they were not excellent writers."

But we also realize that it will take time—more time than a year or a term under our instruction—for students to become the accomplished writers we want them to be. Good writing is multifaceted and requires mastery of a variety of tasks. A statement on the National Writing Project website puts it well: "Writing is essential to success in school and the workplace. Yet writing is a skill that cannot be learned on the spot; it is complex and challenging" (National Writing Project 2008). Hence many districts require a student writing portfolio in which sample pieces of writing are collected and added to each year so that evaluation can inform instruction throughout the student's school career. Most school districts require daily writing as part of a language arts block. Some use a specific writing program. Others engage students in a writing workshop that includes individual and group instruction along with actual writing practice and feedback. Students complete writing assignments ranging from journal entries to essays, reports, and fiction pieces. These practices are good, and they make it clear that writing is so complicated a skill that there is no single way to teach that will help all students become competent writers. And so we are not going to offer *the* single most effective way to teach writing. Rather, our purpose here is to provide busy teachers and others working with children with a resource they can use regardless of how they teach writing: a plethora of excellent children's books and a discussion of some ways in which books in a variety of genres can mentor and stimulate writing. Why suggest books? In *The Power of Reading* (2003), Stephen D. Krashen argues that research strongly points to reading as the primary way to achieve good writing style:

> All the ways in which formal written language differs from informal conversational language are too complex to be learned one rule at a time. Even though readers can recognize good writing, researchers have not succeeded in completely describing just what it is that makes a "good" writing style good. It is, therefore, sensible to suppose that writing style is not consciously learned but is largely absorbed, or subconsciously acquired, from reading. (133)

Frank Smith, too, emphasizes the importance of reading to inform writing: "the subtle style and structure of written discourse, the appropriate organization of sentences and paragraphs, and the appropriate selection of words and tones of voice—are learned through reading" (*Reading without Nonsense*, 2006, 118).

This does not mean that we should not teach writing and leave it to our students to absorb from books how to write well. But it does mean that excellent writers can assist us in our task by providing concrete examples of the writing skills we are trying to teach. Patricia MacLachlan's *Word After Word After Word* (2010) tells the story of a professional writer who remains in residence in a school over six weeks and helps fourth graders understand why writers write and the importance of words, character, and setting. She enables them to see that each of them has a story waiting to be told and empowers them to tell it. Reading this slim book aloud might be a good way to launch younger students on their writing journey. In addition, a good overview of the writing process, including different genres and kinds of writing is available in Esther Hershenhorn's *S Is for Story: A Writer's Alphabet* (2009). Each alphabet letter describes some aspect of books and/or writing. Many have quotes from famous children's writers and writer's tips as well.

We can weave excellent children's books into our curricula as writing models for children, no matter what methods we use or what our school requirements might be. Because the books discussed here range from books for the very youngest children to those for adolescents, teachers at all grade levels can find literature suitable for the abilities and interests of their students and the skills they wish to teach. Having a breadth of excellent children's books at the ready guarantees that students will have writing models available throughout all the years it will require for them to become proficient writers. You will notice that a great number of the books discussed in the following chapters are picture books, many of which are also suitable for middle and even high school students. We focus mainly on picture books because, with time always at a premium, their brevity makes class discussion easier.

One of the best ways to acquire a skill is to study those who perform that skill well. In earlier times, youths were apprenticed to a master of the trade they wished to pursue. Even now, high school and college students engage in apprenticeships during the summer or even for a college term. Ball players and other athletes watch tapes of those who excel in their sport. So it makes sense that if we want students to write well, we put before them the best writers of literature for children and young adults. When we and our students fall in love with a book, we can ask ourselves, "How did the writer do that?" "What caused me to enjoy that story, that piece of non-fiction writing, that poem so much?" "Why did I grow to care so much about what happens to that character?" By actively studying what a writer does, young people can begin to notice and imitate the traits that make for powerful writing. "Authors," write Buzzeo and Kurtz (1999, xi):

> craft the stories that grab our students, the stories that sometimes hug and console young readers, sometimes intrigue or puzzle them, and sometimes shake them inside out. . . . Authors . . . create the informational books that turn students into wide-eyed investigators, bursting with curiosity, tingling with the thrills of learning. . . . Recognizing those resources, schools . . . have been exploring ways to tap into their power.

Although we will discuss a specific aspect of the writer's craft in each of the books featured in the following chapters, it is important to note that authors employ more than a single writing trait in each their works. We group books into specific categories here to provide teachers with multiple examples of a particular skill they may wish to teach. But as children advance through the grades and become more skilled as writers, we should relinquish as much responsibility as possible to them and let them discover for themselves in the books they read facets of an author's writing they may wish to emulate. They may notice things we overlook, and their writing will be all the better for it.

In addition to providing excellent literature for our students, here are some general suggestions for bringing the expertise of any author into the classroom:

1. Set aside enough time for the author study to be meaningful. Times can vary widely, depending upon the extent of the author's body of work, the amount of things you feel this author can teach your students, and the students' interest. In her book *The Girl with the Brown Crayon* (1998), Vivian Gussin Paley describes how she and her kindergarten students studied the works of author Leo Lionni for an entire year and the remarkable writing and discussions that took place during that fruitful experience.
2. Choose an author whose writing you or your students admire and who has a large body of work to study. It is especially helpful if that author has written in more than one genre.
3. Decide what aspects of writing the author can teach your students. Make a list of them and have these things in mind at the outset. As the study progresses, ask students to make their own list of skills the author is teaching them. Does their list coincide with yours? Are there ideas on their lists that go beyond what you had originally thought?
4. Begin by finding out as much as possible about the author's life. Most authors have websites (see http://www.acs.ucalgary.ca/~dkbrown/authors.html, and http://www.acs.ucalgary.ca/~dkbrown/authorsmisc

.html, among others, for lists). Teachingbooks.net website has a great deal of information about many authors as well as guides for discussing their books. The site requires a subscription, but teachers can enter a free trial period to determine whether this website meets their needs. Publishers usually print brochures that include biographical information and even produce DVDs about their authors, and provide these free of charge. Be certain to check out the websites of those publishers who publish your author. In addition to the wealth of information they contain (even video clips sometimes), these sites will often lead you to the author's own website. Some authors are even on Facebook and Twitter. Professional journals (*School Library Journal, Horn Book, Book Links, ALAN Review*, to name just a few) often publish articles on or by authors or interviews with them. Hearing from the authors themselves about their inspiration for writing a particular book can often help students with their own writing choices.

5. Read aloud from the author's works every day. Make books available for children to read individually, in groups, or with partners.

6. During the weeks you spend listening to and studying the author's works, discuss the author's style with the students. What do they notice about how the author begins stories, about his/her sentences, about themes, about language, etc.? The students can discuss this in groups or as a class. Make a chart that lists characteristics of the author's style. You might also want to make a chart that compares the books: how does each begin, what kind of language is used, etc.

7. Compare incidents in the author's life to incidents in the books he or she has written. Are there things from the author's life that find their way into the stories he/she writes? What about setting? Does the author use the place where he/she lives or has spent a considerable amount of time as a setting for a book? Why would an author do this? Jane Kurtz, in her book *Jane Kurtz and You* (2007), tells readers that so many of her novels and folktales are set in Ethiopia because she spent many years there as the child of missionary parents. In the case of non-fiction, is the topic a life-long passion of the author? What triggered this interest? How has the author learned about the topic? (See http://lu.com/showseries.cfm?serid=30 for a list of books published by Libraries Unlimited in which authors discuss their lives and books.)

8. Invite the author for a visit. Of course, a visit in person is the most exciting for students, and Buzzeo's and Kurtz's book *Terrific Connections with Authors, Illustrators, and Storytellers* (1999) is a wonderful resource for making these visits as worthwhile as possible. But such visits can be expensive, and with budgets as tight as they are, there are ways to reduce the cost or to provide experiences that can be almost as wonderful.

   a) Find out the author's speaking schedule from his or her website or the publisher. Often the publisher will provide a packet containing a list of all the authors willing to do school visits, their schedules, fees, and other requirements, etc. If you know when an author will be at a school or conference in your area, you can often share transportation and other costs and arrange for a visit for your students as well.

b) Sometimes local bookstores holding an author appearance will allow classes to come to the event.

c) In addition to free or reasonably priced DVDs available from publishers, many websites provide author videos. A search engine will likely uncover many from which to choose. Here are just a few:
   – http://www.readingrockets.org/books/interviews
   – http://www.readingrockets.org/podcasts/author
   – http://www.kidsread.tv/
   – http://www.bookwrapcentral.com/childrens/

d) Book Bites for Kids (http://www.blogtalkradio.com/bookbitesforkids) features interviews with children's book authors about their books and writing for children.

e) With technology so advanced these days, it is a simple matter to set up a chat, conference call, or even a video conference with an author students have been studying. Many authors are quite willing to do this for a nominal fee because they can talk to students from the comfort and convenience of their own homes. An LCD projector will enable everyone to see and hear a video conference. In her article, "An Author in Every Classroom" (*School Library Journal*, September 2010, 42–44), Kate Messner, teacher and children's book author, talks about the success she has had connecting with students through sessions on Skype. Her blog (kmessner.livejournal.com/106020.html) lists authors who offer free 20-minute Skype visits for classes that have read at least one of their books. In addition, she notes that The Skype-An-Author Network (skypeanauthor.wetpaint.com) is a good source of information about virtual author/illustrator visits.

9. I have had authors willing to remain on call for a specified length of time—a week or two—to answer students' email questions about writing.

10. Give the students oral and written exercises to help them imitate the author's style. Present this as a challenge for fun—just to try something different. If they can do these exercises, then some of what they have learned from the author will likely become part of their own writing. In her book *Lasting Impressions* (1992), Shelley Harwayne reiterates what author Don Murray often suggested: "We learn what makes a writer effective when we attempt to do what that writer has done" (164). A good example of how authors use other authors' writing styles for inspiration is Jonah Winter's picture book biography of Gertrude Stein (Winter 2009). He uses repetitive text throughout the book in imitation of Stein, who was famous for her repetition. Even the title, *Gertrude Is Gertrude Is Gertrude*, is modeled after her often-quoted saying: "Rose is a rose is a rose is a rose."

The books listed and discussed in this volume are by no means exhaustive samples of their given genres. Nor is it likely that you will have access to every book mentioned. These books are merely a sampling of those I have found to be successful with students. Hundreds of new books are published each year, and many more fine examples not included here will be on the shelves by the time this text reaches publication. What matters is that you find some ideas that you can apply to whatever books you have available and/or discover yourself, and that you use the books you and your students love. Students should definitely be involved, if not in the selection of the books the class enjoys together, then certainly in the choice of other books they will be given time to read on their own. In an article entitled "Summer Must-Read for Kids? Any Book" (*New York Times*, August 3, 2010, Science Times D1, D6), Tara Parker-Pope writes: "In a three-year study, researchers at the University of Tennessee, Knoxville found that simply giving low-income children access to books at spring fairs—and allowing them to choose books that most interested them—had a significant effect on the summer reading gap." The 1,300 children in the study were divided into a control group that received only activity and game books and a group that was permitted to select 12 books on their own. After three years of this process, researchers found that the children who had selected books scored significantly higher on tests in the fourth and fifth grade than the control group—the equivalent of attending summer school for three years! Surely such gains would be possible for all children, both in reading and writing.

One last note is in order before we begin. It is important that you keep this caution from renowned author Philip Pullman in mind as you use this book:

> Stories are written to beguile, to entertain, to amuse, to move, to enchant, to horrify, to delight, to anger, to make us wonder. They are not written so that we can make a fifty word summary of the whole plot, or find five synonyms for the descriptive words. That sort of thing would make you hate reading, and turn away from such a futile activity with disgust. . . . Those who design this sort of thing seem to have completely forgotten the true purpose of literature, the everyday, humble, generous intention that lies behind every book, every story, every poem: to delight or to console, to help us enjoy life or endure it. That's the true reason we should be giving books to children.

> —Philip Pullman, Isis Lecture 1 April 2003

So, above all, enjoy the books, get lost in them, discover new insights from them. And if, along the way, you and your students uncover some writing secrets as you sit at the feet of the masters, then a double reward is ripe for the taking.

## References

Buzzeo, Toni, and Jane Kurtz. 1999. *Terrific Connections with Authors, Illustrators, and Storytellers: Real Space and Virtual Links.* Englewood, CO: Libraries Unlimited. ISBN 978-1563087448. The authors discuss how to prepare for and conduct real and virtual author visits.

Charles, S. "Scholarship of teaching undergoing 'sea change'." March 9, 2009. http://www.wabash.edu/news/displayStory_print.cfm?news_ID=6797 (accessed March 15, 2011). This is a discussion of the issues raised during a conference at Wabash College.

Harwayne, Shelley. 1992. *Lasting Impressions*. Portsmouth, NH: Heinemann. ISBN 0-435-8732-0.
   Harwayne explores the role literature plays in inspiring student writing.

Hershenhorn, Esther. 2009. *S Is for Story: A Writer's Alphabet*. Illustrated by Zachary Pullen. Chelsea, MI: Sleeping Bear Press. ISBN 978-1-58536-439-8.
   The author uses each alphabet letter to discuss different aspects of literature and the writing process.

Krashen, Stephen D. 2003. *The Power of Reading*, 2nd ed. Westport, CT: Libraries Unlimited. ISBN 1-59158-169-9.
   Krashen argues that free voluntary reading is the most effective way to increase literacy competency.

Kurtz, Jane. 2007. *Jane Kurtz and You*. Westport, CT: Libraries Unlimited. ISBN 978-1591582953.
   Kurtz discusses the qualities of good writing as exemplified in her books and how her life informs her work.

MacLachlan, Patricia. 2010. *Word After Word After Word*. New York: Katherine Tegen/ HarperCollins. ISBN 978-0-06-027971-4.
   A professional writer spends several weeks with fourth graders helping them to write.

Messner, Kate. 2010. "An Author in Every Classroom." *School Library Journal* 56 (9): 42–44.
   The author discusses the merits of bringing authors and illustrators into the classroom inexpensively through Skype sessions.

Paley, Vivian Gussin. 1998. *The Girl with the Brown Crayon*. Cambridge, MA: Harvard University Press. ISBN 978-0674354425.
   Paley describes the discussions and writing that resulted when she and her kindergarten students studied Leo Lionni's books for a year.

Parker-Pope, Tara. 2010. "Summer Must-Read for Kids? Any Book." *New York Times*, Science Times D1, D6.
   Parker-Pope reports on a three-year study at the University of Tennessee, Knoxville, to determine the effect choosing 12 books for each of three summers would have on low-income children.

Smith, Frank. 2006. *Reading without Nonsense*, 4th ed. New York: Teachers College Press. ISBN 978-0807746868.
   Smith updates his premise that children learn to read by reading.

The National Commission on Writing in America's Schools and Colleges. 2003. "The Neglected 'R': The Need for a Writing Revolution." http://www.collegeboard.com/ prod_downloads/writingcom/neglectedr.pdf, accessed March 15, 2011.
   This is a report on writing in U.S. schools by the National Commission on Writing.

The National Writing Project. 2008. "Writing Is Essential." http://www.nwp.org/, accessed March 15, 2011.
   This home site of the National Writing Project provides information on projects and other resources for the teaching of writing.

Winter, Jonah. 2009. *Gertrude Is Gertrude Is Gertrude Is Gertrude*. Illustrated by Calef Brown. New York: Atheneum. ISBN 978-1-4169-4088-3.
   Winter writes about Gertrude Stein and the writers and artists who regularly gathered in her home.

# 1

# Words: The Heart of Writing

*If you want to write and you're not in love with your language, you shouldn't be writing. Words are the writer's tools.*

—Jane Yolen

*One must be drenched in words, literally soaked in them, to have the right ones form themselves into the proper pattern at the right moment.*

—Hart Crane

"Begin your new construction with twenty-six letters. Hammer a through z into words. Pile your words like blocks into sentence towers," writes Ann Whitford Paul in her book, *Word Builder* (2009), in which she uses building construction as a metaphor for creating a piece of writing. Words are the very heart of writing and the ones we choose and the ways in which we use them greatly affect its quality. "The difference between the right word and the almost right word," said Mark Twain, "is the difference between lightning and the lightning bug."

However, providing lists of vocabulary words for them to define, use in sentences, and commit to memory will most likely not transform students into excellent writers. "Marinating" them in words of all kinds, though: unusual words, words that tickle their ears, words that sound like music, words that surprise and delight, will make it possible for rich vocabulary to slip into their consciousness, into their speech, and eventually, into their writing. When our older son was in the sixth grade, his class was studying Shakespeare's *Macbeth* in preparation for performing the play. The following weekend we were involved in a house renovation project and were anxiously awaiting a friend who had promised to help. After a half-hour had elapsed with no friend in sight, Chris quipped, "Where's Bob? His absence lays blame upon his promise." At first we were stunned, but we really shouldn't have been. Shakespeare's glorious words and phrases had been wafting over him all week and, without effort, he was able to pull a sentence from the play that suited the situation perfectly.

## Well-Crafted Literature: A Gold Mine of Words

One of the best ways we can help students, even our youngest ones, enrich their vocabularies and provide them with examples of ways to arrange words and sentences for greatest effect, is to read aloud to them daily from excellent books—and to point

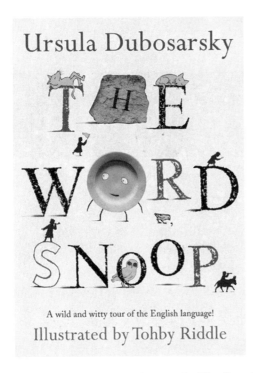

out memorable words and passages when they occur. Although we cannot assume they will always notice these things on their own, with a little encouragement, they can become, like Robert MacNeil, "wordstruck...crazy about the sound of words, the look of words, the taste of words, the feeling for words on the tongue and in the mind" (MacNeil 1989, vii). Our goal should be to help our students move toward the sentiments of the narrator in Ursula Dubosarsky's *The Word Snoop* (2009):

> I love words...I follow words everywhere. I creep down dark hallways, roam wide highways, and sneak along country lanes. I listen to conversations, read over people's shoulders, flip through books, click on websites, and tap out text messages.

or Selig in Roni Schotter's *The Boy Who Loved Words* (2006), a youngster who

> loved everything about words—the sound of them in his ears (*tintinnabulating!*), the taste of them on his tongue (*tantalizing!*), the thought of them when they *percolated* in his brain (*stirring!*), and, most especially, the feel of them when they moved his heart (*Mama!*).

or Max, who was such an avid word collector that his collection "grew too big for his desk," "spread into the hallway," and eventually became a story (Banks 2006), or Neftali, in Pam Muñoz Ryan's *The Dreamer* (2010), a lovely novel of Pablo Neruda's childhood, who "loved the rhythm of certain words, and when he came to one of his favorites, he read it over and over again" (21).

Finally, a most stunning example of a word lover in literature for young people— Melody, a 10-year-old who has cerebral palsy and cannot speak:

> From the time I was really little—maybe just a few months old—words were like sweet, liquid gifts, and I drank them like lemonade. I could almost taste them. . . . By the time I was two, all my memories had words, and all my words had meanings. But only in my head. I have never spoken one single word. (Draper 2010, 2)

The following are a few ideas you can use to prompt such attention to words:

1. Encourage students who become fired up about words through exposure to Dubosarsky's or any of the above-mentioned books to email her about their language questions, word discoveries, comments about words, etc. at wordsnoop@gmail.com.

2. Provide notebooks for all your students, preferably ones small enough for them to carry everywhere. Encourage them to jot down interesting words they hear in conversations and see in print.

3. Have large envelopes with different labels such as "sound words," "weather words," "silly words," etc. available and ask students to contribute applicable words they find. Read the words aloud occasionally and celebrate when they appear in student speech or writing.

4. Encourage students to copy a word they love in their best writing or with an enlarged computer font, create a decorative frame around it, and display it on the classroom wall or bulletin board. Play a "find it" game occasionally, asking different students to find a particular word. Change the words regularly, transferring those that have been up for awhile to a "Favorite Words" book. Ask students to work in committees to create a cover for the book and to create headings for different categories of words. Keep the book in the classroom library for reference during the daily writing workshop.

5. Provide time for students to share the newest words in their notebooks at the end of the week. Are there any words they have in common? Are there words from their classmates' lists students wish to add to their own? Have they used any of these words in their writing? One way to make this sharing especially interesting is to have a space on a white board or bulletin board for students to write their words during the week and to interact with the words others place there. They could draw lines between words with similar meanings, words that begin with the same sound, etc. The Friday discussion would then center around these discoveries.

6. Rather than present a word of the day of your choosing, have a different student write a favorite word from his or her personal list on the board each day.

7. For younger children, create together a chart of favorite words. Add to the chart when applicable after group read-alouds. Say some of the words together occasionally. Talk about their similarities and differences. Include some words, when appropriate, in group chart writing.

### Special Projects to Turn Students into Word Snoops/Lovers

Author/illustrator Debra Frasier is well known for helping teachers and students enjoy her books as thoroughly as possible. Her website, www.debrafrasier.com, is a treasure-trove of ideas and has a special section for teachers. Detailed annotated bibliographies of books that celebrate words and language are on this site. Two of her books are especially geared to invoking in students a curiosity about and love of words. The first is *Miss Alaineus: A Vocabulary Disaster* (2000). Home sick from school, Sage gets the new vocabulary list over the phone from a classmate and mistakenly writes down "Miss Alaineus" instead of the real word *miscellaneous*. When she defines "Miss Alaineus" for the class, they roar with laughter, but she later turns this embarrassing moment into fun by coming to the annual vocabulary parade dressed as "Miss Alaineus." The book is filled with word games, extra assignments, and other ways to

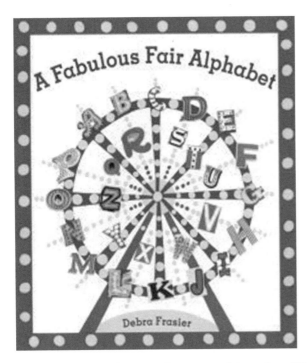

increase students' vocabulary and love of words. Best of all is the suggestion to have a Word Parade. Frasier's website brims with ideas for having such an event, and even provides a list of words that lend themselves to the creation of costumes. Students can take pictures of themselves dressed as their favorite words and send the photos to Debra, display them throughout the school, or turn them into a vocabulary book, each pictured word alphabetically listed. This project is even more effective if you encourage students to choose words that are new to them rather than words that can easily be depicted in costumes. Frasier's newest book at this printing is *A Fabulous Fair Alphabet* (2010). Capitalizing on her love of state fairs, she spent a considerable amount of time photographing the different words she encountered at these fairs. Then she used the photos to single out decorative letters for each of the 26 letters of the alphabet to create her alphabet book. Students can log on to http://www.afabulous fairalphabet.com/ to view a video of Debra at the fair and to print out game cards. The author urges them to go to the fair and use the game cards to write down words they see that begin with each letter of the alphabet. If there is a fair in your town, this would be a wonderful way to combine fair activities with some word snooping. But it would be a great game for any area of town: words they see in the supermarket, at a shopping mall, etc. This game and the word parade described previously are great ways to call students' attention to words, to help them see how much fun words can be, and to turn them into word lovers.

### Books That Contain Superb Language

#### Infants and Young Toddlers

All children, even infants, need books. We are not expecting infants to write, of course, but we can begin surrounding them with the wonderful sounds of language from their earliest days. "New studies . . . demonstrate that babies and very young children know, observe, explore, imagine and learn more than we would ever have thought possible," Alison Gopnik wrote in a piece for the *New York Times* (August 16, 2009, Week in Review, 10). Babies react to sounds, especially the sound of our voice. So it makes sense, because budgets always seem to be tight, to get the biggest "bang for the buck" by making sure that the books we share with our little ones are not only age appropriate, but also have interesting, playful words that will later become part of their speaking and writing vocabulary. Eventually we hope they will echo Pat Mora's sentiments: "Come, words, come in your every color . . . / I'll say, say, say you,/ taste you sweet as plump plums,/ bitter as old lemons" (in Hopkins, sel., 2004, 12).

Fortunately, more and more language-rich books are being published for very young children, making selection a relatively easy task. Clearly, we are far beyond "See Spot run. Run, Spot, run."

### Board Books

Board books are sized perfectly to fit in an adult's hand while cradling a baby and for little fingers to grasp and touch. They are sturdy enough to withstand some gnawing as well. Although we offer a sizeable assortment of board book titles in this section, it is also important to keep in mind that "a baby is hardwired to absorb not just vocabulary, but the rhythms and exchange of conversation and storytelling" (Joosse, "Razzmatazz," 18). It is "fun," therefore, "to improvise and read out loud, with repetition and refrain, and plenty of toe-tapping, lip-smacking sounds—razzmatazz! Even if a baby hasn't yet learned what the words mean, the sound is delicious" (Joosse, 18). So, in addition to the board books below that emphasize marvelous language, and others you love, do not hesitate to read picture books to babies as well, so that they can enjoy their rhythms and drama.

"Chicken grooming, chicken zooming/chicken searching/chickens perching" are some of the delightful word pairs accompanying illustrations of chickens of every feather engaged in the activities described in John Schindel's *Busy Chickens* (2009). The good news is that there is a whole series of these wonderful "busy" books, and each book contains colorful action words that explain what the animals are doing in each illustration. Others in the series are *Busy Birdies* (2010), *Busy Bear Cubs* (2009), *Busy Bunnies* (2008), *Busy Pandas* (2008), *Busy Horsies* (2007), *Busy Barnyard* (2006), *Busy Piggies* (2006), *Busy Doggies* (2004), *Busy Kitties* (2004), *Busy Monkeys* (2004), and *Busy Penguins* (2004).

"Peek-a moo, peek-a zoo" are not the usual peek-a-boo game words, but it is this playful use of words that makes Nina Laden's *Peek-a Who?* (2000) such fun. A die-cut

hole through which the adult and child can "peek" at a visual clue exists, followed by a page turn that reveals the answer. For example, the page on the left says "Peek a . . ." Look at the visual clue, then guide baby's hand into the hole to turn the page and the entire illustration and word are revealed. Alternating pages rhyme as well: "Peek a . . . moo (page turn—cow), peek a . . . boo" (page turn—ghost). The zoo page offers a chance for an animal-naming session as well.

What better way to capture babies' attention than by showing them other babies? Jane Wattenberg's *Mrs. Mustard's Baby Faces* (2007) does just that by depicting colored pictures of seven multi-ethnic babies, each exhibiting two opposite moods: crying/smiling; cranky/happy, etc. The adult can attribute appropriate descriptors to each of the baby faces, thus providing a wide range of emotion words for babies to hear. The book opens like an accordion so that adult and child can get down on the floor and look at the array of expressions together. Older children can try imitating the faces shown.

Lucy Cousins's *Hooray for Fish!* (2008) offers little ones brightly colored fish of every shape, spot, and stripe accompanied by words that are opposites as well as by tongue-tickling alliterative pairs: "twisty/twirly." Many of the fish are fanciful as in "ele-fish," a gray and white fish that sports a tusk and trunk. This book has rhyme, opportunities for counting, great sounds, and saturated colors that will surely attract young children's attention and give their ears a treat. A new paperback edition of this book (2010) contains a DVD storybook animation for older children.

Many opportunities exist to elaborate on the brief text in Leslie Patricelli's *The Birthday Box* (2009) and to engage in fun activities with one child or a small group of toddlers. A diaper-clad toddler receives a box for his birthday and imagines all kinds of things he and the stuffed dog inside can do with it. After reading the book, offer a good-sized carton and play a game of pretend with a child or group. Describe the things the box can become and act them out: a cloth-covered table on which to place a tasty snack; a plane that can soar high in the sky, etc.

"Touch and feel" activities are common in board books. But the few pages in Betsy Snyder's *Have You Ever Tickled a Tiger?* (2009) offer young children especially

fine examples of delicious language. "Have you ever nudged a hedgehog?/She's cute and sharp and kind of prickly./Touch her—is your finger tickly?" The alliteration, rhyme, and catchy words will keep little ones interested through repeated readings. Adults can add to the impact of the book by adding additional descriptors for the scales, feathers, etc. children touch.

Need to get energetic toddlers moving? Harriet Ziefert's *Beach Party!* (2005) is an excellent choice, because youngsters are encouraged to imitate 11 animals as they "slither," "dash," and "twist" their way to the water. After reading the book, call out each verb and act it out with the children. Using their bodies as they hear the words will reinforce for children their sounds and meanings. Not only do Rufus Butler Seder's books *Gallop!* (2007) and *Waddle!* (2009) have rhyming text about moving animals, the animals actually "leap" and "prance" across the pages in a special technique called "Scanimation." A question on the left-hand side asks whether the child can imitate a certain animal movement: "Can you soar like an eagle?" A circle on the right then depicts that animal moving when the page moves, while sound words are written in color underneath. The result is so breathtaking children will not be able to put these books down. *Gallop!* is in black and white, whereas *Waddle!* adds color to an already unique offering.

Tabs, each featuring a leaf, a snowflake, the moon, and other elements of the natural world enable child and adult to turn to a gentle haiku about that element in Snyder's *Haiku Baby* (2008). "a buttercup offers up/yellow nose kisses," while the "wind plays tag with autumn leaf—" in this language-rich, musical book. It would make a fine companion for an exploration of the play yard or a soft-voiced prelude to nap time. Do not be concerned if you feel a child is too young to grasp every poetic image. Just enjoy the sounds together.

Pigs reside in "wallow[s]," pigeons in "rafters," donkeys in "paddock[s]," and they all make delightful sounds in Denise Fleming's *Barnyard Banter* (2008). In addition to

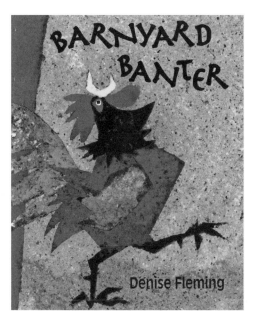

the rhyme, bouncy text, and some unusual farm location names, an elusive goose makes easily spotted appearances to prompt a hide-and-seek game. More animal fun abounds for toddlers who will revel in the myriad ways to describe cats (*Cats*, 2009) and dogs (*Dogs*, 2007) of every size and shape in Matthew Van Fleet's two large board books. "Wrinkly," "sleek," cats with "swishing slinky" tails and "silky," or "shaggy" dogs with "drooly dog sticks" cavort across the pages of these books. And to add to the fun while they repeat the interesting words offered, there are textures to feel and levers to pull that will make the animals do youngsters' bidding.

How many ways can you describe a tail? Matthew Van Fleet answers that question in *Tails* (2003). Tails can be "furry, spiny, rainbow-hued and—shiny." They can "drag" or be "frisky" enough to "wag." The variations in this book are great fun. Sometimes a flap lift is necessary to complete a rhyme. Pulls set some tails in motion and children can feel textured tails as well. Finally, the names of all the animals that appear in the book—some as unusual as "pangolins" and "tamarins"—appear next to their picture with directives to go back and find certain numbers of each animal. Older toddlers can imitate some of the tail motions with their hands. Say, "Show me a dragging tail. Show me a swishing tail," etc. The different parts of animals' heads— heads, necks, ears, mouths, tongues, noses, and eyes—are the focus of Van Fleet's *Heads* (2010). Among the many descriptors for each appendage are "beaked heads," "frilled necks," "floppy ears," "slobber mouths," "scratchy tongues," "tickle noses," and "sly eyes." A large fold-out pictures all the animals together along with their names.

A busy tug boat is a "bounce and bob and float, boat"; a "grab and guide and float, boat"; and much more in Kevin Lewis's *Tugga-Tugga Tugboat* (2009). Little ones will love the bounce and rhyme in this little book, and older toddlers may notice some hints in the illustrations that foreshadow where the little tug is actually doing its work.

It is not too soon to introduce babies to other humans with whom they share the planet, and The Global Fund for Children does just that by proffering *Global Babies* (2009), a book that pictures 17 babies from around the world. The text does not feature special language, for it simply states that wherever babies are, whatever they wear, etc., they are loved. But it does afford the adult an opportunity to introduce all kinds of words. First, each country is named, and so many of these names sound like music if we read them slowly and deliberately: "Guatemala," "Afghanistan," "Malawi." In addition, we can name and describe the distinctive clothing worn by each infant. This gem is a wonderful way to broaden babies' and young children's horizons.

Finally, a word must be said for nursery rhymes, and this is true for every age child, not just the lap set. Children need to hear nursery rhymes from their very earliest days. Of course, they may have no notion of what curds or whey are, or what it means to be contrary, how many peppers are in a peck, or the meanings of so many other

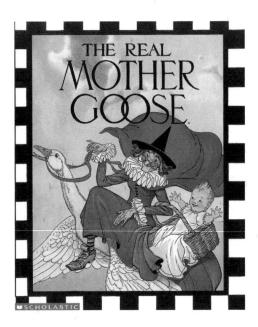

words and phrases we encounter in these rhymes. But they respond to the sound of them, the bounce and rhythm of them, the alliterative sounds in Peter, Peter, pumpkin eater, Tweedle Dum and Tweedle Dee, and so many others. "To read Mother Goose rhymes aloud is to hear the music in language" (Martha V. Parravano, "Books for Babies" in *A Family of Readers: The Book Lover's Guide to Children's and Young Adult Literature*, 13). Several board book editions containing a few rhymes each are available. Among them are: *Mary Engelbreit's Merry Mother Goose* (2008); Lisa McCue's *My First Mother Goose* (2009); *My First Mother Goose* (2009) by Tomie dePaola; Linda Bleck's *A Children's Treasury of Mother Goose* (2009); *Mother Goose* by Kim LaFave et al. (2009); and Blanche Fisher Wright's *The Real Mother Goose Touch & Feel Book* (2001).

## Picture Books

At a meeting of the New England Children's Booksellers Advisory Council, held at The Eric Carle Museum of Picture Book Art in Amherst, Massachusetts, in June 2010, Ken Geist, vice president and editorial director of Orchard Books and Cartwheel Books, made an impassioned plea in support of picture books, which are currently flagging in sales. (See also Julie Bosman's article, "Picture Books No Longer a Staple for Children" in the *New York Times*, Oct. 7, 2010, p. 1.) Obviously some parents, teachers, and even book sellers are not recognizing the value of picture books. Barnes & Noble is even, at this writing, dismantling its picture book section and mixing picture

books in with activity books—a move certain to keep these books from reaching children of all ages who can benefit greatly from the stories, the wonderful art work, and from studying the ways in which picture book authors use language.

The following paragraphs highlight the extreme importance of picture books, not just as a stepping stone to novels, but for all they have to offer in themselves. Because picture books are so short and so much space is usually given over to illustrations, they often contain very few words. When authors of quality picture books are allowed such brief space for text, every word they use has to be carefully considered. Like Noah Webster, they view words as "precious silk threads" (*Noah Webster: Weaver of Words*, Shea, 2009, p. 31) they must choose carefully as they weave their stories. Can they use one strong word in place of two or three weaker ones? Is this sentence or phrase absolutely necessary to the plot? To illustrate, listen to Deborah Freedman, author of *Scribble* (2007) who was hard at work on a new book and facing an imminent deadline. "It only has 160 words," she said, "and I want them to sing. So I'm rewriting the entire beginning" (conversation with the author, Aug. 12, 2010).

A very instructive piece of writing that reveals quite powerfully an author's process in creating a picture book is Mem Fox's explanation of the exhausting process she, with collaboration from her illustrator, Judy Horacek, engaged in over two years to write *Where Is the Green Sheep?* (2004). After numerous drafts, the final version contained only 190 words, but each word entailed many decisions about balance, rhythms, rhyme, and so much more. Sharing Mem's speech about the creation of this book (see http://www.memfox.com/green-sheep-secrets.html) will not only help students see how carefully authors put words together when they write a story, but will also reinforce for those who work with children of all ages the idea that picture books are powerful tools for teaching writing.

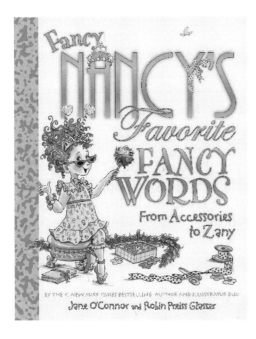

Jonathan London's *I Am a Truck Driver* (2010) gives young children the opportunity to use a variety of onomatopoeic words. A boy and a girl, along with their pet dog or cat, appear on alternate spreads driving a different kind of truck. Rhyming couplets describe what the vehicles do and the sounds they make. Youngsters will have a great time "growling" and "brooming" along with trucks and their drivers.

Fancy Nancy fans (see Jane O'Connor's many books about this extraordinarily fancy young lady) will be delighted to learn that she has created an illustrated book of her very favorite fancy words (*Fancy Nancy's Favorite Fancy Words*, O'Connor, 2008). This book is such fun and so vocabulary-expanding that it may inspire readers to create their own favorite word dictionaries. Although not particularly fancy, the names of many different kinds of light that shine after dark will definitely expand children's concept of the word *light* after they read Susan Gal's *Night Lights* (2009). "Porch light," "headlight," "lantern light," and "firefly light" are just a few "light" words they will encounter. Cookie lovers will enjoy Amy Krouse Rosenthal's *One Smart Cookie* (2010) in which she serves up new words that will not only help youngsters get along with others in school but also help them bake and share a batch of cookies. Pepi, a parrot who loves to sing (Ljungkvist, *Pepi Sings a New Song*, 2010), goes on a search to find things to sing about. In his travels he encounters cooking words such as *whisk* and *decorate*; color words such as *chartreuse* and *umber* and much more—all raw materials for a brand-new song. After enjoying the book with children, post charts around the room with each category of words Pepi discovers and encourage the class to add new words of their own.

How many different words or expressions can your students think of to say "Please keep a secret" or the reverse, "Please spread the news"? The bear in Ian Schoenherr's *Don't Spill the Beans!* (2010) is warned at first: "Don't let it slip!/ Don't give it away!/ Button your lip." But when he can no longer stand it, he is allowed to "blurt," "blab," "alert," and "tip off" his friends. Students might enjoy thinking of as many different words for a particular action as possible. They can brainstorm in groups, or you can put a particular word on the board at the beginning of the day and before lunch or at day's end, they can share whatever words they have jotted in their notebooks. For example, for the word *say*, they might come up with *declare, mention, utter*, etc. Even more challenging for older students would be to have them consider gradations of these words, for example, lining up words in order of emphasis, from *whisper* through *say*, and *declare* until they reach *shout*.

The little girl in Emma Dodd's *I Don't Want a Cool Cat!* (2010) mentions all the kinds of cats she *does not* want. Not for her is a "greedy cat. 'Meow, meow,/ please feed me' cat." Nor is she wild about a "a prize cat./ The best-that-money-buys cat." "Prowlyy," "howly," "yowly," "grunty," or "scowly" cats are not her favorites either. (See also Dodd's *I Don't Want a Posh Dog!* (2008), a book in a similar vein.) On the other hand, the narrator of Sue Stainton's *I Love Cats* (2007) is keen on cats of all kinds. "Bubbly cats, snuggly cats," "bumbling cats," and "tumbling cats" are all her cup of tea. Even though she gets into lots of trouble, who would not love the adventurous kitten in Linda Newbery's *Posy* (2008). She's a "playful wrangler,/" a "knitting tangler"; "a sandwich checker," and a "board-game wrecker!" but charming all the same. Of course, if you do have a pet, it would not do to "tease" or "provoke" or "madden" or "disturb" it. But it would be fine to "pamper" and "dote" on it to your heart's content (Chamberlain, *Please Don't Tease Tootsie*, 2008). Although moose are not quite suitable as pets, the children in Phyllis Root's *Looking for a Moose* (2008) are determined to find

one—a "long-leggy, dinner-diving, branchy-antler moose." So intent are they on finding their quarry that they are willing to "scritch scratch! scritch scratch!" through "brambly-ambly, bunchy-scrunchy,/ scrubby-shrubby bushes" to find one. Another of Dodd's protagonists takes on much smaller creatures in her *I Love Bugs!* (2010). She loves all kinds of bugs: "spiky spiny" ones, "pretty spotty shiny" ones, and even "furry/ whirry/funny" ones. These books are full of humorous and unusual ways to talk about animals. After enjoying them, or the many other word-rich picture books about animals, with your students, provide books and/or magazines about dogs, cats, or other creatures depicted in the books you have chosen and have them work in groups to write clever descriptions of them. Encourage conversation. What particular action or expression is the animal exhibiting that would justify each description? After the groups share what they have written, compile their descriptions into an illustrated book of phrases and expressions about animals. Another way to do this might be to ask students who have pets to bring in pictures of them for groups to describe. A slightly different approach would be to divide older students into groups and ask them to talk about the behaviors of their dogs or the dogs they meet outside or in the homes of relatives and friends. Ask them to make a list of these behaviors such as: begging for food, rolling over to be scratched, chewing bones, chasing balls, wagging tails, etc. Then read *Nobody's Diggier than a Dog* (Bartoletti 2005) in which the author uses coined expressions to describe doggie antics. For example, "Nobody's NAGGIER than a dog—a slurp-your-face dog,/ a let's-play-chase dog." Can the students create their own class book? Each group could choose two or three behaviors on their list and write a three-line description for each one, as modeled by Bartoletti. When the book is illustrated and bound, they can share it with a younger class. If your students are too young to be successful with these activities, work together as a class to describe on a chart pictures you hold up for the group to view. You could also make PowerPoint slides of animal pictures for them to see and do the exercise orally. You can even take them on a walk around the school yard, stopping to observe and describe the insects and other creatures they see.

Young children will enjoy imitating the actions of the different animals in Lindsey Gardiner's *Here Come Poppy and Max* (2000) or the various cuddles in Cabrera's *Kitty's Cuddles* (2007). Or, after listening to Jennifer Merz's *Playground Day!* (2007) they can go out to the playground and use the equipment to transform themselves, like the children in the book, into various animals. When they have experienced these interesting

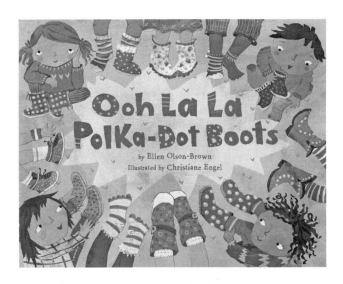

verbs and descriptive words in their bodies, children are more likely to remember them and use them in their writing.

Describing clothing is great fun, and there are many picture books that can spark ideas. Polka-dot boots (Olson-Brown 2010) can make all kinds of clothing look "spiffy," and "snazzy," and "groovy." "Plain coats, zany coats," "fast duds, slow duds"— all benefit with the addition of polka-dot boots. Readers can move flaps to add "splish-splashing" or "rainbow-colored" polka-dot boots to the feet of the children displaying their different outfits. After they enjoy the pairs of unusual opposite kinds of apparel shown on each page, they can continue the book by drawing and labeling other clothing opposites. Challenge them to come up with never-before-encountered pairs.  Eileen Spinelli presents the hats of some well-known people in short, amusing verses in *Do YOU Have a Hat?* (2004): "Igor Stravinsky had a hat,/ a tattered, battered green beret,/ He wore it every single day." In Harriet Ziefert's *Grandma, It's for You!* (2006), Lulu collects bits and pieces of different objects to make the perfect birthday hat for her grandmother. Students can engage in a number of activities after they enjoy these books. Research some people or groups not mentioned in Spinelli's book and create a "Who's Who?" bulletin board featuring drawings or photos of people wearing the hats accompanied by descriptions. Have a hat-decorating contest. Working alone, in pairs, or in groups, ask the students to design as many different kinds of hats as they can. After they have drawn their decorated hats or used actual objects to paste onto paper, have them describe the hats for a sale brochure. They can even take and print out digital pictures of the hats to paste into the brochure. If they design wearable hats, have a fashion show during which students read out colorful descriptions as their hat-wearing classmates parade by.

Children have many occasions to write about the natural world. They may be studying about the seasons or welcoming the arrival of a new one. Perhaps they are investigating the kinds of life in a marsh or other habitat. They might describe a tree, a flower, a body of water, the grass under their feet, or even the day on which their story takes place. Fortunately, there are many beautiful picture books in which carefully chosen words help readers experience the sights and sounds around them in new ways. The aim here is NOT to encourage flowery, descriptive language filled with adjectives. Rather, it is to help students choose the few ear-pleasing, unusual words that will add humor, color, and the unexpected to their pieces.

"Winter will squish squck sop splat slurp melt in mud./Happy mud./Stir it. Stick it./ Dig it. Dance it./" Mary Lyn Ray's *Mud* (2001) is the perfect book to use to usher in spring as the snow melts and young children have the opportunity to make mud pies in the school yard. Encourage the children to talk about their experiences and record their responses on a chart. How does the mud feel on their skin—cool,

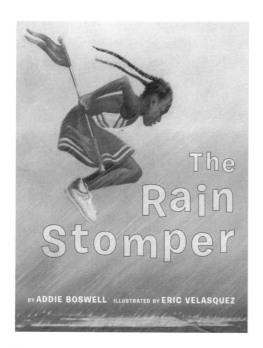

slippery, wet? What are some things they can do with mud? How do creatures use mud?

Rain goes "clatter clatter slap!" and thunder goes "walla boom boom" in Addie Boswell's *The Rain Stomper* (2008), and Jazmin is determined to stomp out this foul weather that threatens to cancel her parade. She hates rain, that old "mud puddler," that "parade wrecker." But the rain actually cheers up the little girl in Jane Kurtz's *Rain Romp* (2002), and she runs out to play in the "little silver worms of rain." For the child in *Puddles* (London 1999), rain makes the needles on the fir trees glisten and leaves sparkle. Best of all, it creates puddles—"pieces of sky on the ground"—just perfect for jumping in as boots make sucking sounds in the mud. What are the students' opinions of rain? Record their responses. Write a list of rain words and sounds together. Talk about London's description of puddles as "pieces of sky on the ground." Why does he say that? Can students come up with some beautiful word pictures such as this one?

"Some words are gay and bright" and others "are just as dark as night" (Rand, *Sparkle and Spin: A Book about Words*, 2006). It is fascinating how choosing just the right words can create a mood. Notice how, in describing the beginning of a snow storm, Bernadette Ford (*First Snow*, 2007) talks about "big flakes softly falling," but as the storm gains momentum, she says the flakes are "swirling, blowing, twirling down." The former description coaxes our reading voices to proceed slowly and softly, and then we can gain volume and speed as the snow comes "swirling, blowing, twirling down." Ask students to read these pages aloud, focusing on what they do with their voices. Talk about words that might describe the height of a storm or a peaceful sunset; a quiet desert or a noisy rainforest. Write their suggestions on charts. Go out into the school yard with notebooks and write a description of the day.

In a perfect fall story, Elizabeth Spurr (*Pumpkin Hill*, 2006) tells how a "lonely only" pumpkin rolls down a hill, splits apart, and scatters its seeds across the hillside. Eventually, masses of pumpkins grow, are blown down the hill by a "mighty wind," and become a "golden avalanche" that "ricochet[s]," "rolls," and "tumble[s]" all over town, turning all the vegetables in the market into "a giant tossed salad." What wonderful word choices this story offers. Read it aloud, lingering over the words "lonely only," so that the children focus on the long "o" sounds that so aptly create a quiet, solitary scene with a lone pumpkin on a hill. Talk about the exciting action words as the story shifts and the pumpkins descend upon the town creating chaos and delight in their wake. Make a list of the students' favorite words and phrases from the story.

Using books that focus on different categories can add to students' store of words in those groupings. For example, although they probably already know what hammers and nails are, even very young children can learn about "levels," "awls," "pliers," and "wrenches" in the very simple *Toolbox Twins* (Schaefer 2006). A more complex book about tools is Marilyn Singer's *Let's Build a Clubhouse* (2006). *Ballerina!* (Sis 2001)

introduces such dance words as *stretch*, *twirl*, and *flutter*, whereas Alexa Brandenberg's *Chop Simmer Season* (1997) offers interesting cooking words like *flambé* and *sauté*. Taro Miura's *Tools* (2005) provides illustrated examples of many different kinds of tools, such as those used by tailors, watch makers, electrical workers, and others. After each two-page spread of different tools, students can decide which category of worker uses those tools before a page turn reveals the answer. After sharing books such as these, divide older students into groups, providing each group with a category with which they may be familiar. Have the groups research and list as many words in that category as they can find, especially those words they have discovered for the first time. They may wish to illustrate the words and turn their different lists into a book modeled after Miura's example. Some possibilities: appliances, machines for cleaning, trucks, boats, etc. Younger children can do this as a class activity.

### Alliteration and Assonance

The famous poet, Eve Merriam, once said:

I've sometimes spent weeks looking for precisely the right word. It's like having a tiny marble in your pocket, you can just feel it. Sometimes you find a word and say, "No, I don't think this is it . . . " Then you discard it, and take another and another until you get it right. (Cullinan and Wooten, *Another Jar of Tiny Stars*, 2009, 35)

One of the very best ways for students to hear alliteration (words in close proximity that begin with the same consonant) and assonance (words in close proximity that have the same internal vowel sound) is to read poetry aloud every day, paying particular attention to the sounds of the words. It is also helpful if the students can see on a chart, a slide, or in the book itself the poem you are reading so that they can become visually aware of the placement of words while their ears are enjoying the sounds they make. Because poems are relatively brief compared to prose, each word is key to the rhythm, music, and imagery of the whole. Fortunately, parents and teachers now have a wide selection of books from which to choose, both in picture and longer book form, to suit all ages. We will discuss only a very few here because poetry is so important and far-reaching a topic it needs a book all its own.

One of the most talented wordsmiths writing poetry for children is Mary Ann Hoberman. Consider the abundance of "b" sounds in her poem "Brother" (*The Llama*

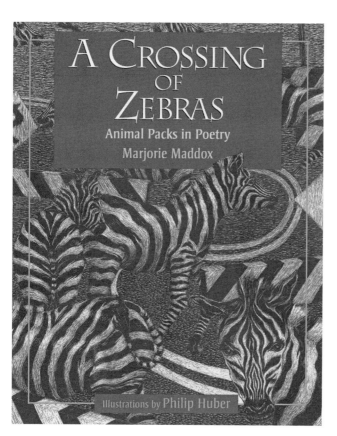

Who Had No Pajama, 10). Or, when reading about a sibling fight in *And to Think that We Thought that We'd Never Be Friends* (Hoberman 2003) listen to the energy in "We thwacked and we whacked and we walloped away." All the short "i" sounds in Dawn Watkins's "Hippo Kisses" (*Every Second Something Happens: Poems for the Mind and Senses*, San José and Johnson, 2009, 27) add to the silliness of the poem, whereas Marjorie Maddox's poem in which "a cartload of monkeys <u>bu</u>mptiously/<u>bu</u>mbled and tumbled..." ("A Cartload of Monkeys" in *A Crossing of Zebras: Animal Packs in Poetry*, 2009, 14) creates a picture of chaos even without seeing the accompanying illustration. An added bonus for using this book is the uncommon collective names such as "scurry of squirrels" introduced.

To get students using their imaginations and playing with collective names, pair *A Crossing of Zebras* with Jacqueline K. Ogburn's *A Dignity of Dragons: Collective Nouns for Magical Beasts* (2010) where they will meet "A sunami of sea monsters," "a blaze of fire-breathers," "a grapple of griffins," and many more fanciful creatures. In addition to describing animals in such alliterative terms as "bamboo bandit" (panda) and "tree-topper" (giraffe), the poems in David Elliott's beautiful *In the Wild* (2010) offer arresting images. Elephants are "Powerful, yet delicate/ as lace." "The jaguar's back is flowering/ with delicate rosettes,/ as if she's grown a garden there,/" and a rhinoceros has a "boot-like face."

Iyengar's *Tan to Tamarind: Poems about the Color Brown* (2009) celebrates the many shades of brown and all the places brown manifests itself in our world. Brown is described as "milk-tea brown," "sepia brown," "sandalwood brown," and so much more. After enjoying these poems with the class, have them take a walk around the school building and the school yard and find different shades of brown. Can they write a description of one of the objects or places they find using that kind of brown? Can they make up other names for brown that have not been mentioned in the poems—names that fit objects in their environment? Open a large box of Crayola crayons and read aloud some of the delicious crayon names. Colors like "Atomic Tangerine," "Blizzard Blue," "Caribbean Green," and "Cerise," sound so marvelous on the tongue. Invite the students to come up with completely new names. Crayola sometimes retires colors and/or changes their names. Submit new and marvelous color names to the company and see if there is any response. The students may also wish to experiment by mixing paints and submitting color samples along with the names. Heidi Mordhorst appropriately begins a winter poem with a succession of "w" sounds: "Just

water/solid water/just water frozen white" in *Pumpkin Butterfly: Poems from the Other Side of Nature* (2009, 15). Fall is a special time when the earth prepares for the long sleep of winter. After displaying their riotous colors, the trees become bare. Birds, having raised their young leave for warmer climes. Listen to the quiet, mournful "o" sounds in Rachel Field's much-loved "Something Told the Wild Geese" as the geese sense a time for goodbyes is a hand: "Something told the wild geese/It was time to go./Though the field lay golden/Something whispered, 'Snow' " (*Poetry by Heart: A Child's Book of Poems to Remember*, Attenborough, 2001, 33). Every curriculum contains study about the natural world, and an especially useful book that can encourage students to write poems and create illustrations about what they are learning is *River of Words: Young Poets and Artists on the Nature of Things* (Michael 2008). Each year River of Words, a nonprofit organization, holds a contest for students from preschool through high school, asking them to send in their poems and illustrations about nature. This volume, consisting of the poems of young people over the past 12 years, has a water theme. Reading other students' work can inspire budding writers with an "I can do that" attitude. Go to www.riverofwords.org to watch videos about the different projects students have done, to find out about new contests and deadlines, and to download a teacher guide.

Sara Holbrook's *Zombies! Evacuate the School!* (2010) contains poems about all aspects of school life: tests, substitute teachers, classmates, etc. Especially valuable are the poet's asides in which she discusses word meanings or a particular poem and its characteristics, and gives students hints for writing a similar kind of poem of their own.

Authors, especially those who write picture books, often use assonance and alliteration to create sentences that "sing." Serfozo provides examples of both literary devices in her delightful *Plumply, Dumply Pumpkin* (2004). Peter wants a perfect pumpkin that is "sunny" and "sumptuous," and he finds it on a "twining vine." This book begs to be read aloud to young children who will surely hear how the consonant and vowel sounds work to bring Peter's special pumpkin to life. Emphasize the crisp initial consonant sounds and linger over the vowels such as those in "plumply dumply." Can the children add to the story as a class by writing additional two-line sentences or phrases using alliteration and/or assonance?

Doreen Cronin's alliterative *Wiggle* (2005) and *Bounce* (2007) call for lots of action as a playful dog wiggles or bounces with toys, in water, with other animals, and in just plain silly antics. Both books can serve as examples of books the class can write together or working in groups. Many possibilities to have fun exist with action words like *jump*, *spin*, *roll*, etc. This might be an oral exercise or chart work for young students. Older students can write and illustrate books and share them with younger children in

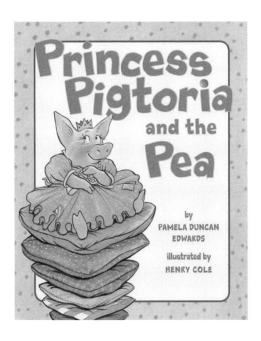

the building. The reproducible page (Chapter 1.1: Alliteration) in Appendix A might help them get started.

Gloria, (Dewdney, *Grumpy Gloria*, 2006) the family dog, is "growly" and "grumpy" when her human pays attention to a new doll. The children try many different ways to cheer her up, but Gloria maintains her grumpy mood until they finally succeed. Young children can brainstorm a string of words to relate how Gloria feels as Dewdney does when she writes that the dog is "Sullen, scowly, sulky, slumpy" or they might write a list of other things they can do to make Gloria happy once again.

Although the alliteration is exaggerated in Edwards's *Princess Pigtoria and the Pea* (2010), *Clara Caterpillar* (2004), *Some Smug Slug* (1998), and Arena's *Sally and Dave a Slug Story* (2007), it is fun for students to see how authors can create stories that have real plots and lots of suspense using this device. The vocabularies in these books are quite sophisticated, making them valuable examples for older students. After enjoying the books, students can write short, original tongue twisters. They have probably all heard "Sally sells sea shells" so a brief reminder will be all they need to get started.

Plenty of trouble ensues when Mabel blows a bubble that carries Baby away (Mahy, *Bubble Trouble*, 2009). All the townsfolk join in the chase in this rhyming, alliterative masterpiece. Read it aloud often, emphasizing the vowel and consonant sounds. Then encourage the children to write a list of ideas for getting Baby down safely.

In Cathryn Falwell's *Scoot!* (2008), the pond is teeming with life, but "six silent turtles sit still as stones" until they unexpectedly speed away. Rhyming sounds abound as the different animals flee from danger. Because Falwell provides notes on the different pond animals readers meet in the story, this book is an excellent companion to a study of pond life. Different children or groups could choose one creature to research in more depth and compile their information into an illustrated book. Use this opportunity to discuss a Table of Contents, headings, etc. It would be wonderful if the children could visit a local pond and take pictures to include in their book.

Margaret Mayo's *Roar!* (2007) combines alliteration and rhyme in a book featuring 11 kinds of animals in their natural environments doing what they do best. Elephants engage in "mud-wallowing, squishy-squashy! Squishy-squashy! Squelching." "Spunky monkeys love swing, swing, swinging, hanging, dangling, tightly clinging." Young children would enjoy acting out the different animals and

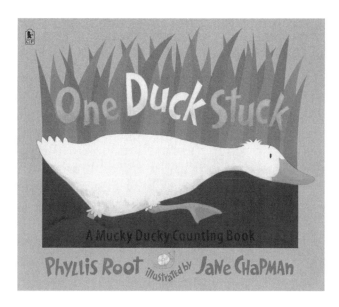

their activities. And trying to do such things as "wallow," "scamper," and "prowl" will certainly help them make these interesting words part of their working vocabularies.

### Word-Rich Concept Books

Before leaving our discussion of picture books, it is important to say a few words about concept books. Most of us use them with young children, and there are an abundance of books from which to choose. But, as previously mentioned, budgets are tight, and it makes sense to center our selections around books that, in addition to the concepts they present, offer rich language as well.

What young child can resist a stinky, smelly backhoe loader that scoops up garbage? The grubby fellow in Kate McMullan's *I'm Dirty!* (2006) has "hydraulic rams" and a "specialized, maximized, giant-sized loader bucket" with which he clears out a dump, all the while counting items in alliterative phrases such a "10 torn-up tires," "9 fractured fans," and on down to "1 wonky washing machine." Can the students think of other items for him to collect? Both familiar and unusual animals "leap," "swirl," and "twirl" their way through a beautiful day in Jeanne Modesitt's alliterative counting book (*Oh, What a Beautiful Day! A Counting Book*, 2009). The creatures in *Animal Antics from 1 to 10* (Wojtowycz 2000), another alliterative counting book, engage in some amazingly improbable activities that will have youngsters laughing while they enjoy hearing the language. More sophisticated for older students are the lovely poems in Jane Yolen's *Count Me a Rhyme* (2006). Several words are paired with each number, along with a poem and striking photograph. For example, the page for "one" contains the numeral along with the words *sole, solitaire*, and *first*. Using this book as a model, older students might engage in a photography project in which they photograph different numbers of things and create a book for their younger schoolmates. They can caption the photos or write accompanying poems as Yolen did. David A. Carter's *One Red Dot* (2004) is a stunning counting book that involves pulls and incredible pop-ups. "Five wiggle-wobble widgets" wave their way across the page while "eight obedient orbs" obligingly pop up at a page turn. Carter and James Diaz have written *Some Words about Playing Elements of Pop Up: A Pop Up Book for Aspiring Paper Engineers* (1999) for older students who want to try their own hand at creating a pop-up book. Different numbers and kinds of animals try to help one unfortunate duck get unstuck from the muck down by the "sleepy, slimy marsh" in Phyllis Root's *One Duck Stuck* (2003). Various animals "splish," "clomp," and "plunk" their way to the duck, but "no luck." He remains "still stuck." This rhyming counting book is a delight, and students will love repeatedly calling for help with the duck. Can they write in other animals to add to the story?

Exhibiting unusual behavior, a curious owl sleeps during the night and awakens at daybreak to a world of color she has never seen. The sky is a "warm and wonderful pink" and "bright orange flowers" open in the sun (Hopgood, *Wow! Said the Owl*, 2009). Although Lucy (Horáček, *A Book of Colors: Butterfly*, 2007) cannot find the butterfly she is chasing, she does discover "spotty red ladybugs scurrying around," a snail "with an orange shell, slithering," and other interesting creatures. Children will enjoy seeing the many insects and the way they are created in the illustrations using die-cut techniques. More insects dance their way through Lindsey Craig's *Dancing Feet!* (2010), their colorful feet slapping and stomping across the pages. "Tippity! Tippity!/ Little black feet!/Who is dancing/ that tippity beat?" Black insect feet and a partial insect body appear on the page to enable children to guess what insect it is before turning the page for the answer. Besides rhythm, delightfully snappy words, and insect names, this book also offers practice in recognizing colors. Concepts of color taught through stories may inspire students to create their own stories or sentences around the colors they are learning. Or begin a group story using a chart. Devote a page to each color, have groups of children illustrate the finished pages, and bind them together into a big book for the library.

In *Big, Bigger, Biggest!* (2009) Nancy Coffelt takes the concept of comparisons to a whole new level. Not only does she mention the three comparative adjectives, she also includes three additional descriptors for each comparison. For example, for "I'm slowest," accompanied by the image of a snail, she also includes "I'm sluggish./ I'm lethargic./I'm lackadaisical!" This simple book is a marvel of vocabulary expansion and can lead to all kinds of comparison games, with children coming up with additional descriptions for different creatures and objects. This is a good opportunity to discuss opposites as well. David Pelham's *Stuff and Nonsense* (2008) has all kinds of "stuff" for students to see and feel: "checked stuff," "scratchy stuff," "velvety stuff," and a surprise pop-up at the end. Create a "stuff" display made up of objects from around the room or brought from home, each accompanied by a descriptive label.

## A Few Words about Play

Perhaps one of the best ways to encourage children to revel in words is just to play with them and to study authors who have fun playing with words in the stories they write. In his article entitled "Playing with Language," Steven Engelfried writes, "a true appreciation [of language] really starts when we begin to take words apart, turn them around, mix up the letters, and look at them sideways. In other words—play" (*School*

*Library Journal*, 2004, 55). *The Word Snoop* (Dubosarsky, 2009), previously mentioned, helps students do exactly that. As the jacket flap states, "there are puzzles to solve, codes to crack, and pun-filled illustrations to decipher!" Older students, who are used to reading high fantasy novels, know that authors are so willing to play with words that they even make up entire new languages for the characters that inhabit their fantasy worlds. (See the works of J. R. R. Tolkien and Peter Dickinson as examples.) They may wish to take up Dubosarsky's invitation (pp. 15–18) to invent their own alphabet—or their own language—for their fantasy stories. Even students who shy away from books will not be able to put *The Word Snoop* down, and they will be creating and learning about words as they go. Companion books that provide even more examples of the word play and games Dubosarsky discusses are several books by Jon Agee such as: *Go Hang a Salami! I'm a Lasagna Hog!: And Other Palindromes* (1994), *Smart Feller Fart Smeller: And Other Spoonerisms* (2006), and *Palindromania!* (2002, 2009). Humorous line drawings will have students laughing as well as eager to take a crack at creating their own language jokes. Agee's *Orangutan Tongs* (2009) might well be discussed in the poetry section because it is a book of poems. But it is a perfect choice when discussing word play as well. Agee's genius shines in poems that are filled with alliteration, tongue twisters, and excellent word choices such as "zither" and "surly." Students will

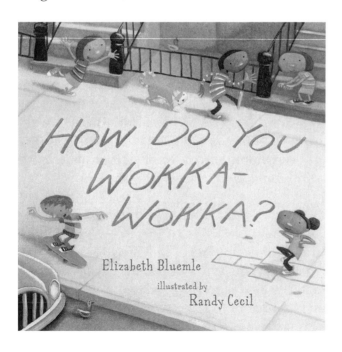

laugh aloud as they drink in these witty gems. In Mark Shulman's *Mom and Dad Are Palindromes* (2006) poor Bob discovers that he is a palindrome and that he is surrounded by palindromes wherever he goes. Children will enjoy uncovering the 101 palindromes hidden within the text and illustrations. If they are alert, they will soon discover that the author has given them very visible hints.

Nonsense words will be easier for younger children to play with than some of the more sophisticated language fun contained in the books discussed in the previous paragraph. In *How Do You Wokka-Wokka?* (Bluemle 2009), a young boy invites his

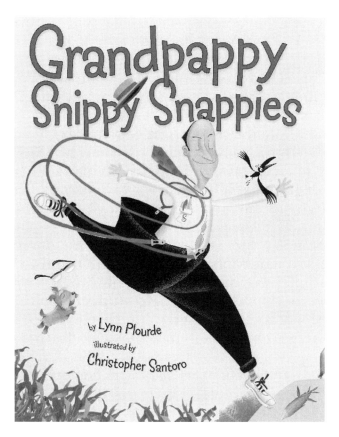

neighbors, "Hey, let's wokka-wokka/ shimmy-shake, and shocka-shocka," and they all proceed to make their fancy moves across the pages. They wokka-wokka like clocks, going "picka-pocka-ticka-tocka"; like "fish-flop" or a door "knocka-knocka" until more and more children join in the wokka-wokka party. Finally, looking right at the reader, the children shout, "Yeh, ya gotta wokka!"—a perfect invitation for children to create their own nonsense words and accompanying movements. Guaranteed fun! More nonsense is afoot in Lynn Plourde's *Grandpappy Snippy Snappies* (2009). When he "snippy snappies" his suspenders, Grandpappy can accomplish marvelous feats like saving derailed trains and getting cows unstuck from the muck. But just when Grandmammy needs rescuing, his suspenders lose their snap and he must resort to another very humorous method. Rhyming text, made-up words—the cows "boing-a-moing-a-mooooooooo" out of the muck, for example—make this a great read-aloud. What other catastrophes can the children think of for Grandpappy to remedy once he gets new suspenders?

Fun awaits students in Helen Lester's *Batter up Wombat* (2008) and Fred Gwynne's *A Chocolate Moose for Dinner* (2005). Both books demonstrate the pitfalls of taking some words and sayings literally. In Lester's picture book, a losing baseball team mistakenly believes a wombat who wanders onto their field is a "whambat" and eagerly sign him on. But the wombat has no idea how baseball is played and takes every word to heart verbatim fearing, for example, that he will actually have to hit somebody when he is told he's the next hitter. Gwynne's comical illustrations depict what a little girl thinks as she hears some of the things the adults around her say. The double-page spread for, "He spent two years in the pen" shows the girl and her dog looking at a man reading the paper inside a giant fountain pen. Read either or both books aloud just for fun so that young students can experience how enjoyable the results can be when an author is brave enough to play with language.

Denise Doyen's *Once Upon a Twice* (2009) is a luscious example of more intricate nonsense that will reach both younger and older students on different levels. Read it aloud once so that they can enjoy the story, a tense adventure in which a young, daring mouse ignores the warnings of his elders and almost becomes a snake's tasty meal. Then read it again, asking students to savor the language, for in this text they will encounter invented words that contain a wealth of meaning. These made-up words are not only music to the ears; they also extend the meaning of the sentences

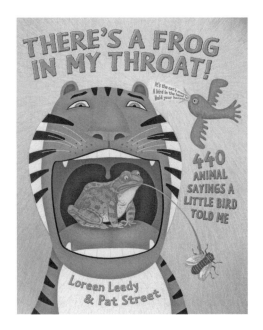

in which they appear—nonsense with a purpose. For example, the mouse who ignores warnings to be careful is dubbed a "riskarascal" and his elders scold, "You brought our scamper to a drag!/ Dropped *preycautions*, raised a flag!" Discuss the word *preycautions* with students. It contains the word *prey*—mice are prey for so many larger creatures—and *caution*—therefore, they must always be cautious. So many other words like this merit being singled out for sheer enjoyment and for the way they enrich the drama of this wonderful story. What is the meaning of the unusual title and the young mouse's name? Use the reproducible entitled Chapter 1.2: Nonsense Words in *Once Upon a Twice* in Appendix A to help students look at these words more closely. They may then wish to work in groups to write a story or paragraph in which they create such words themselves.

Aunt Ant, presently residing at the zoo, sends Deer notes filled with homophones that describe the various animal antics she sees (Barretta, *Dear Deer: A Book of Homophones*, 2007). "Have YOU seen the EWE?/ She's been in a DAZE for DAYS," she observes. Humorous illustrations help readers understand the different meanings of these sound-alike words. Students might enjoy sending illustrated letters to a neighboring class describing their activities, real or imaginary, and using as many homophones as they can. For example, "Mary's WHOLE apple fell in a HOLE at recess."

Idioms are, perhaps, among the most perplexing language puzzles for young children who tend to take in information quite literally, and for second language learners as well. Loreen Leedy's *There's a Frog in My Throat!* (2003) and Will Moses's *Raining Cats & Dogs* (2008) are two books that can help make learning idioms fun and can spark many follow-up activities. Both books contain many idioms with their meanings, examples of how they are used, and humorous illustrations that show the idioms taken literally. After enjoying these books, older students can go to this website: http://www.pride-unlimited.com/probono/idioms1.html to discover the origins of many different idioms. For example, they will learn that "blowing off steam" really means "To enjoy oneself by relaxing normal formalities," and that it is based on the fact that steam-operated systems build up pressure that must be released, "blown off," to prevent explosions—much as humans experiencing pressure must occasionally relax or "blow off steam."

*Crazy like a Fox* (Leedy 2008) is a story made up entirely of similes. For example, it begins, "In the quiet forest, Rufus is sleeping like. . . . " A page turn reveals the completion of the simile: " . . . a log." And the story continues in similar fashion. At the end, Leedy encourages readers to make up their own similes and even turn them into one continuous story. Her full-page author's note gives them a good deal of information to help them get started.

Amy Krouse Rosenthal's *The Wonder Book* (2010) is a combination of poems, palindromes, stories, word games, and just plain fun. It offers all kinds of opportunities

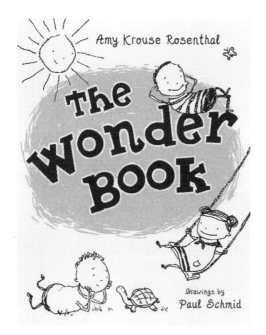

for students to engage in word play. Consider what the author does with the days of the week. For example, Tuesday is written "Twos Day," accompanied by the illustration of a girl seeing her reflection from a rowboat. Students can make their own amusing "Days of the Week" or "Months of the Year" books, working alone or in groups. This is only one example of the many enjoyable writing activities Rosenthal's book can inspire.

Finally, saved for this section are two books that, although they could come under a discussion of poetry, are also examples of the wonders a writer can achieve by being willing to take a risk—to play with words in unusual ways. Absolutely brilliant is Marilyn Singer's *Mirror Mirror: A Book of Reversible Verse* (2010). All the poems are based on fairy tales and can be read beginning from the top or beginning with the last word and reading up. They are reverse images of themselves. It is difficult to praise this book too highly. It would be the perfect book to pair with a unit on fairy tales or to use anytime older students are up for a real challenge. Can they write some mirror poems, either on a single theme that coincides with a unit of study or any topic they wish? This might best be done in groups because it is not an easy task. But the results could be surprising and very satisfying. Several books of acrostic poetry are available; that is, poetry in which a name or word(s) are discovered by reading some letters down the poem. One of the most recent is Avis Harley's *African Acrostics* (2009). Writing acrostic poems is another adventure in word play that older students might enjoy after they have examined several books as examples. In end matter Harley offers some hints about how to create such poems:

Think of a word, phrase, or even a whole sentence that catches your imagination. Then write it vertically. You can use one word per line, or many words—rhymed or unrhymed. A predetermined letter can sometimes spark an unexpected idea, and it's great fun to hide a word or message for your readers!

So let the fun begin. Play with words, arrange and rearrange them, pay attention to how they feel in your mouth; listen to how they sound in your ears; see how they look on the page. Words—wonderful words—are truly the writer's tools, the building blocks of writing that moves us, awes us, and keeps us reading.

## References

Agee, Jon. 1994. *Go Hang a Salami! I'm a Lasagna Hog!: And Other Palindromes*. New York: Farrar, Straus and Giroux, 1994. ISBN 978-0374444730.
   Sixty palindromes accompanied by very funny literal drawings make this book great fun.

Agee, Jon. 2009. *Orangutan Tongs*. New York: Hyperion. ISBN 1423103157.
   Agee's collection of humorous poems has everything: word play, alliteration, tongue twisters, and very funny illustrations.

Agee, Jon. 2009 (reprint ed). *Palindromania!* New York: Sunburst. ISBN 978-0374400255. (Orig. pub. 2002 by Farrar Straus Giroux.)
   Readers will have clues to unlock and even famous personalities to meet as they read the funny stories in this, Agee's fourth collection of palindromes.

Agee, Jon. 2006. *Smart Feller Fart Smeller: And Other Spoonerisms*. New York: Hyperion. ISBN 078683692X.
   Students will learn what a spoonerism is and be treated to many funny examples that are illustrated with humorous cartoons.

Arena, Felice. 2007. *Sally and Dave a Slug Story*. La Jolla, CA: Kane Miller. ISBN 978-1-933605-71-5.
   Sally is far more stunning than Dave, but when the chips are down, she discovers just how sensational he is.

Attenborough, Liz, comp. 2001. *Poetry by Heart: A Child's Book of Poems to Remember*. Various Illustrators. New York: Scholastic/Chicken House. ISBN 978-0439296571.
   This valuable collection, beautifully illustrated by different artists, contains many classics.

Banks, Kate. 2006. *Max's Words*. Illustrated by Boris Kulikov. New York: Frances Foster. ISBN 978-0-374-39949-8.
   Max collects all kinds of words and eventually uses them in a story.

Barretta, Gene. 2007. *Dear Deer: A Book of Homophones*. New York: Henry Holt. ISBN 978-0-8050-8104-6.
   In a letter filled with homophones, an ant writes about what animals are doing in the zoo.

Bartoletti, Susan Campbell. 2005. *Nobody's Diggier than a Dog*. Illustrated by Beppe Giacobbe. New York: Hyperion (o.p. but readily available at this printing at bargain prices). ISBN 0-7868-1824-7.
   The dogs in this delightful book engage in all kinds of antics.

Bleck, Linda. 2009. *A Children's Treasury of Mother Goose*. New York: Sterling Children's Books. ISBN 978-1-402744990.
   Bleck illustrates several popular nursery rhymes.

Bluemle, Elizabeth. 2009. *How Do You Wokka-Wokka?* Illustrated by Randy Cecil. Somerville, MA: Candlewick. ISBN 978-0-7636-3228-1.
   A young boy invites his friends to join him in some wacky moves as they gather for a celebration.

Bosman, Julie. "Picture Books No Longer a Staple for Children." *New York Times*, Oct. 7, 2010, 1.
   Bosman discusses the apparent current unpopularity of chilcren's picture books.

Boswell, Addie. 2008. *The Rain Stomper*. Illustrated by Eric Velasquez. Tarrytown, NY: Marshall Cavendish. ISBN 978-0-7614-5393-2.
   Addie tries to stomp away the rain so her parade can take place.

Brandenberg, Alexa. 1997. *Chop Simmer Season*. San Diego: Harcourt. o.p. ISBN 978-0152009731.
Kitchen workers prepare the food in a restaurant and clean up at the end of the day.

Cabrera, Jane. *Kitty's Cuddles*. 2007. New York: Holiday House. ISBN 978-0-8234-2066-7.
Kitty looks for her favorite kind of cuddle.

Carter, David A. 2004. *One Red Dot*. New York: Little Simon/Simon & Schuster. ISBN 978-0-87769-8.
The amazing pulls and pop-ups in this book turn counting into a wonderful experience.

Carter, David A., and James Diaz. 1999. *Some Words about Playing Elements of Pop Up: A Pop Up Book for Aspiring Paper Engineers*. New York: Little Simon/Simon & Schuster. ISBN 978-0689822247.
The authors offer a history of pop-ups, 50 pop-up models, and photographs showing how pop-ups are made.

Chamberlain, Margaret. 2008. *Please Don't Tease Tootsie*. New York: Dutton. ISBN 978-0-525-47982-6.
Marvelous words paired with humorous illustrations describe how we should and should not treat our pets.

Coffelt, Nancy. 2009. *Big, Bigger, Biggest!* New York: Henry Holt. ISBN 978-0-8050-8089-6.
Comparisons are expanded to include even more descriptions in this marvelous book.

Cousins, Lucy. 2008. *Hooray for Fish!* Cambridge, MA: Candlewich. ISBN 978-0763639181.
All kinds of fish swim throughout the pages of this book.

Craig, Lindsey. 2010. *Dancing Feet!* Illustrated by Marc Brown. New York: Knopf. ISBN 978-0-375-86181-9.
Insects with different colored feet dance their way across these pages.

Cronin, Doreen. 2005. *Wiggle*. Illustrated by Scott Menchin. New York: Atheneum. ISBN 0-689-86375-6.
A lively dog wiggles in many different ways in this alliterative, rhyming book.

Cronin, Doreen. 2007. *Bounce*. Illustrated by Scott Menchin. New York: Atheneum. ISBN 978-1416916277.
A lively dog bounces in many different ways in this alliterative, rhyming book.

Cullinan, Bernice E., and Deborah Wooten, eds. 2009. *Another Jar of Tiny Stars: Poems by More NCTE Award-Winning Poets*. Honesdale, PA: Wordsong/Boyds Mills. ISBN 978-1-59078-726-7.
Some poems written by each of the 15 poets who have received the NCTE Poetry Award appear in this book along with brief biographies of the poets.

dePaola, Tomie. 2009. *My First Mother Goose*. New York: Grosset & Dunlap. ISBN 978-0448451992.
This book has several rhymes accompanied by dePaola's familiar illustrations.

Dewdney, Anna. 2006. *Grumpy Gloria*. New York: Viking. ISBN 0-670-06123-9.
Gloria, a dog, is out of sorts because her owner has received a new doll.

Dodd, Emma. 2009. *I Don't Want a Posh Dog!* Boston: Little Brown. ISBN 978-0-316-03390-9.
A little girl talks about the kinds of dogs she does not want until she finds one that suits her.

Dodd, Emma. 2010. *I Don't Want a Cool Cat!* Boston: Little Brown. ISBN 978-0-316-03674-0.
A little girl talks about all the kinds of cats she does not want until she finds one that suits perfectly.

Dodd, Emma. 2010. *I Love Bugs!* New York: Holiday House. ISBN 978-0-8234-2280-7.
  A little girl talks about all the different kinds of bugs she loves.

Doyen, Denise. 2009. *Once Upon a Twice.* Illustrated by Barry Moser. New York: Random House. ISBN 978-0-85612-9.
  A young mouse ignores his elders' warnings and almost meets his doom.

Draper, Sharon M. 2010. *Out of My Mind.* New York: Atheneum.
  Melody, a girl with cerebral palsy who cannot speak, loves words and manages to find a way to express the brilliant ideas and words locked in her mind.

Dubosarsky, Ursula. 2009. *The Word Snoop: A Wild and Witty Tour of the English Language!* Illustrated by Tohby Riddle. New York: Dial. ISBN 978-0-8037-3406-7.
  This wonderfully readable book traces the history of the English language and involves students in puzzles, codes, games, and much more to explore its inner workings.

Edwards, Pamela Duncan. 1998. *Some Smug Slug.* Illustrated by Henry Cole. New York: Katherine Tegen. ISBN 978-0064435024 (pb).
  A silly slug has no idea about the serious danger he will soon be in.

Edwards, Pamela Duncan. 2004. *Clara Caterpillar.* Illustrated by Henry Cole. New York: HarperCollins. ISBN 978-0064436915 (pb).
  Different insects coax cautious Clara to come out of her egg.

Edwards, Pamela Duncan. 2010. *Princess Pigtoria and the Pea.* Illustrated by Henry Cole. New York: Orchard/Scholastic.
  In this funny take-off on the fairy tale, Princess Pigtoria tries to find a rich prince so she can redecorate her shabby palace.

Elliott, David. 2010. *In the Wild.* Illustrated by Holly Meade. Somerville, MA: Candlewick. ISBN 978-0-7636-4497-0.
  Elliott's 14 poems about wild animals are accompanied by gorgeous double-page woodblock and watercolor illustrations.

Engelbreit, Mary. 2008. *Mary Engelbreit's Merry Mother Goose.* New York: HarperFestival. ISBN 978-0060081287.
  Engelbreit illustrates six classic Mother Goose rhymes.

Engelfried, Steven. 2004. "Playing with Language." *School Library Journal* 50(6): 55.
  The author discusses the importance of word play in developing literacy and cites children's books that feature playing with words.

Falwell, Cathryn. 2008. *Scoot!* New York: Greenwillow. ISBN 978-0-06-128883-8.
  While creatures move around them, six turtles remain sitting silently on a stone.

Fleming, Denise. 2008. *Barnyard Banter.* New York: Henry Holt, 2008. ISBN 978-0805087789.
  Fleming's unique pulp paper art depicts different animals in their homes on the farm along with a rhyming, sound-filled text.

Ford, Bernette. 2005. *First Snow.* Illustrated by Sebastien Braun. New York: Holiday House. ISBN 0-8234-1937-1.
  A bunny family ventures out into the first snow of the season.

Fox, Mem. 2004. *Where Is the Green Sheep?* Illustrated by Judy Horacek. San Diego: Harcourt. ISBN 978-0152049072.
  This book has little ones hunting for a green sheep while delighting in the rhyme, the colors, and the bouncy rhythms that Fox's text provides.

Frasier, Debra. 2000. *Miss Alaineus: A Vocabulary Disaster*. San Diego: Harcourt. ISBN 978-160686192-9.
Sage mistakes a vocabulary word, with hilarious results.

Frasier, Debra. 2010. *A Fabulous Fair Alphabet*. New York: Beach Lane/Simon & Schuster. ISBN 978-1416998174.
The author uses decorative letters photographed at the fair to form words for each letter of the alphabet.

Freedman, Deborah. 2007. *Scribble*. New York: Knopf/Random House. ISBN 978-0375839665.
After drawing a scribble cat on her older sister's drawing of a princess, Lucie follows Scribble into the picture and tries to set things right.

Gal, Susan. 2009. *Night Lights*. New York: Knopf. ISBN 978-0-375-85862-8.
While preparing for bed, a young girl notices the many different kinds of light that shine in the evening.

Gardiner, Lindsey. 2000. *Here Come Poppy and Max*. Boston: Little, Brown (o.p. but readily available at bargain prices at this printing). ISBN 0-316-60346-5.
Different animals engage in all kinds of activities.

The Global Fund for Children. 2001. *Global Babies*. Watertown, MA: Charlesbridge. ISBN 978-1-58089-174-5.
This book introduces babies from 17 different countries around the world.

Gopnik, Alison. 2009. "Your Baby Is Smarter than You Think." *New York Times*, August 16, Week in Review, 10.
Gopnik cites research and experiments that demonstrate how babies and young children learn.

Gwynne, Fred. 2005. *A Chocolate Moose for Dinner*. New York: Aladdin/Simon & Schuster. ISBN 0-689-82827-3. (pb)
Humorous illustrations depict literal interpretations of several expressions.

Harley, Avis. 2009. *African Acrostics*. Photographs by Deborah Noyes. Somerville, MA: Candlewick. ISBN 978-0-7636-3621-0.
Harley provides many acrostic poems about African animals that are accompanied by beautiful photographs.

Hoberman, Mary Ann. 2003. *And to Think That We Thought That We'd Never Be Friends*. Illustrated by Kevin Hawkes. New York: Dragonfly. ISBN 978-0440417767(pb).
Just when fights or disturbances seem unsolvable, someone intervenes to make things better.

Hoberman, Mary Ann. 2006. *The Llama Who Had No Pajama*. Illustrated by Betty Fraser. FL: Sandpiper. ISBN 978-0152055714 (pb).
The poems in this volume have been collected from several of Hoberman's other books. This is a key book for every home and classroom.

Holbrook, Sara. 2010. *Zombies! Evacuate the School!* Illustrated by Karen Sandstrom. Honesdale, PA: Wordsong/Boyds Mills. ISBN 978-1-59078-820-2.
Holbrook writes poems about school life and gives students suggestions for writing their own poems.

Hopgood, Tim. 2009. *Wow! Said the Owl*. New York: Farrar, Straus and Giroux. ISBN 978-0-374-38518-7.
A curious owl awakens during the day to a new world of color.

Hopkins, Lee Bennett, sel. 2004. *Wonderful Words: Poems about Reading, Writing, Speaking, and Listening*. New York: Simon & Schuster. ISBN 0-689-83588-4.
  The marvelous poems in this book are perfect for introducing any lesson on the language arts.

Horáček, Peter. 2007. *A Book of Colors: Butterfly*. Cambridge, MA: Candlewick. ISBN 978-0-76363343-1.
  While chasing a butterfly, Lucy discovers all kinds of colorful insects.

Iyengar, Malathi Michelle. 2009. *Tan to Tamarind: Poems about the Color Brown*. Illustrated by Jamel Akib. San Francisco, CA: Children's Book Press.
  This poetry collection celebrates all the different shades of brown and where they are found in the world.

Joosse, Barbara. 2010. "Razzmatazz: Books That Engage and Delight the Very Youngest listeners." *School Library Journal*, 56(8): 18–19.
  Joosse discusses the kinds of books that appeal to babies and very young children.

Kurtz, Jane. 2002. *Rain Romp: Stomping Away a Grouchy Day*. Illustrated by Dyanna Wolcott. New York: Greenwillow/HarperCollins. ISBN 0-06-029805-7.
  A little girl starts out the day as a grouch but cheers up when she gets to splash in the rain.

Laden, Nina. 2000. *Peek-a Who?* San Francisco, CA: Chronicle Books. ISBN 978-0811826020.
  This rhyming book enables children to guess what will appear on the next page after viewing a visual clue and considering the rhyme.

LaFave, Kim, Marie-Louise Gay, et al. 2009. *Mother Goose*. Toronto, Canada: Groundwood. ISBN 978-0888999337.
  Each of the 16 rhymes in this book is on a double-page spread and illustrated by a different Canadian artist.

Leedy, Loreen. 2003. *There's a Frog in My Throat!: 440 Animal Sayings a Little Bird Told Me*. New York: Holiday House. ISBN 978-0823418190. (pb)
  This book is filled with idioms involving animals, their meanings, and humorous illustrations featuring literal interpretations.

Leedy, Loreen. 2008. *Crazy like a Fox: A Simile Story*. New York: Holiday House. ISBN 978-0-8234-1719-3.
  Leedy writes a story completely in similes about a fox who is up to no good.

Lester, Helen. 2008. *Batter up Wombat*. Illustrated by Lynn Munsinger. New York: Sandpiper. ISBN 978-0547015491. (pb)
  A wombat who knows nothing about baseball takes every directive literally.

Lewis, Kevin. 2006. *Tugga-Tugga Tugboat*. Illustrated by Daniel Kirk. New York: Disney/Hyperion. ISBN 978-1-4231-1581-6.
  Alliterative text describes the activities of a little tugboat.

Ljungkvist, Laura. 2010. *Pepi Sings a New Song*. New York: Beach Lane/Simon & Schuster. ISBN 978-1-4169-9138-0.
  Pepi the parrot discovers new words in his quest to find something new to sing about.

London, Jonathan. 1999. *Puddles*. Illustrated by G. Brian Karas. New York: Puffin. ISBN 978-0140561753 (reprinted paper edition).
  Children delight in playing after a rainstorm.

London, Jonathan. 2010. *I Am a Truck Driver.* Illustrated by David Parkins. New York: Henry Holt. ISBN 978-0805079890.
A boy and girl make all kinds of truck sounds as they drive different kinds of vehicles.

MacNeil, Robert. 1989. *Wordstruck: A Memoir.* New York: Penguin. o.p. ISBN 0-670-81871-2.
The author discusses how growing up in a word-loving family where reading aloud was a daily event made him the "wordstruck" adult he is today.

Maddox, Marjorie. 2009. *A Crossing of Zebras: Animal Packs in Poetry.* Illustrations by Philip Huber. ISBN 978-1-59078-510-2.
Fourteen poems help students learn the collective nouns for different groups of animals.

Mahy, Margaret. 2009. *Bubble Trouble.* Illustrated by Polly Dunbar. New York: Clarion. ISBN 978-0-547-07421-4.
A town tries to rescue Baby when he is carried away in a bubble.

Mayo, Margaret. 2007. *Roar!* Minneapolis, MN: Carolrhoda. ISBN 978-0-7613-9473-0.
Eleven animals engage in their typical behaviors in this rhyming, alliterative text.

McCue, Lisa. 2009. *My First Mother Goose.* New York: Reader's Digest. ISBN 978-0794419318.
This collection of familiar rhymes has a handle so little ones can carry it with them.

McMullan, Kate. 2006. *I'm Dirty.* Illustrated by Jim McMullan. Joanna Cotler/HarperCollins. ISBN 978-0-06-009293-1.
A backhoe loader clears out garbage in this counting book. Also see *I Stink!*, an alphabet book in the same vein, by these authors.

Merz, Jennifer J. 2007. *Playground Day!* New York: Clarion. ISBN 978-0-618-81696-5.
Children imitate different animals as they have fun on the playground.

Michael, Pamela, ed. 2008. *River of Words: Young Poets and Artists on the Nature of Things.* Minnesota: Milkweed. ISBN 978-1571316806.
This is a collection of poems and art work about water done by children of all ages.

Miura, Taro. 2005. *Tools.* San Francisco, CA: Chronicle. ISBN 978-0-8118-5519-8.
Two-page spreads provide illustrated examples of tools used by different kinds of workers.

Modesitt, Jeanne. 2009. *Oh, What a Beautiful Day! A Counting Book.* Illustrated by Robin Spowart. Honesdale, PA: Boyds Mills Press. ISBN 078-1-56397-409-0.
A little girl sees different animals having fun on a beautiful day.

Mordhorst, Heidi. 2009. *Pumpkin Butterfly: Poems from the Other Side of Nature.* Illustrated by Jenny Reynish. Honesdale, PA: Wordsong. ISBN 978-1-59078-620-8.
This is a collection of 23 poems about the natural world.

Moses, Will. 2008. *Raining Cats & Dogs: A Collection of Irresistible Idioms and Illustrations to Tickle the Funny Bones of Young People.* New York: Philomel/Penguin. ISBN 978-0-399-24233-5.
This book contains many idioms, their meanings, examples of their use, and humorous folk art–style illustrations that interpret the idioms literally.

Newbery, Linda. 2008. *Posy.* Illustrated by Catherine Rayner. New York: Atheneum. ISBN 978-1-4169-7112-2.
A kitten gets into all kinds of mischief.

O'Connor, Jane. 2008. *Fancy Nancy's Favorite Fancy Words from Accessories to Zany.* Illustrated by Robin Preiss Glasser. New York: HarperCollins. ISBN 978-0-06-154923-6.
Fancy Nancy makes using fancy words fun.

Ogburn, Jacqueline K. 2010. *A Dignity of Dragons: Collective Nouns for Magical Beasts*. Illustrated by Nicoletta Ceccoli. Boston/New York: Houghton Mifflin Harcourt. ISBN 978-0-618-86254-2.
Readers meet a collection of fanciful creatures. Back matter provides additional information on each of the beasts featured.

Olson-Brown, Ellen. 2010. *Ooh La La Polka-Dot Boots*. Illustrated by Christiane Engel. Berkeley, CA: Tricycle Press. ISBN 978-1-58246-287-5.
All kinds of outfits look better with polka-dot boots.

Patricelli, Leslie. 2009. *The Birthday Box*. Somerville, MA: Candlewick Press. ISBN 978-0763644499.
A toddler receives a box as a birthday gift and the child, along with the stuffed animal inside, uses the box for all sorts of adventures.

Paul, Ann Whitford. 2009. *Word Builder*. Illustrated by Kurt Cyrus. New York: Simon & Schuster. ISBN 978-1-4169-3981-8.
The author shows how using words to make sentences and paragraphs eventually leads to the creation of a book.

Pelham, David. 2008. *Stuff and Nonsense*. New York: Little Simon/Simon & Schuster. ISBN 978-1-4169-5907-6.
All kinds of "stuff" are labeled with interesting descriptive words.

Plourde, Lynn. 2009. *Grandpappy Snippy Snappies*. Illustrated by Christopher Santoro. New York: HarperCollins. ISBN 978-0-028050-5.
Grandpappy can accomplish wonderful rescues when he snippy snaps his suspenders, until they run out of elasticity.

Rand, Ann and Paul. 2006. *Sparkle and Spin: A Book about Words*. San Francisco, CA: Chronicle. ISBN 978-0-8118-5003-2.
Rhythmic, rhyming text sings the praises of all kinds of words.

Ray, Mary Lyn. 2001. *Mud*. Illustrated by Lauren Stringer. Florida: Sandpiper. ISBN 978-0152024611. (pb)
Ray writes beautifully about the start of spring when the snow melts and the earth turns to mud.

Root, Phyllis. 2003. *One Duck Stuck*. Illustrated by Jane Chapman. Somerville, MA: Candlewick. ISBN 978-0763615666. (pb)
Different animals try to get duck unstuck from the muck.

Root, Phyllis. 2008. *Looking for a Moose*. Illustrated by Randy Cecil. Somerville, MA: Candlewick. ISBN 978-0763638856. (pb)
A group of children go through the woods looking for a moose.

Rosenthal, Amy Krause. 2010. *One Smart Cookie: Bite-Size Lessons for the School Years and Beyond*. Illustrated by Jane Dyer and Brooke Dyer. New York: HarperCollins. ISBN 978-0-06-142970-5.
The author discusses such words as *arrogant* and *ponder* as they pertain to getting along with others as well as making cookies.

Rosenthal, Amy Krause. 2010. *The Wonder Book*. Illustrated by Paul Schmid. New York: Harper/HarperCollins.
This book is filled with poems, stories, palindromes, word games, and more.

Ryan, Pam Muños. 2010. *The Dreamer*. Illustrated by Peter Sis. New York: Scholastic. ISBN 978-0-439-24970-4.
A perfect marriage of words and illustration tells the story of poet Pablo Neruda's difficult childhood in Chile.

San José, Christine, and Bill Johnson, sel. 2009. *Every Second Something Happens: Poems for the Mind and Senses*. Illustrated by Melanie Hall. Honesdale, PA: Wordsong. ISBN 978-1-59078-622-2.
This collection of poems helps readers experience the world through their minds and senses.

Schaefer, Lola M. 2006. *Toolbox Twins*. Illustrated by Melissa Iwai. New York: Henry Holt. ISBN 978-0-8050-7733-2.
Vincent and his dad use tools to accomplish different projects.

Schindel, John. 2009. *Busy Chickens*. Illustrated by Steven Holt. Berkeley, CA: Ten Speed Press/Tricycle Press. ISBN 978-1-58246-275-2
Busy chickens engage in a variety of interesting activities. Colorful, uncluttered illustrations accompany each word pair.

Schoenherr, Ian. 2010. *Don't Spill the Beans!* New York: Greenwillow/HarperCollins. ISBN 978-0-06-1724570-2.
A bear receives many different warnings about not giving away a birthday secret.

Schotter, Roni. 2006. *The Boy Who Loved Words*. Illustrated by Giselle Potter. New York: Random House/Schwartz & Wade. ISBN 0-375-83601-2.
Selig has collected so many wonderful words that he travels in search of people who can use them.

Seder, Rufus Butler. 2007. *Gallop!* New York: Workman. ISBN 978-0761147633.
Animals seem to move across the page in a special Scanimation process that produces a stunning result.

Seder, Rufus Butler. 2009. *Waddle!* New York: Workman. ISBN 978-0761151128.
Seder adds color to enhance his moving animals.

Serfozo, Mary. 2004. *Plumply, Dumply Pumpkin*. Illustrated by Valeria Petrone. New York: Aladdin. ISBN 978-0689871351 (pb).
Peter looks for the perfect pumpkin to use for a very special project.

Shea, Pegi Deitz. 2009. *Noah Webster Weaver of Words*. Illustrated by Monica Vachula. Honesdale, PA: Calkins Creek. ISBN 978-1-59078-441-9.
This marvelous biography recounts the amazing life of a man who taught himself many languages and worked tirelessly to create a dictionary that would reflect the richness of the English language.

Shulman, Mark. 2006. *Mom and Dad Are Palindromes*. Illustrated by Adam McCauley. San Francisco, CA: Chronicle. ISBN 978-0-8118-4328-7.
After Bob's teacher tells him he is a palindrome, life is never the same as he discovers palindromes all around him.

Singer, Marilyn. 2006. *Let's Build a Clubhouse*. Illustrated by Timothy Bush. New York: Clarion. ISBN 978-0-618-30670-1.
A group of friends builds a clubhouse.

Singer, Marilyn. 2010. *Mirror Mirror: A Book of Reversible Verse*. Illustrated by Josee Massee. New York: Dutton. ISBN 978-0525479017.

This collection of poems is based on fairy tales that are mirror images of themselves, reading from top to bottom or bottom to top.

Sis, Peter. 2001. *Ballerina!* New York: Greenwillow/HarperCollins. ISBN 0-688-17944-4.
Terry performs some ballet moves.

Snyder, Betsy. 2008. *Haiku Baby.* New York: Random House. ISBN 978-0375843952.
Musical haiku poems celebrate the natural world.

Snyder, Betsy. 2009. *Have You Ever Tickled a Tiger?* New York: Random House. ISBN 978-0-375-84396-9.
Youngsters can feel various parts of animals such as the feathers on an ostrich.

Spinelli, Eileen. 2004. *Do YOU Have a Hat?* Illustrated by Geraldo Valério. New York: Simon & Schuster. ISBN 0-689-86253-9.
Spinelli celebrates famous people's hats in verse.

Spurr, Elizabeth. 2001. *Pumpkin Hill.* Illustrated by Whitney Martin. New York: Holiday House. ISBN 0-8234-1869-3.
A pumpkin's seeds scatter and grow into hundreds of pumpkins that create chaos and excitement in the town.

Stainton, Sue. 2007. *I Love Cats.* Illustrated by Anne Mortimer. New York: HarperCollins/Katherine Tegen Books. ISBN 978-0060851545.
Cats of all descriptions are the objects of this narrator's delight.

Sutton, Robert, and Martha V. Parravano. 2010. *A Family of Readers: The Book Lover's Guide to Children's and Young Adult Literature.* Forward by Gregory Maguire. Somerville, MA: Candlewick Press.
The authors and various contributors discuss the various genres of children's and young adult literature and criteria for choosing the best of each category.

Van Fleet, Matthew. 2003. *Tails.* San Diego: Harcourt Inc, 2003. ISBN 978-0152167738.
This rhyming book describes all kinds of tails and provides activities with flaps and pulls.

Van Fleet, Matthew. 2007. *Dogs.* Photography by Brian Stanton. New York: Simon & Schuster. ISBN 978-1-4169-4137-8.
Interesting words describe the many dogs in this interactive board book.

Van Fleet, Matthew. 2009. *Cats.* Photography by Brian Stanton. New York: Simon & Schuster, 2009. ISBN 978-1-4169-7800-8.
Interesting words describe the many cats in this interactive board book.

Van Fleet, Matthew. 2010. *Heads.* New York: Paula Wiseman/Simon & Schuster. ISBN 978-1-4424-0379-6.
Van Fleet depicts many different kinds of animal heads and their appendages.

Wattenberg, Jane. 2007. *Mrs. Mustard's Baby Faces*, rev. ed. San Francisco, CA: Chronicle Books. ISBN 978-0811859677.
This accordion-shaped board book presents seven babies, each displaying two different emotions.

Wojtowycz, David. 2000. *Animal Antics from 1 to 10.* New York: Holiday House. ISBN 0-8234-1552-X.
In this alliterative counting book, animals at a resort engage in amusing activities.

Wright, Blanche Fisher. 2001. *The Real Mother Goose Touch & Feel Book*. New York: Scholastic/ Cartwheel. ISBN 0-439-25481-7.

> Children can touch parts of the animals depicted in these rhymes and even smell the cake in "Pat-a-Cake."

Yolen, Jane. 2006. *Count Me a Rhyme*. Photographs by Jason Stemple. Honesdale, PA: WordSong/Boyds Mills. ISBN 978-1590783450.

> Poems, beautiful photographs, and several words for each number grace this beautiful counting book.

Ziefert, Harriet. 2005. *Beach Party!* Illustrated by Simms Taback. Maplewood, NJ: Blue Apple/ Chronicle. ISBN 978-1593540678.

> Eleven animals slither and slide as they make their way to the water.

Ziefert, Harriet. 2006. *Grandma, It's for You!* Illustrated by Lauren Browne. Maplewood, NJ: Blue Apple/Chronicle. ISBN 978-1-59354-109-5.

> Lulu creates the perfect hat for her grandmother. Add activities and games occasionally and you engage students in a variety of ways that will surely make an impact.

# 2

## Taking Some of the "Chore" Out of Writing

*People on the outside think there's something magical about writing, that you go up in the attic at midnight and cast the bones and come down in the morning with a story, but it isn't like that. You sit in back of the typewriter and you work, and that's all there is to it.*

—Harlan Ellison

Ann Mazer says, "Writing is some of the hardest work in the world. I call it 'mental rock breaking'" (Mazer and Potter, *Spilling Ink*, 2010, 241). Donald Murray was a Pulitzer Prize winner, an author of several books as well as a column in the *Boston Globe* for two decades, and taught writing at the University of New Hampshire. Yet, just five days before his death at age 82, this mentor to countless aspiring writers wrote, "Each time I sit down to write I don't know if I can do it. The flow of writing is always a surprise and a challenge. Click the computer on and I am 17 again, wanting to write and not knowing if I can" (In Marquard, *The Boston Globe*, 2006). Yes, writing *is* hard work. Mem Fox, the brilliant Australian writer whose books for children have won numerous awards, is fond of saying that she loves being a writer but HATES writing—simply because it is so difficult. We saw in Chapter 1 how writing the small number of words contained in her book *Where Is the Green Sheep?* (2004) took her over two years. Author Deborah Wiles, in a blog written on August 1, 2010, expresses both the agony and ecstasy of the writing experience:

> I've spent the entire week in this pink chair (covered with an old quilt for summer comfort), next to the cold fireplace, STEEPED, I tell you, STEEPED in 1964 Freedom Summer and Book Two of the Sixties Trilogy. I have barely come up for air. These are the days when I must remember to eat, bathe, converse, those days of long, long hours with a story, trying to keep it together, of-a-piece, when it seems so unwieldy, and when so much is unknown. And, as much as this place is frustrating, it is also thrilling—thrilling. I'm making connections left and right, up and down, over and under. I'm scrambling to keep up with them, I'm shouting *A-HA!* and grinning with delight. I'm groaning and tearing my hair out. I'm moving forward, back, stalled, forward again.

Writing will likely be even more difficult for our students, no matter what their ages, because they are still relatively new to the process. But there are things we can do, models we can offer, that will make the way a bit smoother for them. This chapter will offer books that can help students who are stuck for ideas by providing topics they will be interested in writing about; books with marvelous beginnings that can serve as models for students struggling with ways to start their pieces; and patterned books that can provide a template for our youngest writers and young children learning English as a second language.

## Book Topics That Can Spark Ideas for Writing

So often our students feel they must have had exotic experiences in order to have something to write about. They must have taken a marvelous trip, performed a brave deed, seen something extremely unusual. Janet Wong's book, *You Have to Write* (2002), expresses just such sentiments in the voices of youngsters trying to write: "Boy, how the others shine./She's got a story,/She's been to France . . ." but then she reminds them: "No one else can say/what you have seen/and heard/and felt/today." Read this book aloud at the beginning of the year to encourage your young writers as they struggle to find the stories only they can tell.

Many children's books, especially picture books, are about the ordinary "stuff" of every day—things that resonate with children as they take their place in the family constellation, go to school, strive to make and be a friend, overcome difficulties, or just notice the many things in the world around them. The best of these books can help students write about similar happenings in their own lives.

*The Wonder Book* (Rosenthal, 2010), discussed at the end of the first chapter, is also a treasure trove of topics for writing. There is an "I Wonder" page peopled with children whose thought balloons reveal the things they wonder about: "I wonder who left something under the tooth fairy's pillow when she was little." Because these wonderings are so short, they make fine writing starters for very young writers. Each child can contribute a page containing his or her own speculation, accompanied by an illustration, to a class book. Or the child can state what he or she wonders about orally for a class chart or individual dictations that can then be illustrated and displayed. *The Wonder Book* also contains musings about what you can and cannot run with and what does and does not grow on trees—both fun topics for student writing. The latter two can expand into even more topics: what you can and cannot do in the school yard; what you can and cannot do in church; what you can and cannot see in your school locker, etc. An entire picture book in this vein is

Meredith Gary's *Sometimes You Get What You Want* (2008). A short sentence relates a time when a young boy and girl get what they want while another short sentence relates a time when they do not. For example, "Sometimes your friends want to do what you're doing. Sometimes they want to do something else." Both *The Wonder Book* and Gary's picture book offer models that are easily imitated, and opportunities for some humorous pieces.

Very simple rhyming text celebrates the four seasons in Saltzberg's *All Around the Seasons* (2010). The section on spring begins, "Chicks are hatching;/Cool melting snow./Digging a garden,/seeds in a row." Concentrating on the season currently in progress, brainstorm with children some of the things they can do in that season, what the weather is like, etc. Then using their ideas, write a chart story together. Saltzberg's work can also serve as a model for a class book, with each of the children's ideas becoming an illustrated page.

For the narrator of Dan Yaccarino's *Every Friday* (2007), Friday is his favorite day because he and his dad have breakfast together at a local diner, rain or shine, before they go off to work and school. In matter-of-fact language, the youngster describes what they see on the way, whom they greet, and his eager anticipation to share a meal and good talk with his dad. " 'C'mon, I say./Only one more block to go." Most children in the class will have a favorite day or activity. Use the reproducible in Appendix A entitled Chapter 2.1: Favorite Day/Activity to help them start writing about their own special times.

*I Am a Backhoe* (Hines 2010) is a marvelous little book for young children in which a small boy pretends he is different vehicles used in construction. He describes the things he does with his hands and body and readers have to guess the vehicle. A page turn reveals the answer. "Down on my knees,/I make my hands/into a blade./Scrape. Push. Plow./I make a pile./I am ... a bulldozer." After reading the book aloud, invite the children to mimic each of the boy's actions. Using their bodies to pretend they are different vehicles will help them understand how they move and the different kinds of work they perform. This is excellent preparation for writing that can go beyond a

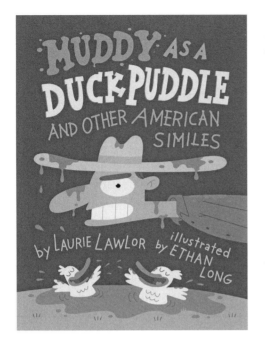

simple statement of fact such as "A flatbed truck carries things." Using *I Am a Backhoe* as a model, you can have the children do similar pretend activities with many categories of objects or creatures, depending upon what the class is studying: a river, a growing plant, etc. Getting to know a thing kinesthetically will make their writing much more interesting. A spin-off of this idea is for children to consider how the different ways their bodies move can be similar to the movements made by a dancer, a racer, even a favorite animal. A good model for this kind of thinking and subsequent writing is Pat Lowery Collins's *I Am a Dancer* (2008). Child narrators compare themselves to dancers when they engage in certain activities. The language itself is a graceful ballet: "I am a dancer when I bend like/grass in the wind/ or lean against it, not giving in,/ or when I flop down and turn myself into a dash or a dot." After enjoying this book, engage in a class chart writing activity. Help ideas flow by providing a chart template such as: "I am a _____ when I _____."

Michael Hall's *My Heart Is Like a Zoo* (2010) is awash with content that will not only spark writing topics but will also enrich curriculum studies. The text explores different heart feelings by comparing them to the actions or attributes of various zoo animals. The similes, filled with alliteration and imaginative language, are accompanied by collage illustrations of the animals. All the illustrations consist of hearts arranged in ways to represent the animal described. This is a perfect book to use in a unit on feelings, shapes, or colors, and the idea can be expanded to different topics as well. Enjoy the book and its innovative illustrations, and then continue the conversation using comparisons with jungle animals or sea creatures or insects—whatever the class might be studying. Or use a different part of the body such as hands. "My hands are as busy as _____." On a large sheet, each child can write a simile accompanied by a collage illustration made up of shapes cut from construction paper. Display the sheets in the room or turn them into a big book. Another book that can fuel this project is Laurie Lawlor's *Muddy as a Duck Puddle and Other American Similes* (2010).  In this alphabet book, each simile begins with a different letter, and their accompanying illustrations add to their humor. Americans from different regions and walks of life contributed the expressions, and the author provides information on the location and origin of each. Researching additional regional similes and expressions could be a rewarding project for interested individuals or groups of students. They might interview relatives to ascertain what sayings these adults heard during their childhood years. Related to the idea of well-known American sayings is Janet Wong's book of poems entitled *Knock on Wood: Poems about Superstitions* (2003). "Hair: Eat the crust of fresh baked bread/ for curly hair upon your head—/ brush, don't comb, your hair at night,/ and you won't hear a nasty fight—/." Superstitions involving all areas of daily living inspire these poems and may inspire students to write their own verses about superstitions observed in their families.

David A. Johnson's *Snow Sounds: An Onomatopoeic Story* (2000) offers a wealth of inspiration for those children whose writing is still largely illustration. This book is almost wordless except for the few sound words on each page that are connected to a winter snow storm: the "crash, crush, clank" of the snow plow; the "beep, beep, beep" it makes as it backs up; the "chug, chug, whoosh" of the snow blower, and much more. Enjoying this book aloud will surely lead to a discussion of sound words. From there, you might make a chart with the children, categorizing different kinds of sounds: vehicle sounds, kitchen sounds, animal sounds, etc. Then youngsters can choose a favorite kind of sound, draw a series of pictures related to that category, and label them with appropriate sound words.

Unfortunately, Tobi Tobias's brilliant book, *Serendipity* (2000), is currently out of print, but used copies are available. *Serendipity* means unexpectedly making a pleasant or advantageous discovery. In brief statements the youngsters depicted in Tobias's book talk about unanticipated events that gave them special delight. "Serendipity is when you have to go/ to your grouchy Aunt Bea's house,/ and—guess what!—/ her dog, Banjo, just had puppies." For younger children, this could be an opportunity to contribute writing to a special bulletin board in the classroom or a display in the hall or school lobby. Cut out and center large decorative letters saying "Serendipity is . . . " on a wall or bulletin board. Then ask children to write paragraphs or even single sentences about a serendipitous event in their lives and display the results around the centered letters. Older children might wish to interview teachers or other students in the school and compile a book of such events. *Serendipity* was recently voted the favorite word of the people of Great Britain. In a wonderful video on YouTube (www.youtube.com/watch?v=E0DUhneaGO8) a British woman mentions this vote and then recounts a fantastic incident in which she unexpectedly had the opportunity to play with a killer whale. What makes her story so wonderful is how she tells it, describing the quiet of the place, her surprise, and then delight. If you and your students can watch this short video, it might inspire them to write even longer pieces filled with the joy they experienced in their serendipitous moments. The students can also engage in a research writing project. Many inventions or scientific discoveries are the result of serendipity—while working on something, sometimes for many years, the scientist or inventor accidentally discovers something else or comes across something unforeseen that will make the invention or science work—and has the sense to explore it. *With a Little Luck: Surprising Stories of Amazing Discoveries* (2006) by Dennis B. Fradin is a great collection of stories about such unexpected breakthroughs and would make an excellent resource for research. *Lucky Science: Accidental Discoveries from Gravity to Velcro, with Experiments* (1995) by Royston Roberts and Jeanie Roberts is another useful tool.

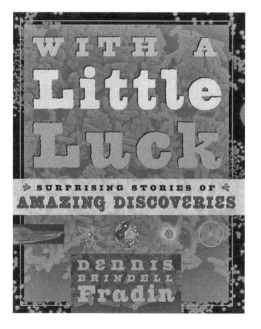

*Billy & Milly Short & Silly* (Feldman 2009) is a seemingly simple picture book consisting of very few words. But on closer reading, it is clear that the 13 four-word stories it contains required some creative thinking and a willingness to play with ideas. Scene: On a page bearing the word *ape*, a girl stands trailing her cape behind her as she views an ape in a cage. The next page says *cape*, and the ape is now wearing the girl's cape. On the final page of the story, the word *escape* appears, and the ape has burst through the roof of its cage and is flying away one paw raised, much like Superman, with his cape flying behind him. All of the stories have a surprise twist like this at the end, and all of them rhyme. The illustrations are great fun as well. Older students could work in groups to come up with three- or four-word rhyming stories complete with illustrations and then compile them into a book for a younger class that is working on rhyming sounds. This exercise will not provide an opportunity to write well-crafted sentences that extend into lovely paragraphs, but it will require working at excellent word choice that will capture the attention of the youngsters to whom they give their book. It could also get reluctant writers started on a productive project.

In our discussion of word play in the previous chapter, we saw how much fun nonsense words can be and how they can develop a love of language. What about an entire story based on nonsense? Two such stories may be just the thing to entice students to write. No matter what activity a young boy undertakes, be it a picnic or simply reading a book, it is interrupted by creatures such as "Sneeps" or "Snooks" or "Grullocks" or "Floons" or "Knoos" (Pym, *Have You Ever Seen a Sneep?*, 2009). And no matter what uses an elephant devises for the red "thingamabob" he has found, none of them work until it starts to rain (Na, *The Thingamabob*, 2010). Either of these books can spark some humorous stories. The two reproducibles: Chapter 2.2: Story Featuring a Nonsense Creature and Chapter 2.3: Story Featuring a Nonsense Object, provided at the end of this book, can help more hesitant students get started, but most may just want the freedom to run with their own ideas.

In her book *Blood on the Forehead: What I Know about Writing* (1998), M. E. Kerr offers this advice: "What if triggers most ideas for novels. It is often the very heart of fiction. You take something real and add to it" (97). Asking "What if . . . " is a good way to get students thinking and writing creatively. The wealth of fantasy novels, many of them hundreds of pages, currently overflowing our shelves likely began with just such a question in the author's mind. What if there were a parallel universe; what if creatures could talk; what if a young boy or girl had magical powers—and on and on. High fantasy that helps young people enter into these "what-if" worlds and think about the qualities of true heroes and how to use power for good are some of the most valuable books we can offer students. Upper elementary and young adult readers may already be hooked on these fantasy or science fiction novels, and their reading may already have spilled over into the writing of their own fantasy stories. We need to nurture and encourage them. But as we all face that daily struggle against the clock, it is good to know that a number of children's picture books also play with that "what if" idea. These books, although not nearly as deep or rich as the novels, can, nevertheless, ignite students' thinking and ultimately provide ideas for writing. They can plant the seeds for more involved imagining to come. Probably most youngsters have engaged in wishful thinking about what their lives would be like if only things were different. The narrator in Caralyn Buehner's *Snowmen All Year* (2010) speculates about what his life would be like if the snowman he builds in winter could remain with him all year. Jon Agee's hilarious *The Retired Kid* (2008) recounts Brian's life as a retired

Yes! It's by Amy Krouse Rosenthal & Tom Lichtenheld!

eight-year-old in the Happy Sunset retirement community. Fed up with the pressures of school, music lessons, sports, and other aspects of his busy days, Brian checks out life as a retiree. But prune juice smoothies, knitting, operation stories, and swing dancing eventually help him realize life as a kid is not so bad after all. What would life be like if every request were answered with a resounding "YES!" (Rosenthal, *Yes Day!*, 2009)? Pizza for breakfast, making all the food choices in the supermarket, food fights, staying up until all hours—what bliss! Maybe it would be even more fun to be able to turn yourself into any animal you wish, "for just one day" (Leuck, *For Just One Day*, 2009); or to be just about anything like a "cheek-to-cheek grinner" or "dizzy-dance spinner" (Spinelli, *I Can Be Anything*, 2010); or to have your very own garden where the "flowers could change color . . . even patterns" and you could plant things like jelly beans and sea shells and they would actually grow (Henkes, *My Garden*, 2010). These and many more "what if" picture books present topics for students to explore in their own writing. Or the books can prompt youngsters to ask "what if" questions of their own. Before they begin writing, it might be worthwhile to discuss the true consequences of some of their speculations so that students can carry the idea to its realistic conclusion in their stories—just as Brian eventually comes to recognize that retirement at age eight might not be such a great idea. What would be the result, for example, if everyone could do what he or she wished all the time?

Goodbyes, some more permanent than others, are part of everyone's life. Many different "goodbye" occasions are recounted in Doughty's simple *Oh No! Time to Go! A Book of Goodbyes* (2009) along with different ways to take one's leave: "gotta split"; "g'bye, y'all"; or "toodle-oo." The book ends with the sad departure of friends in a moving van. Students can write about the happy or sad goodbyes in their lives and how they dealt with them.

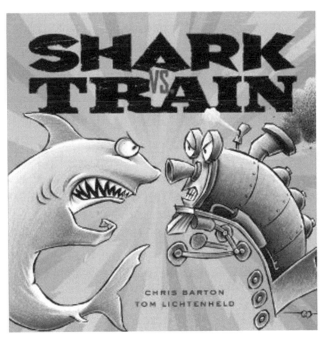

Two boys each grabs his favorite toy from a toy box in Barton's *Shark vs. Train* (2010) and the argument about which is best begins. Of course, it depends upon the venue or activity. Shark is better at eating, but burping is train's forté, hands down. After enjoying this humorous book, students could write about similar contests: bees vs. ants; vacation in the mountains vs. one at the beach, etc. They will likely have to do research to make their stories ring true.

In Betsy Rosenthal's *My House Is Singing* (2004), a poem entitled "The Smoke Detector" reads: "Why is it that/ whenever I make my toast/ a little crispy,/you tell on me?" This is only one of the wonderful poems about different objects in the home. If you can obtain this out-of-print book from a library or second hand, it is well worth it. When students see that everyday things like clothes dryers and kitchen smells can become the subjects of a poem, it may encourage them to look at the objects around them with a writer's eye. They can branch out to write about objects in the classroom, the school, etc.

Fourteen children's book artists answer the title question: *Why Did the Chicken Cross the Road?* (Frazee et al. 2006). Some artists answer with just an illustration, whereas others provide a sentence and illustration. The result is an absolutely hilarious book that will certainly appeal to older students. They might wish to work individually with the same question or come up with a different one to challenge their creativity and sense of humor. Even the most reluctant writers will not be able to resist joining in the fun.

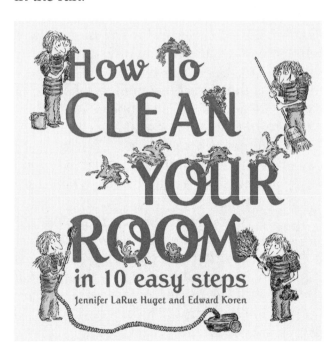

"How To . . . " books make great topics for student writing. Each student is likely good at something and can write with confidence about how to do that thing. To get them started, read Josh Lerman's very funny *How to Raise Mom & Dad* (2009). Students will love such tongue-in-cheek suggestions as "it's our job to tire out Mom and Dad so they'll get a good night's rest." Another hilarious "how to" picture book is Jennifer LaRue Huget's *How to Clean Your Room in 10 Easy Steps* (2010). Such sage advice as "Half-finished cups of milk may be placed in the hamper. (Don't worry: the clothes in there need washing anyway.)" will keep students asking for more of the author's delightful suggestions. Their own "How To . . . " books can be funny or serious, and they can even have a specific purpose—a book for a younger child on how to brush teeth, or how to care for a particular kind of pet, for example.

Since the late 1990s, Scholastic has been publishing the *Dear America* series, books written by well-known authors in diary form, supposedly by a young girl living in a particular historical period. Now the company is giving them a new look and adding titles. These books enable middle grade readers, especially girls, to live history by reading the stories of children their own age. By combining these fictional works with a unit of study, teachers can bring history to life and spark writing projects as well. In imitation of the book character, students can write a diary that includes information they are learning about during that period in history. By going to www.scholastic.com/ dearamerica, students can explore interactive scrapbooks for each Dear America character, participate in a blog, post stories about their own lives, view a digital gallery of historical artifacts, and much more. The website www.scholastic.com/teachdearamerica has historical information from the Library of Congress and many ways teachers can use the books.

Graphic novels, that is, books in comic format that are about the size of the usual novel for children or adolescents, might be just what reluctant writers need for motivation to get started. This genre has taken off in recent years, continually gaining in importance and recognition. Comics have long attracted young people, and the very best graphic novels combine a good story, comic book–style dialogue, and fine artwork. So many good graphic novels are on the market today that it would be difficult to cull even a few for this chapter. It is far more useful to provide a list of sources for you to explore. Perhaps, after perusing some of these resources, you can recommend some of your favorite titles for purchase if your school or public library does not already own them. The following resources provide lists, reviews, and award-winning titles:

*Library Journal*—publishes graphic novel reviews every other month.

*Publishers Weekly*—in addition to reviews, publishes an annual graphic novel list.

*School Library Journal*—publishes articles about graphic novels and has a graphic novel supplement.

Scholastic Publishers—provides extensive information about graphic novels, how to evaluate and use them with students, and a list of recommended titles. Go to: www2.scholastic.com/browse/collateral.jsp?id=1399.

The Cooperative Children's Book Center—provides a list of recommended graphic titles by age. Go to: www.education.wisc.edu/ccbc/books/detailList Books.asp?idBookLists=192.

The Young Adult Library Services Association—has published an annual list of great graphic novels for teens since 2007. Go to: www.ala.org/ala/mgrps/divs/ yalsa/booklistsawards/greatgraphicnovelsforteens/gn.cfm.

Go to: www.education.wisc.edu/ccbc/links/links.asp?idLinksCategory=15 for a listing of graphic novel websites.

Find links to articles about graphic novels at: www.education.wisc.edu/ccbc/ books/graphicnovels.asp.

Finally, some challenges for older students. Candace Fleming's second book in a series about children in Aesop Elementary School, now fifth graders (*The Fabled Fifth Graders of Aesop Elementary School*, 2010), contains stories about classroom happenings. Each story exemplifies one of Aesop's fables, complete with moral at the end. The best

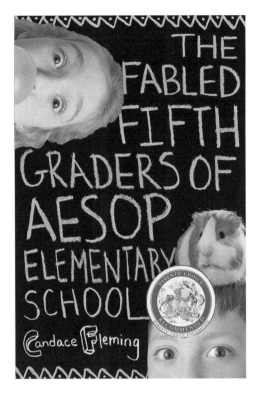

way for students to experience this book is to hear it aloud. The chapters are short enough for brief daily read-aloud sessions, after which the class can discuss the event and how the children's actions connect with a particular fable. Reading the actual fable from Aesop would be important as well. Then divide the students into groups and ask each group to come up with a story that connects to an Aesop fable. They need not use the same fables Fleming uses in her novel. Once everyone has enjoyed the stories, bind them into a book and display it alongside Aesop's Fables in the classroom or school library. Perhaps a project that would be a bit easier is modeled in Greg Tang's *Lessons that Count: Math Fables* (2004). In this book, he explains, via short rhymed fables, the different ways numbers can be grouped together. Students might want to try their hand at writing math fables of their own.

Many older students will, of course, be familiar with fairy tales featuring princesses—princesses who wait for their prince to come, princesses who are rescued from towers, kissed from sleep by true love, etc. But the princesses in Fiona Waters's *Don't Kiss the Frog!: Princess Stories with Attitude* (2008) are the rebellious sort who do not follow the rules—princesses who do the kissing and the rescuing. Read these very humorous stories aloud and then challenge students to create their own princesses or princes who operate outside the rules. Jane Yolen's *Not One Damsel in Distress* (2000) also presents some feisty females.

### Great Beginnings

Jack Cappon of The Associated Press once wrote, "Every story must have a beginning. A lead. Incubating a lead is a cause of great agony. Why is no mystery. Based on the lead, a reader makes a critical decision: Shall I go on?" (In Scanlan, *The Power of Leads*, 2003, http://www.poynter.org/how-tos/newsgathering-storytelling/chip-on-your-shoulder/11745/the-power-of-leads/)

Certainly, figuring out just how to begin a piece can be very challenging. The lead not only helps the author break the ice and get going on a piece of writing. It also captures readers' interest and, as Cappon asserts, either entices them to keep reading or convinces them to stop right there. Fortunately, many children's books can serve as models for students struggling with effective ways to begin their pieces. In his excellent book, *What a Writer Needs* (1993, 81–90), Ralph Fletcher suggests there are several different kinds of beginnings. Among those he discusses are: The Dramatic Lead; Starting in the Middle of a Scene; Leisurely Leads; Beginning at the Ending; and Introducing the Narrator. The books that follow represent a variety of ways to begin writing. Some will shock, others will amuse, still others will surprise. All of them can provide students with just the spark they need to move from the blank page or computer screen into that first attention-grabbing sentence. In addition to sharing some of these beginnings with a class or group, you can point individual children to particular kinds of leads depending upon the kinds of stories they want to write. Even younger children who could never read or understand some of the novels themselves can learn from listening to their opening lines. The reproducible page entitled Chapter 2.4: Great Beginnings provided for this section may help individual students get started (see Appendix A).

### The Humorous Beginning

A good laugh can always hook readers. Your students will likely be familiar with the movie *Shrek* and its sequels. But what they may not know is that this film is based on William Steig's book of the same name. Fortunately, Farrar, Straus, and Giroux has reissued the book in hard cover (2010) so that new generations of children can delight in Steig's marvelous language and sense of humor. What youngster could resist this beginning:

> His mother was ugly and his father was ugly, but Shrek was uglier than the two of them put together. By the time he toddled, Shrek could spit flame a full ninety-nine yards and vent smoke from either ear. With just a look he cowed the reptiles in the swamp. Any snake dumb enough to bite him instantly got convulsions and died.

*The Best Christmas Pageant Ever* (1995), Barbara Robinson's funny and moving classic, begins:

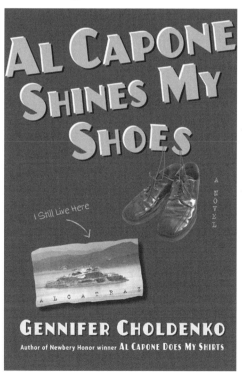

> The Herdmans were absolutely the worst kids in the history of the world. They lied and stole and smoked cigars (even the girls) and talked dirty and hit little kids and cussed their teachers and took the name of the Lord in vain and set fire to Fred Shoemaker's old broken-down tool house.

While life close to criminals on Alcatraz (Choldenko, *Al Capone Shines My Shoes*, 2009) is indeed challenging, it has its funny side as readers note right from the start:

> Nothing is the way it's supposed to be when you live on an island with a billion birds, a ton of bird crap, a few dozen rifles, machine guns, and automatics, and 278 of America's worst criminals—"the cream of the criminal crop" as one of our felons likes to say.

Sonnenblick's *Dodger for Sale* (2010) begins with a promise of high adventure and just the brand of gross humor middle graders crave:

> Look, if I'm going to tell you **everything** that happened with Dodger's strange transformations, Amy's disappearance, and our secret battle with the dreaded leprechauns, you have to promise **you won't tell**. And you won't get totally grossed out—even by the parts that are completely **disgusting**.

The fun begins with the very first sentence in Doreen Cronin's humorous picture book, *Click, Clack, Moo: Cows that Type* (2000): "Farmer Brown has a problem. His cows like to type."

### Starting in the Middle of a Scene

Readers leap right into the action with these exciting leads:

"Luke took the key out of the sideboard drawer in the dining room, took a rifle and put the key back very carefully." (Brown, *Black Angels*, 2009)

"'Where's Papa going with that axe?' said Fern to her mother as they were setting the table for breakfast." (E. B. White, *Charlotte's Web*, 2006)

> The videotape of my father was never meant to be seen by me, and were it not for a chow mix ripping apart half my face, the man might have remained only a mysterious void. But it was that day when I was five, that day of growls and blood and pain and screams, when I first heard my father's voice. (Bodeen, *The Gardener*, 2010)

> So Mom got the postcard today. It says *Congratulations* in big curly letters, and at the very top is the address of Studio-15 on West 58th Street. After three years of trying, she has actually made it. She's going to be a contestant on *The $20,000 Pyramid*. (Stead, *When You Reach Me*, 2009)

"A big cloud of dust came winding down our road, like a tornado on wheels. More mail? I wondered. That was strange. We never got mail twice a day." (Nolen, *Pitching in for Eubie*, 2007)

"'Don't be scared, Sareen. It'll be all right,' my twin brother, Desmond, whispers to me. I grip his hand as we settle onto one of the many benches in the yard." (Hanson, *A Season for Mangoes*, 2005)

Joan Bauer's novels, known for their humor, sharp dialogue, and poignant themes, usually get readers off to a rollicking start. Here are just two examples:

> I leaped onto the sliding ladder in the back room of Gladstone's Shoe Store of Chicago, gave it a shove, and glided fast toward the end of the floor to ceiling

shelves of shoeboxes. My keen retailer's eye found the chocolate loafers, size 12. (*Rules of the Road*, 2005)

Somehow I knew my time had come when Bambi Barnes tore her order book into little pieces, hurled it into the air like confetti, and got fired from the Rainbow Diner in Pensacola right in the middle of the lunch time rush. She'd been sobbing by the decaf urn, having accidentally spilled a bowl of navy bean soup in the lap of a man who was, as we say in the restaurant game, one taco short of a combo platter. (*Hope Was Here*, 2005)

Marcus Zusak's Printz Honor book for older readers, *I Am the Messenger* (2005), features Ed Kennedy, a 19-year-old cab driver, whose life is uneventful until he receives mysterious messages that send him on missions to help people in need. Zusak plunges readers headlong into the bank robbery that kicks off Ed's unusual life of service:

> The gunman is useless.
> I know it.
> He knows it.
> The whole bank knows it. (1)

Patricia Polacco's picture book, *Pink and Say* (1994), is about two boys fighting in the Civil War, and brings readers right into the aftermath of a battle: "I watched the sun edge toward the center of the sky above me. I was hurt real bad."

The idyllic summer evening described in Jonathan London's *When the Fireflies Come* (2003) begins, literally, with a bang: "The screen doors slam. Slam-bang. Slam-bang."

Sheila A. Nielson's *Forbidden Sea* (2010), a novel about a young girl who must choose between what might be an exciting life under the sea and her difficult life on land, begins:

> Pelting rain battered against me, stinging my skin and eyes, almost driving me backward. Forcing myself to continue, I felt my way down the slick rock face one foot at a time. I clung to the cliff face a moment, crying into the dark squall raging around me.

### The Dramatic or Shocking Beginning

Some stories begin with a sentence or paragraph that hits the reader in the gut. They start with sentences that almost force the reader to go back and read them again

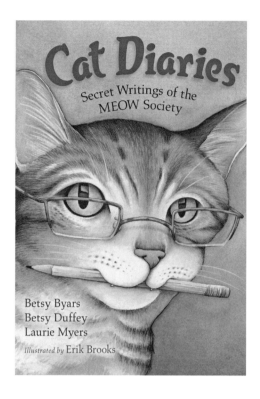

and then keep going to find out what comes next. Betsy Byars's *Cat Diaries: Some Writings of the MEOW Society* (2010) begins: "It was the third full moon of the year when cats around the world began to disappear." Nikki Grimes starts *The Road to Paris* (2008), her novel about a biracial foster child, like this: "Ask Paris if a phone call can be deadly. She'll tell you. She learned the truth of it last night." "I'm an island in the middle of the hall. Kids stream around me on either side. I don't remember getting here, and I don't have the energy to break through the flow and escape," begins Taylor Rose, the narrator in Drew Lamm's *Bittersweet* (2003). Franny Chapman, the heroine of Deborah Wiles's ground-breaking documentary novel about living in fear of nuclear annihilation in 1962, begins the story of her community's search for sanity in a world gone crazy this way: "I am eleven years old, and I am invisible" (*Countdown*, 2010). We learn from the very beginning about 11-year-old Fadi's dangerous plan to find his little sister left behind in a Pakistani refugee camp: "It's a perfect night to run away, thought Fadi, casting a brooding look at the bright sheen of the moon through the cracked backseat window" (Senzai, *Shooting Kabul*, 2010). Neal Shusterman's *Full Tilt* (2003) starts with this shocking line: "It began the night we died on the Kamikaze." Han Nolan's *A Summer of Kings* (2006 is about a family

who takes in an African refugee and how 14-year-old Esther, overshadowed by her siblings, gains the courage to join Martin Luther King, Jr., in his 1963 march. Esther's opening words are, "Last summer a murderer came to live with us." Rather than encourage youngsters to read his book, Lemony Snicket starts *A Bad Beginning* (1999) with the opposite injunction: "If you are interested in stories with happy endings you would be better off reading some other book."—an opener guaranteed to make them keep reading. "When Jamie saw him throw the baby, saw Van throw the little baby, saw Van throw his little sister Nin, when Jamie saw Van throw his baby sister Nin, then they moved." Although this beginning from Carolyn Coman's *What Jamie Saw* (2008) is indeed shocking, middle grade readers are not exposed to graphic domestic violence, and they will come to celebrate Jamie's and his mother's resilience and courage. Susan Campbell Bartoletti wrote her gripping novel, *The Boy Who Dared* (2008), after being captivated by a teen she encountered while researching her non-fiction book about Hitler youth. Helmuth Hübener, the 17-year-old hero of the story, defied Nazi rules and paid with his life. Readers sense his terrible fate from the first paragraph:

> It's morning. Soft gray light slips over the tall redbrick wall. It stretches across the exercise yard and reaches through the high, barred windows. In a cell on the ground floor, the light shifts dark shapes into a small stool, a scrawny table, and a bed made of wooden boards with no mattress or blanket. On that bed, a thin, huddled figure, Helmuth, a boy of seventeen, lies awake. Shivering. Trembling.
> It's a Tuesday.
> The executioner works on Tuesdays.

In Valerie Zenatti's *A Bottle in the Gaza Sea* (2008), Naïm, a Palestinian living in Gaza, and Tal, an Israeli living in Jerusalem, come to grips with the hatred and violence that continually erupts between their two cultures. It begins, "It's a time of darkness, sadness, and horror. The fear's back again."

Georgina Hayes is desperate to earn some money so her family can live in an apartment again instead of in their car. Barbara O'Connor's poignant book *How to Steal a Dog* (2007) thrusts readers immediately into her puzzling and surprising plan: "The day I decided to steal a dog was the same day my best friend, Luanne Godfrey, found out I lived in a car."

Kathryn Erskine's *Mockingbird (mok'ing-bûrd)* (2010) is the amazing story of a young girl with Asperger's syndrome who must deal with her beloved older brother's death in a school shooting. Young readers will be touched by her courage and goodness and drawn in immediately by the dramatic and strange first paragraph:

> It looks like a one-winged bird crouching in the corner of our living room. Hurt. Trying to fly every time the heat pump turns on with a click and a groan and blows cold air onto the sheet and lifts it up and it flutters for just a moment and then falls down again. Still. Dead.

Deborah Wiles could have begun *Each Little Bird that Sings* (2005) by explaining that 10-year-old Comfort Snowberger's family runs a funeral home. It would have been a perfectly acceptable start to a great novel filled with memorable characters—but hardly attention-getting. Instead, Comfort says, "I come from a family with a lot of dead people"—a sentence that hits readers between the eyes and keeps them turning the pages.

Young readers will immediately want to argue with author George Shannon when they read the title of his picture book, *White Is for Blueberry* (2005). "No, that can't be. Blueberries are blue," they might say. But they are in for even more surprises when they read the first line: "Pink is for crow" on a page with a picture of a black crow. Really curious now, they MUST turn the page where they see a spread depicting four pink baby birds and the words, "when it has just hatched from its egg." From first line to last, this creative book shocks youngsters into thinking again about how the author's assertions can be true. Can students think of other examples of statements that appear to be false but aren't?

The title alone of Brad Sneed's picture book, *Deputy Harvey and the Ant Cow Caper* (2005), promises a humorous read. Yet there is drama as well, right from the start:

> Way out West at the foot of an old cottonwood, there is a sleepy little town by the name of Ant Hill. Nothing much ever happens there, and that is just fine with most folks, especially Deputy Harvey. But this morning was different.

Mountains are such seemingly solid masses that we might not think of them as capable of movement, which makes the title and lyrical opening statement of Thomas Locker's picture book, *Mountain Dance* (2001), all the more dramatic:

> Mountains rise through the clouds
> In a slow dance that goes on and on
> For millions of years.
> Every mountain moves in its own way.

"I will always remember when the stars fell down around me and lifted me up above the George Washington Bridge," is the dramatic way the narrator of Faith Ringgold's lovely picture book *Tar Beach* (1996) begins recounting the pleasant experiences she shares with her family on the roof of their building in Harlem during the Depression.

### Introducing the Narrator

Fourth-grader India McAllister introduces herself immediately in the first chapter entitled "Me—India McAllister":

> My name is India McAllister, and I'm nine and a half years old. I live in Wolfgang, Maine, where there are no wolves, but the coyotes grow almost as big. You can hear them calling to each other at night. (Angell, *The Accidental Adventures of India McAllister*, 2010)

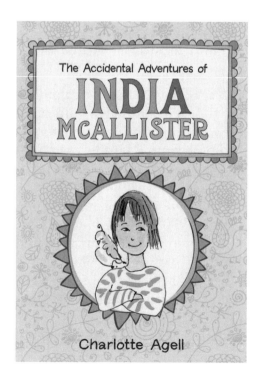

Fourteen-year-old Toby Walsgrove tells readers about his unusual entrance into the world (Knight, *The Last Words of Will Wolfkin*, 2010):

> My name is Toby Walsgrove, and before I begin to tell you my story, I should give you a short explanation of who I am.
>
> I was born at the Royal Free Hospital in Hampstead, London, England, fourteen and a half years ago. I was named by the nurses there. Apparently one of the nurses had a cat called Toby, and when I was first born, my ears were slightly pointy like her cat's ears, so they named me Toby. But it's okay. I'm not in

the least bit bitter. I like cats. A cat saved my life once, but I will tell you about that later. (3)

Phineas Listerman MacGuire (Dowell, *Phineas L. MacGuire Gets Slimed!*, 2010) starts his tale by focusing on his unusual name:

> My name is Phineas Listerman MacGuire.
> Most people call me Mac.
> My Sunday-school teacher and my pediatrician call me Phineas.
> A few people, mostly my great-uncle Phil and his cockatiel, Sparky, call me Phin.
> Nobody calls me Listerman.
> Nobody.
> I mean not one single person.
> Everybody got that? (1–2)

An unusual narrator introduces himself in Jan Fearnley's *The Search for the Perfect Child* (2006): "I am Fido Farnsworth,/the **cleverest,/sharpest,/coolest/**dog detective in the whole world."

When Beatrice learns her favorite fantasy series is being cancelled, she must travel back and forth from her real world to the world of Imaginalis to rescue her fantasy friends from oblivion. Here's how readers meet her in the first paragraph:

> My name is Mehera Beatrice Crosby, I'm twelve years old, and I've never even been on an airplane. Five steps up a ladder and I freak out. I wouldn't go on a roller coaster if you paid me a gazillion dollars. So what the heck was I doing . . . sailing over the North Carolina woods, riding a *winged lion* across the sky? (DeMatteis, *Imaginalis*, 2010)

In Judy Blume's *Going, Going, Gone! with the Pain & the Great One* (2008), a brother and sister take turns introducing each other:

> My sister's name is Abigail. I call her the Great One because she thinks she's so great. She says, "I don't think it, I know it!" Then she gets mad. It's fun to make her mad. Who cares if she's in third grade and I'm just in first? (1)
>
> My brother's name is Jacob but everyone calls him Jake. Everyone but me.

I call him the Pain because that's what he is. He's a first-grade pain. And he will always be a pain—even if he lives to be a hundred. (3)

### Beginning at the End

Two children's books begin in almost the same surprising way. David LaRochelle's picture book, *The End* (2007), turns a fairy tale upside down. It starts "They all lived happily ever after," whereas Cynthia Voigt's novel *Dicey's Song* (2003) begins, "They lived happily ever after." Arthur Yorinks, in his picture book *Louis the Fish* (1986), tells the story of a man who was forced to work as a butcher but really loves fish. His life is miserable until one day he turns into a fish and is happy ever after. But instead of revealing this transformation chronologically, Yorinks begins, surprisingly, with the end result and almost forces readers to continue reading to discover how this amazing event came about: "One day last spring, Louis, a butcher, turned into a fish. Silvery scales. Big lips. A tail. A salmon." Scott William Carter's *The Last Great Getaway of the Water Balloon Boys* (2010), a powerful novel for young adult readers, reveals, in the very first sentence, the end result of a series of bad decisions: "If I'm going to tell you how I killed this kid, I can't start on the day it happened." They will surely want to keep reading to find out how the narrator got into so much trouble and to learn how his situation is finally resolved.

**Success for Beginning Writers and Young Students Learning English as a Second Language—Following a Pattern**

Our youngest writers are often so caught up in the mechanics of forming letters and words that actually producing writing in any genre can be a difficult task. So it may be a good idea to offer them models, from time-to-time, that follow a predictable pattern that they can easily imitate. This may seem unoriginal and not like "real" writing at all, but it provides a template for children to use that will enable them to feel successful as writers while they hone their mechanical skills. And, just as Frank Smith told us long ago (*Reading Without Nonsense*, 2005) that feeling like a reader enables a child to consider him or herself a member of the "Reading Club," so feeling successful, considering oneself a

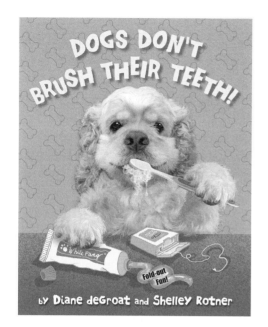

writer, is a powerful confidence-builder and a motivator to seek ever-greater writing challenges. Depending upon their ages and abilities, students may not be able to follow the patterns exactly at first—write in rhyme, for example, but they will be able to continue the repetitive plot and include a recurring phrase. Initially, it would be beneficial to undertake patterned writing as a class, with children supplying a plot element that could come next in a story and the teacher adding that element on a chart. What follows is just a small sample of the many patterned books available.

An excellent way to begin with the very youngest writers is Diane deGroat's *Dogs Don't Brush Their Teeth!* (2009). In this lift-the-flap book, the pictures indicate the very simple sentences children need to write. For example, only the words "Dogs do . . . " appear above a dog holding a stick in its mouth. The children can write individually or via a group write on a chart: "Dogs do carry (or fetch) a stick." Lift the flap and two dogs are pictured with baseballs, glove, and bat. The words on the page are: "Dogs don't!" Children can supply the rest of the sentence: "Dogs don't play baseball." The book continues in this vein, picturing different kinds of dogs doing what real-life dogs can and cannot do. This simple format is sure to provide a successful experience for young writers and some laughs as well.

In addition to the pleasure of touching the different kinds of wings pictured in Salina Yoon's *Wings* (2010), even preschool children can successfully follow the text pattern in this simple board book. The same question appears on each double-page spread, the only change being the animal name. For example, "What kind of wings do bumblebees have?" In each case, the answer contains three words—a texture word such as *sparkly* or *fuzzy*, a color word appropriate to the creature, and the word *wings* as in "sparkly silver wings." Work with the children to continue the story on a chart. Have them decide which creature to write about next and write the question using that creature's name. Then take suggestions from the group for the three-word answer.

Another very simple book is Leonid Gore's *Mommy, Where Are You?* (2009). A little mouse wakes up, wonders where his mommy is, and runs outside to find her. "There you are!" he says, as he sees a gray shape behind a fence. But a page turn reveals only "silvery fountain grass." He keeps declaring "There you are!" as he searches behind each object—only to discover he is wrong. The language is repetitive in each instance. Ask the children to add hunting places before the final resolution. They will enjoy drawing additional objects hiding gray shapes and may even want to turn their pages into a book.

In Scott M. Fischer's delightful *Jump!* (2010), creatures of increasing size are sleeping peacefully until a larger predator arrives. Then the animal jumps and the predator sleeps until a larger one appears, and so on. "Well,/I'm a bug./I'm a bug./I'm a snug little bug,/and I'm sleeping on a jug./Until I see a frog, and I . . . JUMP!" Children can write their own books or stories following this pattern on the reproducible (Chapter 2.5:

Pattern for Fisher's *Jump!*) in Appendix A as a guide if they wish. Or, rather than write a completely new story, they can insert other animals into the existing one before the larger creatures appear toward the end of the book.

A girl and her younger sister camp out in their yard overnight in Wendy Orr's *The Princess and Her Panther* (2010). In a repeated plot pattern enhanced by delightful language, the sisters hear different scary sounds during the night but "the princess was brave, and the panther (her younger sister) tried to be." They hear the "too-whit-too-whooing, [the]screechy hoo-hooing of an owl-witch," and the "deep, throaty moaning, [the] croakety groaning of a frog-monster roaming." Continue this story on a chart, with students contributing other nocturnal animal sounds to fill the girls' night. Encourage them to think of sounds that ring with the alliteration, rhyming, and assonance that make the original text such a pleasure to read aloud.

Cumulative text provides an easy pattern for children to follow, and because there are so many phrases and sentences that keep repeating, their stories will be quite long and they will feel very accomplished. Combine cumulative text with a tune they know, and youngsters will be eager to add their own writing to the mix. Eye-catching, color-saturated illustrations and a text patterned after "I Know an Old Lady Who Swallowed a Fly" introduce readers to a monster with similar problems in the Emberleys's *There Was an Old Monster!* (2010). "Scritchy-scratch" noises are made by ants dancing in his

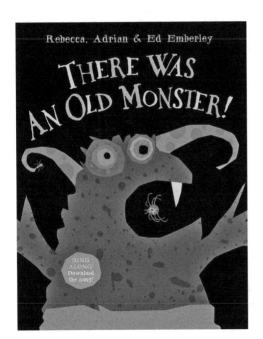

pants, rhyme, and all-out nonsense to entice children to add on to the story before the monster's eventual demise. Another wonderful cumulative text is Karla Kuskin's *A Boy Had a Mother Who Bought Him a Hat* (2010). Young writers can add more humorous objects for the ever-shopping mom to buy her son. If the class is studying pond life, a perfect book to read aloud is Betsy Franco's *Pond Circle* (2009). One after another, pond creatures in ever-increasing size eat the animal that came before it until the food chain extends to larger animals in the surrounding landscape. The book concludes with some non-fiction facts about the animals introduced in the story. This book can serve as a model for a cumulative story about pond life or any other curriculum topic.

The youngsters in David Elliott's *And Here's to You!* (2004) find delight in all the creatures in

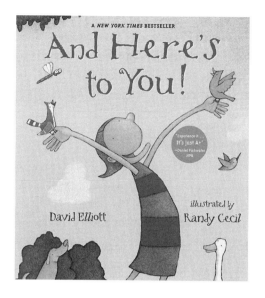

their world, from tiny bugs to huge cows and on to people. This is a celebration of creation with language that brims over with alliteration and catchy descriptions: "Here's to the bugs!/ ... Here's to the sting-y ones,/The weird and the wing-y ones." Invite students to write their own poems of praise for creatures they admire. A reproducible (Chapter 2.6: Poems of Praise for Creatures) found in Appendix A follows Elliott's pattern and may help them get started. Children can work individually or in groups and combine their pages into a book.

A young girl keeps adding on descriptors for her exceptional dog, Lyle, in Jennifer P. Goldfinger's *My Dog Lyle* (2007). He's "smart, howling, burping" and much more. The girl describes what her dog does, sums it up in one word, and adds that word to the next account of the dog's behavior. For example, "My/snuggly,/smart,/howling,/burping,/slurping/dog Lyle sometimes is/surprised by skunks." Children may enjoy adding adventures and descriptors.

Besides patterned text, stories can be shaped in a particular pattern. We are familiar with folktales that have a circular shape or pattern—the characters end where they began but are changed by their experience. *The Fisherman and His Wife* is a good example. Children's picture book stories sometimes have a circular pattern as well, and both young and older students can try their hand at creating them. If the class is studying the life cycle of trees, a perfect book to read is *A Grand Old Tree* by Mary Newell DePalma (2005). The story opens with an old tree and the creatures for whom she provided a home. When she dies and decays, she continues to provide life, and shoots from her seeds grow to begin the cycle once again. Little Jane's rubber duck falls off the bathroom windowsill

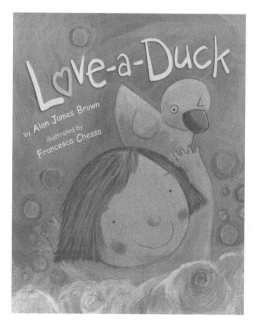

while she is bathing, lands outside, and through a series of coincidences, ends up in a baby carriage, a park, a pond, and eventually back in the same bathtub where Jane is once again taking a bath (Brown, *Love-a-Duck*, 2010). "Frankie works the night shift" are both the opening and closing words of Peters's book, *Frankie Works the Night Shift* (2010) that describes a cat's nightly adventures around town. In Karen Ritz's *Windows with Birds* (2010), a cat, unhappy with a move away from its familiar home with birds outside the windows, hides from its young owner until it discovers that the new house indeed does have birds outside its windows. Two more stories you might want to read to help students understand how a circular pattern works are: *The Blue Stone* by Jimmy Liao (2008) and *When the Shadbush Blooms* by Carla Messinger with Susan Katz (2007).

Indeed, writing *is* hard work. But by giving our students books that treat topics they might be interested in exploring in their writing; providing our youngest writers with examples of patterned writing and plots they can expand upon in their individual writing and as a group; and reading aloud different kinds of leads that might inspire them to put down that difficult first sentence, we can help make their writing tasks a bit easier and more enjoyable.

## References

Agee, Jon. 2008. *The Retired Kid*. New York: Hyperion/Disney Book Group. ISBN 978-0-142319314-1.
 Tired of his life as a kid, Brian heads to the Happy Sunset retirement community.

Agell, Charlotte. 2010. *The Accidental Adventures of India McAllister*. New York: Henry Holt. ISBN 978-0-8050-8902-8.
 India talks about a year of changes in her life as a fourth grader.

Bartoletti, Susan Campbell. 2008. *The Boy Who Dared*. New York: Scholastic. ISBN 978-0439680134.
 A 17-year-old distributes pamphlets about Nazi atrocities and pays with his life.

Barton, Chris. 2010. *Shark vs. Train*. Illustrated by Tom Lichtenheld. Boston: Little Brown. ISBN 978-0-316-00762-7.
 A toy shark and train argue over which one is best.

Bauer, Joan. 2005. *Hope Was Here*. New York: Penguin. ISBN 978-0142404249-02. (pb)
 When 16-year-old Hope and her aunt move from Brooklyn to Mulhoney, Wisconsin, to work as waitress and cook in the Welcome Stairways diner, they become involved with the diner owner's political campaign to oust the town's corrupt mayor.

Bauer, Joan. 2005. *Rules of the Road*. New York: Penguin. ISBN 978-0142404256-02. (pb)
 Sixteen-year-old Jenna agrees to drive the elderly woman who owns Gladstone Shoes across the country in an effort to stop her son from taking over and destroying the business.

Blume, Judy. 2008. *Going, Going, Gone! with the Pain & the Great One*. Illustrated by James Stevenson. New York: Delacorte/Random House. ISBN 978-0-385-73307-6.
 Jake and Abigail's adventures include a trip to the beach with Grandma.

Bodeen, S. A. 2010. *The Gardener*. New York: Feiwel and Friends. ISBN 978-0-312-37016-9.
 When high school sophomore Mason finds a beautiful but catatonic girl in the nursing home where his mother works, the discovery leads him to revelations about a series of disturbing human experiments that have a connection to his own life.

Brown, Alan James. 2010. *Love-a-Duck*. Illustrated by Francesca Chessa. New York: Holiday House. ISBN 978-0-8234-2263-0.
 Jane's rubber duck has a series of adventures before he lands back in her tub where he started.

Brown, Linda Beatrice. 2009. *Black Angels*. New York: Putnam/Penguin. ISBN 978-0-399-25030-9.
 Eleven-year-old Luke leaves home to join the Union army, but he meets needy children along the way and feels responsible for them.

Buehner, Caralyn. 2010. *Snowmen All Year*. Illustrated by Mark Buehner. New York: Dial/Penguin. ISBN 978-0-8037-3383-1.
  A child describes the different things he could do with his snowman if the snowman could remain with him all year.

Byars, Betsy, et al. 2010. *Cat Diaries: Secret Writings of the MEOW Society*. Illustrated by Erik Brooks. New York: Henry Holt. ISBN978-0-8050-8717-8.
  One night every year, cats in the Memories Expressed in Our Writing society gather to read from their diaries and hear a variety of stories.

Carter, Scott William. 2010. *The Last Great Getaway of the Water Balloon Boys*. New York: Simon & Schuster. ISBN 978-1-4169-7156-6.
  When 16-year-old Charlie, an excellent student, and his former best friend embark on a road trip, the choices they make have profound consequences.

Choldenko, Gennifer. 2009. *Al Capone Shines My Shoes*. New York: Dial/Penguin. ISBN 978-0-80373460-9.
  Life on Alcatraz, where his father works as a guard, has its challenges for Moose and his family.

Collins, Pat Lowery. 2008. *I Am a Dancer*. Illustrated by Mark Graham. Minneapolis: Millbrook Press. ISBN 978-0-8225-6369-3.
  Children compare their various movements to those of a dancer.

Coman, Carolyn. 2008. (reprint ed.) *What Jamie Saw*. Honesdale, PA: Front Street/Boyds Mills. ISBN 978-1590786390. (Orig. pub. 1995 by Front Street.)
  Jamie and his mom leave when her live-in boyfriend becomes abusive and learn to survive on their own.

Cronin, Doreen. 2000. *Click, Clack, Moo: Cows That Type*. Illustrated by Betsy Lewin. New York: Atheneum. ISBN 978-0689832130.
  Farmer Brown's typing cows demand all kinds of creature comforts from their harried owner.

deGroat, Diane. 2009. *Dogs Don't Brush Their Teeth!* Illustrated by Shelley Rotner. New York: Orchard/Scholastic. ISBN 978-0-545-08064-4.
  In this lift-the-flap book, dogs are pictured doing activities they can and cannot do.

DeMatteis, J. M. 2010. *Imaginalis*. Katherine Tegen/HarperCollins. ISBN 978-0-06-17286-7.
  Twelve-year-old Beatrice attempts to save the land of Imaginalis and its inhabitants.

DePalma, Mary Newell. 2005. *A Grand Old Tree*. New York: Arthur A. Levine/Scholastic, 2005. o.p. ISBN 0-439-62334-0.
  This story presents the circular life cycle of an old tree.

Doughty, Rebecca. 2009. *Oh No! Time to Go!: A Book of Goodbyes*. New York: Schwartz & Wade/Random House. ISBN 978-0-375-84981-7.
  This book features the many different ways to say goodbye.

Dowell, Frances O'Roark. 2010. *Phineas L. MacGuire Gets Slimed!* Illustrated by Preston McDaniels. New York: Atheneum. ISBN 978-1-4169-0775-7. (pb)
  When his best friend decides to run for class president, fourth-grade science whiz Mac agrees to be his campaign manager in exchange for help with his latest experiment.

Elliott, David. 2004. *And Here's to You!* Illustrated by Randy Cecil. Somerville, MA: Candlewick. ISBN 978-0-7636-4126-9. (pb)
Children praise the creatures around them.

Emberley, Rebecca, Adrian, and Ed. 2010. *There Was an Old Monster!* New York: Orchard/Scholastic.
A monster keeps swallowing ever larger creatures to get rid of the animals already inside him.

Erskine, Kathryn. 2010. *Mockingbird (mok'ing-bûrd)*. New York: Philomel/Penguin. ISBN 978-0-399-2564-8.
Caitlin, who has Asperger's syndrome, struggles to understand emotions and make friends at school even while she must find closure in dealing with her brother's death.

Fearnley, Jan. 2006. *The Search for the Perfect Child*. Cambridge, MA: Candlewick. ISBN 978-0-7636-3231-1.
Fido, a dog detective, enumerates the traits of the perfect child for whom he is searching.

Feldman, Eve B. 2009. *Billy & Milly Short & Silly*. Illustrated by Tuesday Mourning. New York: G.P. Putnam's Sons. ISBN 978-0-399-24651-7.
Each of the 13 rhyming stories in this book contains only three or four words.

Fischer, Scott M. 2010. *Jump!* New York: Simon & Schuster. ISBN 978-1-4169-7884-8.
Creatures jump away when a predator threatens them.

Fleming, Candace. 2010. *The Fabled Fifth Graders of Aesop Elementary School*. New York: Schwartz & Wade/Random House. ISBN 978-0-375-86334-9.
Fifth graders engage in activities related to Aesop's Fables.

Fletcher, Ralph. 1993. *What a Writer Needs*. Portsmouth, NH: Heinemann. ISBN 0-435-08734-7.
Fletcher discusses the writer's craft and those things the writer needs to learn to be successful.

Fox, Mem. 2004. *Where Is the Green Sheep?* Illustrated by Judy Horacek. San Diego: Harcourt. ISBN 978-0152049072.
This book has little ones hunting for a green sheep while delighting in the rhyme, the colors, and the bouncy rhythms that Fox's text provides.

Fradin, Dennis Brindell. 2006. *With a Little Luck: Surprising Stories of Amazing Discoveries*. New York: Dutton. ISBN 978-0-525471967.
The author describes 11 scientific breakthroughs made by accident.

Franco, Betsy. 2009. *Pond Circle*. Illustrated by Stefano Vitale. New York: Margaret McElderry. ISBN 976-1-4169-4021-0.
Cumulative text describes the food chain in a pond.

Frazee, Marla, et al. 2006. *Why Did the Chicken Cross the Road?* New York: Dial. ISBN 0-8037-3094-2.
Different children's book artists answer the title question via word and illustration.

Gary, Meredith. 2008. *Sometimes You Get What You Want*. Illustrated by Lisa Brown. New York: HarperCollins. ISBN 978-0-06-114015-0.
A young boy and girl talk about when they do and do not get their way.

Goldfinger, Jennifer P. 2007. *My Dog Lyle*. New York: Clarion. ISBN 978-0-618-63983-0.
A young girl thinks her dog is truly exceptional.

Gore, Leonid. 2009. *Mommy, Where Are You?* New York: Ginee Seo Books/Atheneum. ISBN 978-1-4169-5505-4.
A little mouse keeps mistaking gray shapes for his "lost" mother.

Grimes, Nikki. 2008. *The Road to Paris.* New York: Puffin. ISBN 978-0142410820. (pb)
Paris, a biracial foster child, longs for a normal life, but even when she is placed with a loving foster family, she faces grave difficulties.

Hall, Michael. 2010. *My Heart Is Like a Zoo.* New York: Greenwillow/HarperCollins. ISBN 978-0-06-191510-9.
Different feelings are compared to the attributes and activities of 20 zoo animals.

Hanson, Regina. 2005. *A Season for Mangoes.* Illustrated by Eric Velasquez. New York: Clarion. ISBN 978-0-618-15972-7.
A young Jamaican girl experiences her country's custom of sitting up all night and telling stories to honor a deceased person.

Henkes, Kevin. 2010. *My Garden.* New York: Greenwillow/HarperCollins. ISBN 978-0-06-171517-4.
A little girl imagines all the wonderful things she could grow in a fantastical garden of her own.

Hines, Anna Grossnickle. 2010. *I Am a Backhoe.* Berkeley: Tricycle Press. ISBN 978-1582463063.
A young boy pretends to be different construction vehicles.

Huget, Jennifer LaRue. 2010. *How to Clean Your Room in 10 Easy Steps.* Illustrated by Edward Koren. New York: Schwartz & Wade/Random House. ISBN 978-0-375-84410-2.
A young girl offers 10 tongue-in-cheek suggestions for making room cleanup easy.

Johnson, David A. 2000. *Snow Sounds: An Onomatopoeic Story.* Boston: Houghton Mifflin. ISBN 978-0-018-47310-0.
Beautiful illustrations depict the aftermath of a snow storm, complete with the sound words the activities pictured bring to mind.

Kerr, M. E. 1998. *Blood on the Forehead: What I Know about Writing.* New York: HarperCollins. o. p. ISBN 0-06-027996-6.
Using her own writing as examples, Kerr offers readers advice about becoming successful writers.

Knight, Steven. 2010. *The Last Words of Will Wolfkin.* New York: Walden Pond/HarperCollins. ISBN 978-0-06-170413-0.
Fourteen-year-old Toby, paralyzed since birth and raised in a convent, suddenly finds himself capable of movement and speech when his longtime companion, a cat, takes him on a magical and mysterious journey to Iceland.

Kuskin, Karla. 2010. *A Boy Had a Mother Who Bought Him a Hat.* Illustrated by Kevin Hawkes. New York: HarperCollins. ISBN 978-0-06-075330-6.
A mother keeps buying her son different items of clothing and other objects, resulting in some humorous situations.

LaRochelle, David. 2007. *The End.* Illustrated by Richard Egielski. New York: Arthur A. Levine/Scholastic. ISBN 978-0439640114.
This book begins with a wedding between a knight and princess—the "happily ever after" with lots of adventures in between that bring them to "once upon a time."

Lamm, Drew. 2003. *Bittersweet*. New York: Clarion. ISBN 0-618-16443-X.
    Taylor Rose is a talented artist, but the teen loses her desire to create when the grandmother who is bringing her up is struck by illness.

Lawlor, Laurie. 2010. *Muddy as a Duck Puddle and Other American Similes*. Illustrated by Ethan Long. New York: Holiday House. ISBN 978-0-8234-2229-6.
    This is a collection of American similes, each beginning with a different letter of the alphabet.

Lerman, Josh. 2009. *How to Raise Mom & Dad*. Illustrated by Greg Clarke. New York: Penguin. ISBN 978-0-525-47870-6.
    A boy's older sister gives him humorous suggestions for bringing up Mom and Dad.

Leuck, Laura. 2009. *For Just One Day*. Illustrated by Marc Boutavant. San Francisco: Chronicle. ISBN 978-0-8118-5610-2.
    A child imagines turning himself into different creatures.

Liao, Jimmy. 2008. *The Blue Stone*. Transl. by Sarah Thompson. Boston: Little Brown. ISBN 978-0316113830.
    A large blue stone is cracked in half and while one half remains in the forest, the other is sculpted into many different things, each time breaking apart with longing for its forest home. The story comes full circle when both halves of the stone are reunited.

Locker, Thomas. 2001. *Mountain Dance*. San Diego: Harcourt. ISBN 978-0152026226.
    Locker describes in beautiful language how mountains are formed.

London, Jonathan. 2003. *When the Fireflies Come*. New York: Dutton/Penguin. o.p. ISBN 0-525-45404-7.
    London's picture book celebrates, in lyrical language, the joys of a summer evening.

Marquard, Bryan. "Columnist Donald Murray Dies at 82." *The Boston Globe*, December 31, 2006, B3.
    In a moving tribute, Marquard gives an account of Donald Murray's life and work.

Mazer, Anne, and Ellen Potter. 2010. *Spilling Ink*. Illustrated by Matt Phelan. New York: Roaring Brook. ISBN 978-1-59643-514-8.
    Two professional authors share their writing processes with young adult writers.

Messinger, Carla, and Susan Katz. 2007. *When the Shadbush Blooms*. Illustrated by David Kanietakeron Fadden. Berkeley, CA: Tricycle Press. ISBN 978-1582461922.
    A young Lenni Lenape Indian child describes her family's life through the seasons, beginning and ending with early spring. The child's ancestors' lives are contrasted with life in the present.

Na, Il Sung. 2010. *The Thingamabob*. New York: Knopf/Random House. ISBN 978-0375861062.
    En elephant cannot figure out what a "thingamabob" is for until it begins to rain.

Nielson, Sheila A. 2010. *Forbidden Sea*. New York: Scholastic. ISBN 978-0-545-00734-5.
    When a mermaid attempts to lure her into the sea, 14-year-old Adrienne, who lives in a superstitious island community, must choose between the promise of an underwater paradise and those she loves.

Nolan, Han. 2006. *A Summer of Kings*. San Diego: Harcourt. ISBN 978-0152051082.
    After her family takes in an African American teen accused of murder, Esther learns about the Civil Rights movement and joins Martin Luther King, Jr., in his 1963 march.

Nolen, Jerdine. 2007. *Pitching in for Eubie*. New York: Amistad/HarperCollins. ISBN 978-0688149178.
   An African American girl's family pitches in to help her go to college.

O'Connor, Barbara. 2007. *How to Steal a Dog*. New York: Frances Foster/Farrar, Straus and Giroux. ISBN 978-0-374-33497-0.
   To get enough money to move her family out of the car in which they live and into an apartment, Georgina persuades her younger brother to help her steal and dog and then claim the reward.

Orr, Wendy. 2010. *The Princess and Her Panther*. Illustrated by Lauren Stringer. New York: Beach Lane/Simon & Schuster. ISBN 978-1-4169-9780-1.
   Two young girls face scary sounds bravely as they camp overnight in their yard.

Peters, Lisa Westberg. 2010. *Frankie Works the Night Shift*. Illustrated by Jennifer Taylor. New York: Greenwillow/HarperCollins. ISBN 978-0-06-009095-1.
   Frankie the cat has many nighttime adventures.

Polacco, Patricia. 1994. *Pink and Say*. New York: Philomel. ISBN 978-0399226717.
   A Caucasian and an African American boy fighting on opposite sides during the Civil War strike up a surprising friendship.

Pym, Tasha. 2009. *Have You Ever Seen a Sneep?* Illustrated by Joel Stewart. New York: Farrar, Straus and Giroux. ISBN 978-0374328689.
   Every time a boy tries to do something, he is interrupted by a monster.

Ringgold, Faith. 1996. *Tar Beach*. New York: Dragonfly. ISBN 978-0517885444.
   Beautifully illustrated with reproductions of Ringgold's quilts, this is the story of a young girl growing up in Harlem during the Depression.

Ritz, Karen. 2010. *Windows with Birds*. Honesdale, PA: Boyds Mills. ISBN 978-1-59078656-7.
   A cat adjusts to its new home when its sees some familiar things.

Roberts, Royston and Jeanie. 1995. *Lucky Science: Accidental Discoveries from Gravity to Velcro, with Experiments*. New York: Wiley. ISBN 978-0-471009542.
   The authors discuss discoveries that were seemingly made by accident and suggest experiments for students to undertake.

Robinson, Barbara. 1995. *The Best Christmas Pageant Ever*. New York: HarperCollins. ISBN 978-0060250430.
   When the worst family in the school participates in the Christmas Pageant, the community comes to know the true meaning of Christmas.

Rosenthal, Amy Krouse. 2009. *Yes Day!* Illustrated by Tom Lichtenheld. New York: Harper Collins. ISBN 978-0-06-115259-7.
   A child imagines that the answer to every request is "Yes!"

Rosenthal, Amy Krouse. 2010. *The Wonder Book*. Illustrated by Paul Schmid. New York: Harper/HarperCollins. ISBN 0-06-142974-0.
   This book is filled with poems, stories, palindromes, word games, and more.

Rosenthal, Betsy R. 2004. *My House Is Singing*. Illustrated by Margaret Chodos-Irvine. San Diego: Harcourt. o.p. ISBN 0-15-216293-3.
   This is a collection of poems about different objects and places in the home.

Saltzberg, Barney. 2010. *All Around the Seasons*. Somerville, MA: Candlewick. ISBN 978-0-7636-3694-4.
Rhyming text celebrates the four seasons.

Scanlan, Chip. "The Power of Leads." *Poynter Online*. http://www.poynter.org/how-tos/newsgathering-storytelling/chip-on-your-shoulder/11745/the-power-of-leads/ (accessed March 16, 2011).
Scanlan discusses the importance of beginning a piece well and quotes several authors to support his point.

Senzai, N. H. 2010. *Shooting Kabul*. New York: Paula Wiseman/Simon & Schuster. ISBN 978-1-4424-0194-5.
Eleven-year-old Fadi and his family settle in San Francisco after escaping Taliban-controlled Afghanistan in 2001, but Fadi plans to return to the refugee camp in Pakistan where his little sister was accidentally left behind.

Shannon, George. 2005. *White Is for Blueberry*. Illustrated by Laura Dronzek. New York: Greenwillow/HarperCollins. ISBN 978-0-06-029275-1.
The author makes a series of seemingly untrue statements until readers turn the page for an explanation.

Shusterman, Neal. 2003. *Full Tilt*. New York: Simon & Schuster. ISBN 978-0689803741.
To save his comatose brother, Blake must survive seven horrendous carnival rides.

Smith, Frank. 2005. *Reading Without Nonsense*, 4th ed. New York: Columbia College Press. ISBN 978-0807746868.
Smith advocates teaching reading naturally without emphasis on drills and phonics.

Sneed, Brad. 2005. *Deputy Harvey and the Ant Cow Caper*. New York: Dial. ISBN 978-0803730236.
One morning Ant Hill's herd of ant cows turns up missing and Deputy Harvey has to solve the mystery.

Snicket, Lemony. 1999. *A Bad Beginning*. Illustrated by Brett Helquist. New York: Harper Collins. ISBN 978-0064407663.
Three children suffer continuous misfortunes.

Sonnenblick, Jordan. 2010. *Dodger for Sale*. New York: Feiwel and Friends. ISBN 978-0-312-37795-3.
In this final book of a funny series, a school project and the genie, Dodger, help fifth-grader Willie, his friend, Elizabeth, and his younger sister, Amy, save a local forest from developers.

Spinelli, Jerry. 2010. *I Can Be Anything!* Illustrated by Jimmy Liao. Boston: Little Brown. ISBN 978-0-316-16226-5.
A boy muses on the many things he can be.

Stead, Rebecca. 2009. *When You Reach Me*. New York: Wendy Lamb/Random House. ISBN 978-385-73742-5.
As her mother prepares to be a contestant on the 1970s game show, *The $20,000 Pyramid*, Miranda tries to make sense of a series of mysterious notes received from an anonymous source that seem to defy the laws of time and space.

Steig, William. 2010 . *Shrek!* New York: Farrar, Straus and Giroux. ISBN 978-0374368791.
Shrek, a truly ugly but loveable guy, sets out to find his true love.

Tang, Greg. 2004. *Lessons That Count: Math Fables*. Illustrated by Heather Cahoon. New York: Scholastic. ISBN 0-439-45399-2.

Tang explains different ways numbers can be grouped together with original rhyming fables.

Tobias, Tobi. 2000. *Serendipity*. Illustrated by Peter H. Reynolds. New York: Simon & Schuster. o.p. ISBN 0-689-83373-3.
Young children talk about unexpected delights in their lives.

Voigt, Cynthia. 2003. *Dicey's Song*. New York: Atheneum. ISBN 978-0689863622. (pb)
This award-winning second book in a series recounts the story of the Tillerman children after they arrive at their grandmother's house.

Waters, Fiona. 2008. *Don't Kiss the Frog!: Princess Stories with Attitude*. Illustrated by Ella Furfoot. New York: Kingfisher/Holt ISBN 978-0753459539.
Six princesses obtain their hearts' desire, but they do not play by the usual rules to do it.

White, E. B. 2006 (reprint ed). *Charlotte's Web*. Illustrated by Garth Williams. New York: Harper-Collins. ISBN 978-006-1124952.
Charlotte, the spider, saves Wilbur, the pig, from a terrible fate.

Wiles, Deborah. 2005. *Each Little Bird that Sings*. San Diego: Harcourt/Gulliver. ISBN 978-0152051136.
Comfort's family owns a funeral home, but death becomes even more personal when she suffers the loss of loved ones and even the apparent death of a friendship.

Wiles, Deborah. 2010. *Countdown*. New York: Scholastic. ISBN 978-0-545-10605-4.
This documentary novel, interspersed with footage from 1962, captures the fear of an 11-year-old girl and her community caught in the grip of a nuclear threat.

Wong, Janet S. 2002. *You Have to Write*. Illustrated by Teresa Flavin. New York: Margaret K. McElderry. ISBN 0-689-83409-8.
This book encourages youngsters struggling for a topic to write about.

Wong, Janet S. 2003. *Knock on Wood: Poems about Superstitions*. Illustrated by Julie Paschkis. New York: Margaret McElderry. ISBN 0-689-85512-5.
This is a delightful collection of 17 poems about superstitions.

Yaccarino, Dan. 2007. *Every Friday*. New York: Henry Holt. ISBN 978-0-8050-7724-7.
A young boy talks about his special breakfast with his dad every Friday.

Yolen, Jane. 2000. *Not One Damsel in Distress*. Illustrated by Susan Guevara. San Diego: Harcourt. o.p. ISBN 0-15-202047-0.
The 13 folktales in this collection feature strong females from different parts of the world.

Yoon, Salina. 2010. *Wings*. New York: Little Simon/Simon & Schuster. ISBN 978-1-41698956-5.
Different creatures' wings are described in this simple touch-and-feel board book.

Yorinks, Arthur. 1986. *Louis the Fish*. Illustrated by Richard Egielski. New York: Farrar, Straus and Giroux. ISBN 978-0374445980.
Forced to work as a butcher, Louis is miserable until he turns into a fish.

Zenatti, Valerie. 2008. *A Bottle in the Gaza Sea*. New York: Bloomsbury. ISBN 978-1599902005.
A Palestinian and Israeli teen struggle to understand the hatred and violence they must live with every day.

Zusak, Markus. 2005. *I Am the Messenger*. New York: Knopf. ISBN 978-0375830990.
After Ed foils a bank robbery, he begins to receive messages that send him on missions to help people.

# 3

# Making Stories Unique

*Caress the detail, the divine detail.*

—Vladimir Nabokov

*Don't tell me the moon is shining; show me the glint of light on broken glass.*

—Anton Chekhov

We teachers have probably all experienced student writing that is so general it might even have been possible to substitute one writer's name for another's with little notice. One child's "bed-to-bed" account of a typical school day reads much like his or her classmate's. Yet, "writing becomes beautiful when it becomes specific" (Linda, a teacher, to Ralph Fletcher in *What a Writer Needs*, 1993, 47). It is that unusual pattern in the sidewalk, that chance encounter in the hall, that funny episode in the cafeteria, that turn what was once an ordinary day into a story that comes alive and makes readers notice. Our students are surrounded by little happenings: sounds, tastes, smells, encounters that constantly insert themselves into their daily lives—happenings that could have a powerful impact on their writing if only they were awake to what is going on around them. We tell our students to write from their own lives, but when we try to get them started by asking, "What's happening?" the answer is often "Nothing." Donald Graves (speech entitled "Learn to Read the World and Write It Joyfully," IRA Convention, 1995) says "we go through the world, but the world does not go through us." "Kids," he continues, "are connected to a shadow world over there . . . rather than the world that's under their noses. And it's going by." But, Graves asserts, "writing is a way of seeing the detail, reading the world, and bringing it in." Or, as Ferris Bueller would say, "Life moves pretty fast. You don't stop and look around once in a while, you could miss it."

The main character of Emily Smith Pearce's easy reader, *Slowpoke* (2010), echoes Graves's view. Fiona is so slow that she sometimes misses the school bus, so her parents send her to Speed School. Now she can "eat an ice-cream cone before you could say 'lickety-split'" and "shower in five seconds flat" (21). But "Fiona could not taste her ice cream. She could not enjoy a soak in the tub" (23). Eventually, she convinces her family to slow down a bit while she speeds up some. The result: her father actually tastes the meatloaf her mom had been serving forever. Her mother actually notices the flowers she had never noticed before. Perhaps if we slow our students down just a bit, they will notice things they, too, have never noticed before.

An excellent way to help our students "read" their world is to devote considerable time to TALKING. That is a hard saying in these days of ever-expanded amounts of the school day being given over to drill and test preparation. But we can never underestimate the power of talk to help bring the world into consciousness. We teachers can talk about the details we notice on our way to school, our walk from the parking lot to the classroom, our time in the school yard and the cafeteria. We can take our students on "read the world" walks in the neighborhood or school yard or even within the school and talk about what we have seen, smelled, and heard when we return to the classroom. To initiate such a walk, you might wish to read Elvira Woodruff's *Small Beauties: The Journey of Darcy Heart O'Hara* (2006), a picture book about a young girl whose family is forced to leave Ireland and come to America because of the failure of the potato crop. To comfort herself later during the trying transition to a new world, Darcy brings out the little things she had col-

lected before the family embarked on its journey. For "Darcy was different. She was a noticer. She stopped to notice small beauties wherever she went." We can ask our students to be alert to unique moments, "small beauties," as they wait on the lunch line or interact at recess. We can give them miniature pads they can keep in their pockets to jot down those special small moments they experience throughout the day—the sun's reflection on the slide, someone's unusual walk, a quirky remark, etc. All these and more can be grist for a story or work their way into an interesting description later on.

After enjoying a "read the world" walk and discussion, introduce the reproducible, Chapter 3.1: Reading the World, available in Appendix A. It might be a useful way to launch older students into a writing project that will help them become more aware of what is around them. With younger students, you may wish to answer the questions on the reproducible orally together and then engage in a piece of writing on a chart as a class.

Along with talk and the previous exercise, we should fill our read-aloud times with children's books that model detailed writing—stories that capture the writer's or the writer's character's unique world and help the reader experience it with all of his or her senses. The books discussed next provide wonderful examples of such writing.

### Pay Close Attention to the Particulars and Add Details

Begin consideration of particulars and details, even with older students, by sharing two picture books by Elisha Cooper: *Beach* (2006) and *Farm* (2010). When you ask

students to conjure up a day at the beach, perhaps their mental pictures will contain only sand, water, people, and, perhaps, food. But with a minimum of words and tiny vignette paintings, Cooper helps readers see all the things that are actually happening on a particular stretch of sand. "A woman lathers on sunscreen and reaches for a spot that cannot be reached." "A boy and girl ride their parents in a crab race." After turning a few pages, students will likely be amazed at all they never noticed during a beach outing. No wonder their vacation stories about time at the shore are often so lackluster! Cooper's *Farm* is also a gem of detail: "Inside the tractor the farmer drinks coffee and listens to the weather reports on the radio. Every once in a while, he turns in his seat to check the tiller." How different that is from simply saying "The farmer plowed the fields in his tractor."

In a stroke of brilliance, Russell Freedman describes what Abraham Lincoln had in his pocket on the day of his death (*Lincoln: A Photobiography*, 1987):

> The morning he died, Lincoln had in his pockets a pair of small spectacles folded into a silver case; a small velvet eyeglass cleaner; a large linen handkerchief with A. Lincoln stitched in red; an ivory pocketknife trimmed with silver; and a brown leather wallet lined with purple silk. The wallet contained a Confederate five-dollar bill bearing the likeness of Jefferson Davis and eight newspaper clippings that Lincoln had cut out and saved. All the clippings praised him. (130)

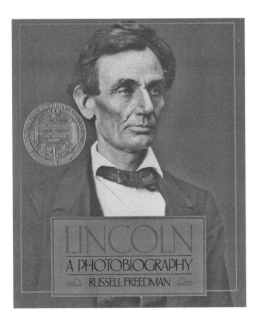

What an extraordinary picture of Lincoln, the man, this description of pocket contents offers readers.

A perfect book to read as spring approaches is Steven Schnur's *Spring Thaw* (2009). As the sun rises, Schnur recounts its effect on the snow collected on the roof: "Water trickles from the roof, drop by drop. . . . By midmorning thin streams of water snake down the windowpanes. . . . And later in the day, . . . . a thousand tiny streams run from the roof like a curtain of crystal beads." Another seasonal book is Cynthia Rylant's *In November* (2000). She describes the bare tree branches "spreading their arms like dancers"; the chilly air, the animals hunkering down to sleep, the different food smells. The refrain "In November" repeats its music throughout this lyrical heralding of fall.

A family sets off on a drive (Rosen, *A Drive in the Country*, 2007) with no particular destination in mind, and so they can take time to notice everything around them: "roads with dips and bumps. . . . smells of hay and poop from pigs . . . sprinkled rain on sun-baked roads . . . yellow lines disappearing just at the top of a hill."

One of the major tasks of the writer of fantasy is to create a setting, a world, that is so real the reader believes, right to the last page, that such a world exists and such things can really happen. Animals can talk, children can fly around on brooms, people can become invisible. Perhaps one of the most beloved works of fantasy is E. B. White's *Charlotte's Web* (2006). His description of the barn in which the farm animals live is so detailed, so real, that of course, readers will believe this barn's inhabitants can actually talk and help alter poor Wilbur's destiny:

> The barn was very large. It was very old. It smelled of hay and it smelled of manure. It smelled of the perspiration of tired horses and the wonderful sweet breath of patient cows. It often had a sort of peaceful smell—as though nothing bad could happen ever again in the world. It smelled of grain and of harness dressing and of axle grease and of rubber boots and of new rope. And whenever the cat was given a fish-head to eat, the barn would smell of fish. But mostly it smelled of hay, for there was always hay in the great loft up overhead. And there was always hay being pitched down to the cows and the horses and the sheep. (13)

Gary Provost (*Make Your Words Work: Proven Techniques for Effective Writing—For Fiction and Nonfiction*, 2001) advises writers to make their details work for them so that they are not simply presenting a picture to the reader. Rather, an effective detail makes the reader look at a particular object, scene, or character "in a certain way." An effective detail reveals more than just what the eye can see. He gives several examples, among them, how the simple change of one word, that is, from "He came in wearing *blue* jeans" to "He came in wearing *eighty-dollar* jeans" can convey a more specific idea of the kind of person the jean-wearer is (105). You can find a wonderful example of this kind of description in the world of children's books if you are fortunate enough to obtain a copy of *Like Butter on Pancakes* (London, 1995) from a library or used book seller. It is well worth the effort. In a beautiful text that comes full circle, London describes a day from the birds' first call in the morning to the birds' sleep that night. We follow the narrative into a young child's bedroom where "First light melts/like butter on pancakes,/spreads warm and yellow/across [his] pillow." London could have described the sun as coming through the window and shining on the boy's pillow or warming his pillow. But he's counting on the reader's prior experience with pancakes and how putting butter on a warm stack causes that butter to melt and run from the middle across and down the sides. So, from his text, the reader can feel the gradual movement of the sun across a pillow. It does not fall on the pillow all at once, but proceeds in stages as it changes position in the sky.

Another outstanding example of effective description is Patricia Thomas's *Nature's Paintbox: A Seasonal Gallery of Art and Verse* (2007). In it she captures the essence of each of the four seasons by describing a medium most appropriate for depicting that season. For example, because winter is largely devoid of color, she wants to sketch it "in pen and ink . . . /black and white;/sharp and clear and fine;/no colors to blur the line." She wants to draw spring in pastels "warm-as-sunshine colors; gentle baby colors." In

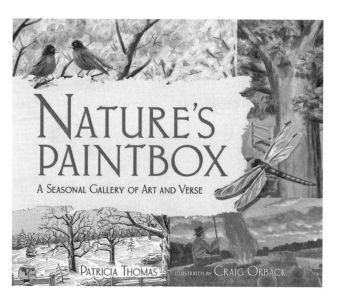

each instance, her description of the medium conjures up for the reader the *essence* of the season, not simply a mental picture of what they might see on a winter or a spring day.

## Help Readers Enjoy the Story with Their Senses

The authors of the following books include details that help readers experience their stories with multiple senses:

Linda Sue Park begins *Project Mulberry* (2005) with her heroine, Julia, recounting how she met her best friend, Patrick, because of a Korean specialty called kimchee. She describes the long, leaf cabbage from which kimchee is made. And she especially describes its smell: "it has a really strong smell. Even though it's stored in jars, you can still smell it, right through the jar and the refrigerator door. It sends out these feelers through the whole house" (2).

Ten-year-old Comfort Snowberger says, "My parents smell like a mixture of gardenias and embalming fluid, even in the evenings after their showers. I think the smells of their jobs (they run a funeral home) have permanently soaked into their skins" (Wiles, *Each Little Bird that Sings*, 2005, 17).

Deborah Hopkinson's picture book about the building of the Empire State building

(*Sky Boys: How They Built the Empire State Building*, 2006) treats readers to the feel of the icy wind of winter; the sounds of "rumbling flatbed trucks" carrying steel to the building site, and the hammering of rivets, "two rivets a minute, five hundred rivets a day"; the smell of the hot beef stew the men eat at lunch time; and the glorious sight of the skyscraper as it grows day by day.

Patricia Polacco (*An Orange for Frankie*, 2004) calls on three senses in one sentence as she summons up the memory of a very special brother: "Every time I peel an orange and inhale the scent of it and feel the mist that sprays from its skin, I think of a very special Christmas and a flaxen-haired boy who lived many years before I was ever born."

In a beautiful, complex novel for older readers Siobhan Dowd (*Bog Child*, 2008) tells parallel stories: the struggle in Northern Ireland in the 1980s and the subsequent hunger strike endured by some IRA prisoners, and the uncovering of the 2,000-year-old body of a young girl discovered preserved in a bog. The story of the girl's sacrifice for her people and the sacrifices of the IRA prisoners weave together in a fascinating tale. On the morning that the main character, Fergus, and his uncle discover the body, Dowd describes the scene this way:

> The sky was like dark glass, reluctant to let the light through. The only sound was the chudder of the van skirting the lough. The surface of the water was colourless. The hills slumped down on the far side like silhouettes of snoozing giants. Fergus yawned. It was still before five as they turned off up the mountain road. Uncle Tally chewed on nothing as the tyres lumbered over the ruts. Fergus cradled the flask of sweet black tea. (3)

Karla Kuskin captures the sights, sounds, and smells of dawn in Jerusalem (1990) in her opening paragraphs:

> The bread is baked before sunrise. I have seen a loaf that looks like a pair of eyeglasses. And another in the shape of a ladder. Every morning sixty-four kinds of bread are baked here. Every day in these narrow old streets seventy languages are spoken. This is not a very large city. It is far, far away from many that are much larger and newer. Then why should so many people come from everywhere to here? And why should they have been coming here for more than three thousand years?
>
>   Sit beside me. The sky is getting lighter. The sun comes up behind that ridge. It puts gold on the crescents and stars on the mosques, gold on the crosses of the churches

### Tell a Big Story by Writing about a Small Incident

Some stories are so big, or so devastating, that it is impossible to capture their full import in an overview. For example, writing about 6,000,000 Jews who were exterminated by the Nazis reveals a horror beyond measure. But that horror is really brought home to the reader, makes the reader care deeply in his or her mind and heart and gut, if the author writes about one particular person or group of people who suffered atrocities during Hitler's regime. That is why Anne Frank's story so captivates and why so many books for children have been written about her. We can never underestimate the power the story of a single person, a single event, or a single picture can have to touch the emotions of the reader or viewer and even to change public opinion and effect change.

During the Depression, the Farm Security Administration sent photographer Dorothea Lange to photograph migratory farm workers. Her pictures, especially the one here, caused federal officials to realize how desperate the needs of these people were, and help followed.

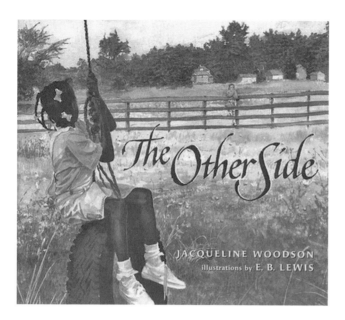

Perhaps one of the most famous photos in the world is that of Kim Phuc, a young girl who fled naked and burning during the Vietnam War. That picture aroused so much public feeling that it actually contributed to the ending of that war.

Children's book authors know the power of presenting a big topic or idea through a single person or even an object. Here are some models to share with students:

Jacqueline Woodson uses the metaphor of a fence (*The Other Side*, 2001) to describe the segregation of African Americans and Whites in the South: "That summer the fence that stretched through our town seemed bigger. We lived in a yellow house on one side of it. White people lived on the other. And Mama said, 'Don't climb over that fence when you play.' She said it wasn't safe."

An Australian and a Japanese soldier fight along the Kokoda Track in the Papua, New Guinea, jungle during World War II (Wolfer, *Photographs in the Mud*, 2007). Each has left beloved family behind to fight for his country. The soldiers encounter one another after both are wounded, and during the long night they spend together, they share family pictures. In the morning, only one soldier remains alive, and those pictures are found stuck together in the mud. Here readers face the real tragedy of war—that it is fought by human beings who are so very like one another yet forced to become enemies, and who are lost to their families forever. And this message whispers its powerful truth in the form of simple pictures carried lovingly by soldiers far from home.

Two children's picture books show young readers the ravages of the war in Iraq, each by focusing on the activities of one individual. In her very simple *Librarian of Basra: A True Story from Iraq* (2005), Jeanette Winter tells how a simple librarian and her friends moved 30,000 books into her and their homes and hid them there at great risk to themselves to keep them from being destroyed when the library was bombed. With very few words and a sky depicted in ever-darkening colors, Winter conveys the fear and destruction that war brings. Young Ali (Rumford, *Silent Music: A Story of Baghdad*, 2008), who lives in Baghdad and loves many of the things young readers of his story would enjoy: playing soccer with friends, music, dancing—finds comfort from the fear of war by practicing calligraphy much as his hero, Yakus, also found respite from war through calligraphy 800 years before. Ali observes how some words, like "HARB–war," flow easily from the pen, whereas others, like "SALAM–peace," are more difficult to form—just as differences are more difficult to settle peacefully than through violence. This is a beautifully illustrated book that sheds light on life in a war-torn country through the actions of a boy and his pen.

In her book for older readers, *No Choirboy: Murder, Violence and Teenagers on Death Row* (2008), Susan Kuklin tells the stories, often in their own words, of four teens who committed murder before the age of eighteen and are condemned to death row. She also presents one of the victims' families and the work of an attorney who fights to end the death penalty. The teens talk about the foolish decisions that brought them to this moment, their regrets, and their wasted lives. In one section, Kuklin brings the horrors of life on death row home to the reader by focusing on a number:

> My number is 999163. That's not my identification number; that's my death number. This number is based on the order in which you come to death row. A lot of times, they try to kill you in that order. It's your death number, right? They make me recite it all day. You gotta put it on your mail. You gotta say it every time they come to count you. You gotta say it to get trays–999163. It replaces me being Nanon. They ask for the number half the time before they ask you your name. (90)

A young girl expresses her close relationship with her mother by talking about her mother's voice in Joanne Ryder's *My Mother's Voice* (2006): her mother's cheering voice at ball games, her comforting voice, her calling voice. By presenting the different intonations of her mother's voice depending upon the situation, the girl reveals both the joyous and more trying times she and her parent share.

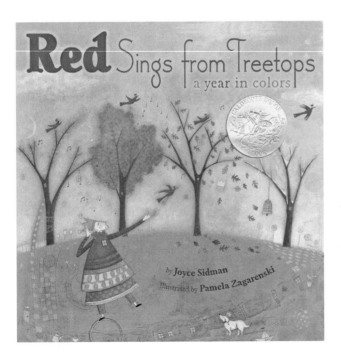

A close examination of some of the books discussed previously should help students become more aware of the ways in which authors use details in their writing when they read on their own. And, of course, we want them to try to include the details that will make their own writing sparkle. They can try their hand at crafting meaningful details by using the reproducible entitled Chapter 3.2: Colors in the Seasons/Classroom found in Appendix A. First, read Joyce Sidman's beautiful Caldecott Honor book *Red Sings from Treetops: A Year in Colors* (2009) and talk about it together. Then distribute the reproducible and ask older students to work on it alone or in groups. Share the results aloud. You might want to engage younger students in the activity by reading the example on the reproducible aloud, determining together what space or season and color the class would like to write about, and then writing a few lines about the color on a chart following the pattern on the reproducible.

### Writing with a Unique Voice

Voice is one of the most important ways a writer makes a piece unique. In fact, asserts Jane Kurtz, it is "the writer's job to find the right voice for each piece of writing." "Just as people can be entertaining and compelling to listen to when they talk,"

she continues, "people can be entertaining and compelling to listen to when they write" (*Jane Kurtz and You*, 2007, 8). Finding one's voice, however, is, perhaps, the most difficult writing challenge of all. In her article entitled "Ten Steps to Finding Your Writing Voice" (2007), Holly Lisle says that writing with voice "means you have to put yourself on your page. Voice is style, plus theme, plus personal observations, plus passion, plus belief, plus desire." Yes, writing with voice involves all that, and yet, laments Trip Gabriel in his piece entitled "The Almighty Essay" (*NY Times Education Life*, January 7, 2011, ED 6), college admissions officers "have made a fetish of the personal essay." Even though many professional authors do not succeed in crafting "prose in which an author's voice emerges through layers of perfectly correct sentences," admissions personnel expect teenagers to do just that in the essays they write for college admission. Certainly, then, we should do all we can to help our students find their writing voices during their elementary and high school years.

We will meet some characters with resounding voices in the next chapter, and non-fiction that is filled with passion and voice in Chapter 5. But here, we can consider how to help young writers find that all-important aspect of writing—their own voice—when they write personal narratives and poems. Excellent examples of what writing with voice, passion, and emotion sounds like are two picture books: Holly Hobbie's *Everything but the Horse* (2010) and Jane Yolen's *Elsie's Bird* (2010). Hobbie tells the story of a special time in her childhood—her family's move from a house in a

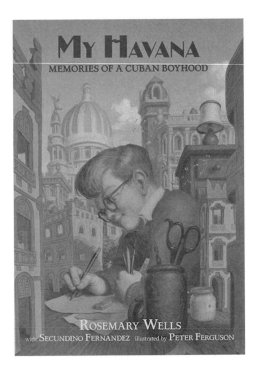

neighborhood "packed with kids" to a lonely farm in the country. But she soon falls in love with the place and, especially, with the animals. Her fondness for them shines through in her words as she describes "talk[ing] softly to the chickens" and learning to milk the "beautiful Guernsey cow." Her longing for one animal in particular, though, begins to grow when she first sees "Sarah Wilcox on her tall, glossy horse." "I was swept away," she writes. She talks about "long[ing] to watch the Dowd Morgans galloping on their hill." She says "a horse was the one and only thing [she] wanted more than anything in the world." And she shows readers that desire in action. Holly pictures herself in the saddle. She even collects manure and scatters it in the barn so it smells like her horse is in there. Yolen's narrator tells Elsie's story from her point of view. After her mother's death, Elsie's father decides to move from her beloved Boston with its "cozy harbor," "busy streets," and her many friends to the Nebraska prairie where "the only sea . . . was a sea of grass," and "the nearest neighbors lived miles away." Elsie cries at night, she "huddle[s]. . . . in the cool dark of the sod house," she "dream[s] of Boston cobbles and bells," and refuses to listen to the prairie sounds. But when she must chase her pet bird across "the tall prairie grass," a whole new world of sound and beauty opens to her. A longer personal narrative or memoir is one Rosemary Wells wrote with the man whose story it is, Secundino Fernandez, who is now an architect in New York. In *My Havana: Memories of a Cuban Boyhood* (2010) Fernandez describes his ardent feelings for Havana, land of his birth, his dismay when the family has to move to Spain to help an uncle who had an accident, and, worse, when they had to leave Havana permanently in 1959 to escape a dictator. Exhibiting artistic talent at a very young age, Secundino draws pictures of Havana buildings while in Spain to curb his homesickness. He relates his emotions when the family returns to Havana, though he is unaware at the time it will not be permanent: "I wander the streets with my head up like a tourist. 'I will never leave you again,' I whisper to my city" (35). Forced to leave for good a few years later, however, Secundino tells us he went through the streets saying goodbye to the buildings he loved. "I wanted," he says, "to listen one last time to the wind in the palms that circled the harbor facing El Palacio Presidencial" (46). These books are suitable read-alouds for students of all ages. After reading any or all of them, prompt students to listen for words and actions that express true feelings, passion. Make a list of these words and phrases together. Then ask the students to think of something they themselves want more than anything else. It does not have to be a material thing. It could be peace, a certain kind of food in the cafeteria, a special friend, a school project, etc. What words might best express this desire? What actions could demonstrate that the writer's desire is real? Challenge students to write down words and phrases that might eventually be incorporated into a narrative or poem. In a very brief YouTube video (see http://www.youtube.com/watch?v=Nmxiba53w-I&eurl=http%3A%2F %2Ftechnorati%2Ecom%2Fvideos%2Fyoutube%2Ecom%252Fwatch%253Fv%253DNm xiba53w%2DI&feature=player_embedded) of a school visit, children's book author Deborah Wiles speaks of the importance of exposing children to many personal narrative stories. To help them get started on their own writing, she asks them to list things that make them angry, sad, happy, or frightened and begin from there. Watching this clip with students might help them find their voices as they begin their own pieces.

Another way to foster writing with voice is to encourage journal writing, for when students write in a journal or diary, they are most themselves. In this kind of informal writing, they express their ideas, their desires, their frustrations, their problems, their plans, etc. It is out of such passionate writing, out of such emotions, that their natural voices come through. It is a good idea to provide some journal writing time each day and to ask students to read their journals regularly, circling sections that could be the germ of a piece of writing they truly care about. We can also offer them children's books in which the characters write in a journal or diary. A few good examples are: Jessica Green's *Diary of a Would-be Princess* (2007); Jeff Kinney's *Diary of a Wimpy Kid* (2007) and others in this series; Kevin Henkes's *Olive's Ocean* (2005); Sherman Alexie's *The Absolutely True Diary of a Part-time Indian* (2007) and Saci Lloyd's *The Carbon Diaries 2015* (2009) and its sequel for older students; and Doreen Cronin's picture book, *Diary of a Worm* (2003) and others in this series.

## References

Alexie, Sherman. 2007. *The Absolutely True Diary of a Part-time Indian*. Boston: Little Brown. ISBN 978-031601368-0.
    Arnold Spirit writes in his diary about the trials of growing up on the res, leaving, and being the only Indian in his high school.

Cooper, Elisha. 2006. *Beach*. New York: Orchard, 2006. ISBN 978-0439687850.
    The author provides delightful details in words and pictures about activities at the beach.

Cooper, Elisha. 2010. *Farm*. New York: Orchard. ISBN 978-0545070751.
    Cooper describes in detail the activities of a farm family from March to November.

Cronin, Doreen. 2003. *Diary of a Worm*. Illustrated by Harry Bliss. New York: HarperCollins ISBN 978-006000150-6.
    A young son in the worm family writes a diary about the ups and downs of being a worm. See other books in this wonderful series.

Dowd, Siobhan. 2008. *Bog Child*. New York: David Fickling/Random House. ISBN 978-0385751698.
  While his brother is enduring a hunger strike in prison in Northern Ireland in the 1980s, Fergus and his uncle uncover the 2,000-year-old body of a young girl who had also made a great sacrifice for her people.

Fletcher, Ralph. 1993. *What a Writer Needs*. Portsmouth, NH: Heinemann. ISBN 0-435-08734-7.
  Fletcher discusses the writer's craft and those things the writer needs to learn to be successful.

Freedman, Russell. 1987. *Lincoln: A Photobiography*. New York: Clarion/Houghton Mifflin. ISBN 978-0899193809.
  Freedman's Newbery award-winning biography presents Lincoln in period photos as well as text.

Gabriel, Trip. "The Almighty Essay." *New York Times Education Life*, January 7, 2011, ED 6.
  Gabriel laments the importance college admissions officers place on the personal essay.

Graves, Donald. 1995. "Learn to Read the World and Write It Joyfully." Anaheim, CA: International Reading Association Convention.
  In this speech, Graves maintained that their writing lacks detail because students do not notice the world around them.
  He advocates giving students many opportunities to "Read the World."

Green, Jessica. 2007. *Diary of a Would-be Princess*. Cambridge, MA: Charlesbridge. ISBN 978-158089167-7. (pb)
  Jillian, a fifth grader and an unpopular girl, is looked down upon by the "princesses" in her class. In fact, there is so much backstabbing and bullying going on that she invites everyone to her birthday party to try to bring the class together. She writes of her many adventures in a diary that is sure to keep you laughing out loud.

Henkes, Kevin. 2005. *Olive's Ocean*. New York: Greenwillow. ISBN 978-0060535452.
  Olive dies in a car crash and her mother gives Martha a page of the dead girl's journal in which she talks about Martha as "the nicest girl in our class." Martha learns more from Olive's writing than she ever did from the girl herself. This is a beautiful coming-of-age novel.

Hobbie, Holly. 2010. *Everything but the Horse: A Childhood Memory*. New York: Little Brown. ISBN 978-0-316-07019-5.
  The author recalls a time when she desperately wanted a horse and received a bicycle instead.

Hopkinson, Deborah. 2006. *Sky Boys: How They Built the Empire State Building*. Illustrated by James E. Ransome. New York: Schwartz & Wade/Random House. ISBN 0-375-83610-1.
  Hopkinson recounts, through the eyes of a young boy, the building of the Empire State Building in New York during the Depression.

Kinney, Jeff. 2007. *Diary of a Wimpy Kid*, 3rd ed. New York: Amulet/Abrams. ISBN 978-0810993136.
  Greg writes in a diary throughout a year of middle school and accompanies his writing with funny illustrations. This wildly popular series has many other books.

Kuklin, Susan. 2008. *No Choirboy: Murder, Violence and Teenagers on Death Row*. New York: Holt, 2008. ISBN 978-080507950-0.
  This is the harrowing account of four teens on death row and one of their victim's family.

Kurtz, Jane. 2007. *Jane Kurtz and You*. Westport, CT: Libraries Unlimited. ISBN 978-1-59158-295-3.
   Kurtz describes the things good writers do and gives examples from her own books.

Kuskin, Karla. 1990. *Jerusalem Shining Still*. New York: Trophy. o.p. ISBN 978-0064432436.
   Kuskin discusses the history of Jerusalem and the three religions that seek to claim the city.

Lisle, Holly. 2007. *Ten Steps to Finding Your Writing Voice*. http://hollylisle.com/fm/Articles/wc1-6.html, accessed March 16, 2011.
   The author offers 10 suggestions writers can use to develop their unique writing voice.

Lloyd, Saci. 2009. *The Carbon Diaries 2015*. New York: Holiday House. ISBN 978-0823421909.
   Laura Brown, a teen living in London, chronicles in her diary life during the first year of the government's carbon rationing. She includes newspaper clippings and other items in her account. See also *The Carbon Diaries 2017*.

London, Jonathan. 1995. *Like Butter on Pancakes*. Illustrated by G. Brian Karas. New York: Viking/Penguin. ISBN 0-670-85130-2.
   London describes the passing of a day from early morning to sleep in the evening.

Park, Linda Sue. 2005. *Project Mulberry*. New York: Clarion. ISBN 978-0-618-47786-9.
   While working on a school project, Julia, a Korean American, and her friend, Patrick, learn about silk worms and also about tolerance, prejudice, friendship, patience, and more.

Pearce, Emily Smith. 2010. *Slowpoke*. Illustrated by Scot Ritchie. Honesdale, PA: Boyds Mills. ISBN 978-1-59078-705-2.
   Fiona is very slow and her family is very fast. Eventually, they learn to enjoy their lives more with a bit of compromise.

Polacco, Patricia. 2004. *An Orange for Frankie*. New York: Philomel/Penguin. ISBN 978-0399-24302-8.
   Polacco recalls a special Christmas during the Depression and the generosity of her brother.

Provost, Gary. 2001. *Make Your Words Work: Proven Techniques for Effective Writing—For Fiction and Nonfiction*. Bloomington, IN: iUniverse. ISBN 978-0595174867.
   This book is filled with ideas for authors who wish to make their writing effective.

Rosen, Michael J. 2007. *A Drive in the Country*. Illustrated by Marc Burckhardt. Cambridge, MA: Candlewick. ISBN 978-0-7636-2140-7.
   A family takes a drive in the country and notices many things along the way.

Rumford, James. 2008. *Silent Music: A Story of Baghdad*. New York: Roaring Brook. ISBN 978-1-59643-276-5.
   Ali finds refuge from war as he practices the graceful art of calligraphy.

Ryder, Joanne. 2006. *My Mother's Voice*. Illustrated by Peter Catalanotto. New York: HarperCollins. ISBN 978-006029509-7.
   A girl expresses her love for her mother by talking about all the different intonations of her mother's voice.

Rylant, Cynthia. 2000. *In November*. Illustrated by Jill Kastner. San Diego: Harcourt. ISBN 0-15-201076-9.
   In lyrical language, Rylant describes the signs of autumn in nature, animals, and people.

Schnur, Steven. 2009. *Spring Thaw*. Illustrated by Stacey Schuett. New York: Viking/Penguin. ISBN 0-670-87961-4.
   Schnur describes the signs of spring on a farm.

Sidman, Joyce. 2009. *Red Sings from Treetops: A Year in Colors*. Illustrated by Pamela Zagarenski. New York: Houghton Mifflin Harcourt. ISBN 978-0547014944.
    Sidman explores, in a very unique way, the different colors of each season.

Thomas, Patricia. 2007. *Nature's Paintbox: A Seasonal Gallery of Art and Verse*. Illustrated by Craig Orback. Minneapolis, MN: Millbrook/Lerner. ISBN 978-0-8225-6807-0.
    The author captures the essence of each season by rendering it in an appropriate medium.

Wells, Rosemary, with Secundino Fernandez. 2010. *My Havana: Memories of a Cuban Boyhood*. Illustrated by Peter Ferguson. Somerville, MA: Candlewick. ISBN 978-0-7636-4305-8.
    Secundino Fernandez recalls his love for his beloved Havana and his pain at having to leave the city of his birth.

White, E. B. 2006. *Charlotte's Web*. Illustrated by Garth Williams. Reprint, New York: Harper-Collins. ISBN 978-0739477076.
    Facing eventual slaughter at market, Wilbur the pig's life is saved by Charlotte, the spider.

Wiles, Deborah. 2005. *Each Little Bird That Sings*. San Diego, CA: Gulliver/Harcourt. ISBN 0-15-205113-9.
    Comfort's family owns a funeral home, but she is not prepared for the deaths that strike too close to her heart.

Winter, Jeanette. 2005. *The Librarian of Basra: A True Story of Iraq*. San Diego: Harcourt. ISBN 978-0- 152054458.
    Alia Muhammad Baker, chief librarian of Basra's Central Library, saves thousands of books by hiding them in her home and the homes of friends before the bombs drop in Iraq.

Wolfer, Diane. 2007. *Photographs in the Mud*, 2nd ed. Fremantle, WA: Fremantle Press. ISBN 978-192136104-3.
    Two wounded enemy soldiers, a Japanese and an Australian, spend the night together in the muddy jungle and share family pictures.

Woodruff, Elvira. 2006. *Small Beauties: The Journey of Darcy Heart O'Hara*. Illustrated by Adam Rex. New York: Knopf/Random House. ISBN 978-0-375-82686-3.
    The small things Darcy notices and collects from her home in Ireland comfort her and her family when they emigrate to America.

Woodson, Jacqueline. 2001. *The Other Side*. Illustrated by E. B. Lewis. New York: Putnam/Penguin. ISBN 978-0039923116-2.
    An African American girl and a White girl dare to climb over a fence and play together in the segregated South.

Yolen, Jane. 2010. *Elsie's Bird*. Illustrated by David Small. New York: Philomel/Penguin. ISBN 978-0-399-25292-1.
    Young Elsie misses her Boston home when her father moves them to the Nebraska prairie after her mother's death.

# 4

# Creating Memorable Characters

*A writer's job is to create people who are not "generic," but instead people who are distinctive in the ways they talk and move and fight and play.*

—Jane Kurtz

We all know that the books that resonate with us long after we turn the last page are those with memorable characters. These characters are REAL to us, people whose needs are like ours, whose fears are like ours, whose passions are like ours. We either love or hate them, but we cannot remain indifferent to them. Their voices ring in our ears, making us laugh, cry, or even shudder in fear. According to Orson Scott Card (*Characters & Viewpoint*, 1988),

> Readers want . . . characters to seem like real people. Whole and alive, believable and worth caring about. Readers want to get to know . . . characters as well as they know their own friends, their own family. As well as they know themselves. (4)

Very often though, and this is especially true for students or less experienced readers, a first reading of a story or novel centers around plot. We turn the pages to find out what happens next. Although we grow to care deeply about the main characters, we do not focus on why this is so. We do not stop to figure out how the author has created such a character and what it is about that character that strikes a chord with us as readers. We teachers need to slow our students down, to encourage rereading if not entire books, at least certain pages and paragraphs so that we can focus on the author's craft. The books offered in this chapter are especially suited to such scrutiny and discussion, because the characters in them are rich and multi-faceted. Of course, this is only the barest sampling, because most of the hundreds of books, and certainly all the novels, allotted precious space on my shelves contain such characters. To present them all here would be impossible, and you will, at any rate, wish to focus on some favorites of your own.

## Making Characters Memorable

### Meet Your Character before He or She Appears in the Story

My students let out a collective gasp when talented children's book author, Joan Bauer, visited and showed them the 30-page biography she had written for her main character before she even began work on her book. She needed, she said, to know her character inside and out; to discover what she had been doing before this particular story begins; to understand her character's family, friends and possible enemies, her joys, fears, challenges. She needed to hear her character's voice—how she talked and responded to the people and events in her life. Above all, she wanted to know her character's burning passion, because it would be this passion that would drive her actions and decisions. It was, Joan, admitted, a considerable amount of work to create this prior life for her character. But it was work that paid off handsomely once Joan placed that character in a setting and gave her a set of problems to solve. Because she knew her so well, Joan could figure out how her character would navigate through both the good and bad days of her life.

To help students see how helpful considering a character's earlier life in a biographical sketch is, encourage them to try one. If you have read a novel in common, one with a powerful main character who resonated with the students, that would be a good choice. Picture books for younger and older children can work as well. A few I highly recommend are Patricia Polacco's *Mrs. Katz and Tush* (2009), Laura E. Williams's *The Can Man* (2010), or Karima Grant's *Sophie and the City* (2006). Kevin Henkes has written several picture books with strong characters (as we shall see in detail later with his Lilly). Divide older students into small groups and ask them to write a series of questions they can ask the character in an interview to find out more about that person's life and personality. Younger students would probably find it easier to work together on a chart. In *Spilling Ink* by Anne Mazer and Ellen Potter (2010), Potter lists 15 questions (see p. 27) to consider. The answers the group or class comes up with should be similar to what they know of the character after reading the book. They can then work the answers

into a brief biographical piece. This, of course, is working backwards because they have already read the book and know how the character lives and acts. But this exercise will pave the way for the much more difficult task of creating their own characters. At the very least, it will certainly help students understand a character in a particular book more thoroughly, and therefore, make them better readers.

### Give the Character a Distinctive Name

Authors spend a good deal of time choosing just the right name for their characters. A name can reveal a character's personality, ethnicity, and much more. M. E. Kerr (*Blood on the Forehead: What I Know about Writing*, 1998) says, "When a writer chooses names for characters, she has to believe they couldn't be called anything else. Frankenstein could never be called Anderson. Dr. Jekyll and Mr. Hyde could never be called Dr. White and Mr. Smith. Mickey Mouse wouldn't make it as Walter Mouse" (231).

Gary D. Schmidt's name for the hero of *The Wednesday Wars* (2007) is a great example of the important role a character's name plays. Holling is different from all of his seventh-grade classmates. Half of them are Jewish and go to Hebrew School every Wednesday afternoon. The other half are Catholic and go to Catechism class at St. Adelbert's on that same afternoon. But Holling is neither. His family is Presbyterian, and he goes nowhere on Wednesday afternoons. And this means his teacher, instead of having free time, must stay in the classroom with him. Holling's full name? Holling Hoodhood—a name so different it embodies Holling's unique classification as the only Protestant in class. It encapsulates not only the weekly agony of, in his view, punishing his teacher, but also the agony of constantly having to apologize for his name.

Ask students to think of some distinctive character names from children's books they love. How do these names especially fit that character's personality and/or situation? Discuss such names as Ferdinand (Leaf, *The Story of Ferdinand*, 1936), *Fancy Nancy* (O'Connor 2005), Curious George (Ray, *The Complete Adventures of Curious George, Anniversary Edition*, 2001), The Grinch (Seuss, *How the Grinch Stole Christmas*, 1957), Winnie-the-Pooh (Milne, *The Complete Tales of Winnie-the-Pooh*, 1996), Stanley Yelnats (Sachar, *Holes*, 2008), Winn-Dixie (DeCamillo, *Because of Winn-Dixie*, 2000), and others. You may wish to ask students to fill out the top part of the reproducible entitled

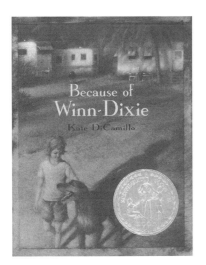

Chapter 4.1: Distinctive Character Names, available in Appendix A. Those students who are planning to write a story with a main character can fill out the bottom part as well to help them name a character of their own creation.

### Describe the Character's Appearance

Children's book author Ann Turner and I were chatting in my living room when she stopped in the middle of a sentence and focused on a picture among a collection of framed photos on display. "Well, that's just more proof," she said pointing to a picture of my grandparents standing in front of their Model-T. "Proof for what?" I asked. "I've been observing women for six months and now I'm convinced that heavy-set women stand with their arms twisted so that their elbows are pointing out." And sure enough, there was my buxom grandmother standing exactly that way. I was overwhelmed by Ann's statement—she had been observing women for *six months*! Her research would likely find its way into one sentence of a character description. Such is the great care excellent authors take to get things right. These are the authors we want to put before our students.

In Deborah Wiles's *Each Little Bird that Sings* (2005), Comfort Snowberger describes her young cousin, Peach:

> Now, Peach didn't act orderly, but he was the most orderly-*looking* person you would ever want to meet. Every single day he looked like he had just walked out of Sunday school: Every thin yellow hair on his pinhead was perfectly cut and licked to a gloss. He wore a white button-down shirt and long brown pants, with shiny brown shoes. He was scrubbed so clean, his pale skin seemed to glow. (105)

Lloyd Alexander's description of Rizka (*Gypsy Rizka*, 1999) tells us as much about the girl as it does about her appearance:

> She was skinny as a smoked herring; long-shanked, bright-eyed, with cheekbones sharp enough to whittle a stick. She had nothing, but was generous with it. She preferred laughing to crying; she could whistle every birdsong, and the birds whistled back at her. She lived by her wits and, since they were very quick wits, she lived not too badly. (4)

Richard Peck, author of over 18 novels for young people and winner of the prestigious Margaret A. Edwards Award for his contributions to the field, is a master of characterization and humor. Often he combines both in his descriptions of the people who inhabit his books. He peppers *On the Wings of Heroes* (2007) with hilarious descriptions of the many characters within its pages:

A black shape stood in the barn door against the sunlight. The figure held a shotgun. . . . It was a dried-up woman with a face like a walnut. She'd lowered her blunderbuss . . . The gun hung broken open in the crook of her wrinkled arm. (67–68)

In that bed was a woman that time had forgot. She had a face like the Grand Canyon. She was bigger than Miss Titus, and somewhat balder. . . . Strange smells wafted out of the bed. We were close enough to see all the craters in her nose. (72)

Meet Grandma Dowdel, heroine of Peck's *A Long Way from Chicago* (1997) and of two later novels, *A Year Down Yonder* (2000) and *A Season of Gifts* (2009). From *A Year Down Yonder:*

My goodness she was a big woman. . . . And taller still with her spidery old umbrella held up to keep off the sun of high noon. A fan of white hair escaped the big bun on the back of her head. She drew nearer till she blotted out the day. You couldn't call her a welcoming woman, and there wasn't a hug in her. . . . Nobody had told Grandma that skirts were shorter this year. Her skirttails brushed her shoes. I recognized the dress. It was the one she put on in hot weather to walk uptown in. (5)

Descriptions of Georgie Bishop, a fourth grader who is a dwarf, appear throughout Lisa Graff's *The Thing about Georgie* (2007). He has "stubby little fingers" and cannot "hold his pencil like any regular person and make it move where he want[s]" (20). He was "born with a big head, a stuck-out forehead, arms that barely reached his waist, and legs that bowed at the knees" (23–24). And just to make sure we fully understand Georgie's challenges, a chummy narrator occasionally interrupts the story to make a request and tell us something else Georgie cannot do. Before he even allows the reader to begin, this mysterious narrator says:

Stretch your right arm high up to the sky. Now reach across the top of your head and touch your left ear. Did you do it? Good. Go find a mirror and look at yourself. . . . Did you know you could do that?
Well, Georgie can't.
I thought you should know that before you started. (1)

Georgie will never be a great musician like his parents, strangers often stare at him, and his classmate, Jeanette Wallace (alias Jeannie the Meanie), constantly taunts him. Georgie is an upbeat kid, though, and he does not focus on these things. He has loving parents who consider him "the completion of [their] song," and a best friend, Andy, with whom he shares everything, including a successful dog-walking business. But then Georgie's parents announce they are having a baby, a normal, healthy baby who will soon grow taller than Georgie; he has a falling-out with Andy; and, horrors, he must partner with Jeanie to portray Abraham Lincoln in a class play. This is a wonderfully funny and entertaining look at a serious disability with a winsome protagonist who will help young people see his accomplishments along with his limitations. An added delight: the surprise identity of that bossy narrator at the end.

### Describe What a Character Does

In *What a Writer Needs* (1993) Ralph Fletcher talks about how providing "telling detail," describing a specific action, can "bring a character to life." He gives an example of what he means by quoting from *Miss Maggie* (1983) a picture book by Cynthia Rylant:

> Sometimes Miss Maggie rode to the grocery store with Nat and his grandfather. Nat would wait in the truck when Miss Maggie went into the store, because she always had a wad of tobacco in her jaw and she'd spit it just anywhere she pleased. Nat was afraid people might think she was a relative. (*What a Writer Needs*, 59)

That action of spitting tobacco just anywhere reveals a great deal about the kind of person Miss Maggie is—someone removed from polite society and unaware of social graces.

In *Rules of the Road* (Bauer 1998), Jenna describes the president of the shoe company, Mrs. Gladstone's, reaction when Jenna's drunk father comes into the shoe store: "Mrs. Gladstone snapped her long, bony fingers at Murray to do something. . . . Her gray eyes blasted through me. She stood rigidly erect, every thick, snowy curl in place" (9). Clearly Mrs. Gladstone is a very proper lady who brooks no untoward behavior in one of her establishments!

Even before she knows Dustfinger is a character who once inhabited a book and has now come with terrible news, Meggie fears him because of his unusual stoicism as he stands in the pouring rain:

> the stranger was little more than a shadow. Only his face gleamed white as he looked up at Meggie. His hair clung to his wet forehead. The rain was falling on him, but he ignored it. He stood there motionless, arms crossed over his chest as if that might at least warm him a little. And he kept on staring at the house. (Funke, *Inkheart*, 2009, 2)

In Sarah Weeks's *As Simple as It Seems* (2010), Verbina Colter finds out, at age 11, that she is adopted. Worse, her birth mother was an alcoholic, responsible for causing Verbina to be born with fetal alcohol syndrome—a condition that makes academic learning extremely difficult for her. Worse still, her father is in jail for killing a man, and Verbina is convinced that she is intrinsically evil and will do something terrible one day. Her adoptive parents are very loving and put up with her terrible moods, but Verbina is now uncomfortable with them, with the world, and most of all, with who she is. "A person's habits and patterns of behavior are definitely a part of who he is—especially if those habits drive you crazy" (Card, 1988, 11). So

repeatedly throughout the book, Weeks gives readers evidence of her character's unease by saddling her with a nervous mannerism. She "push[es] [her] glasses up with a bent knuckle and then pull[s] them partway back down [her] nose again" (29, 60, 68, 110, 122). Verbina is a marvelously drawn character who grows remarkably as the story progresses.

### Voice

The way you craft your characters will decide their *voice*, and whether they become powerful, jump-off-the-page characters, or pale, fade-into-the-text nonentities. Your story is seen, told and experienced, through the eyes, ears, and senses of your main character. It takes a main character with a powerful voice, to grab a reader by the scruff of the neck, and keep him reading until THE END.

—Margot Finke

In the previous chapter, we discussed voice in student writing. Their personal narratives and poems should encompass topics they choose so that the pieces ring with their own emotions and unique voices. In fiction writing, voice comes through in the kind of narration the author employs. Several different choices are available, of course, depending upon who tells the story. Will a main character tell the story in the first person from his or her point of view? Will a narrator tell the story from a single character's point of view or tell the reader about several characters' thoughts and actions? *Duck! Rabbit!* (Rosenthal 2009), a very simple picture book, can help even young children understand the concept of point of view. Two people, both unseen, look at the image of a creature with a pointed snout and long appendages. "Hey, look! A duck!" says one. "That's not a duck. That's a rabbit!" counters the other. And they continue in this vein, giving explanations for their opinions. One declares the two long appendages are a bill and therefore, the creature is a duck. The other insists they are ears and belong to a rabbit. Readers can see these two equally valid points of view. In another picture book, Melita Morales's *Jam & Honey* (2011), a little girl goes with her mother to pick blueberries. For her, the berries mean "sweet jam on toast" for a tasty treat. In the second half of the book, while on her berry-picking expedition, the girl encounters the bee, who sees the berry bush as a source of nectar from which it will make "sweet honey to fill our honeycomb." Older students can see different points of view in action in Marilyn Singer's masterful poetry book, *Mirror Mirror* (2010). As mentioned in Chapter 1, each of these poems involves classic fairy tale characters. Read top to bottom, they express one character's point of view. Read bottom to top, the exact same words express another character's point of view. The poems make fascinating reading.

Ellen Potter gives a very readable explanation of different points of view and narrative voices along with examples in *Spilling Ink* (Mazer and Potter, 2010, 66–76). You may wish to discuss these distinctions with older students. Certainly, it would be too confusing for younger children. For all students, perhaps the best thing we can do is give them many examples of powerful voices in both picture books and novels and discover together with them what makes these voices continue to resound in our ears long after we have finished reading. We can hear these voices in the dialogue of the characters and in the language the narrator uses to tell the story. The books discussed in the following paragraphs are excellent resources. Because voice is best discovered through one's ears, read as many of them aloud as you can. Play audio versions of them and/or make audio books available to the students so they can listen on their own. Phyllis Levy Mandell's article "Heard Any Good Books Lately?" (32–38) in the August 2010 issue of *School Library Journal* discusses the best audio books available for middle and high school students. You can also go to http://www.randomhouse.com/audio/listeninglibrary/for an extensive list of audio books put out by Listening Library, now part of Random House Children's Books and even hear excerpts on the site. These productions are all excellent and most of the narrators are professional actors. In addition, many other publishers put out audio versions of their books. Their websites provide information about their offerings.

Three excellent examples of narrative voice are Kate DiCamillo's *Tale of Despereaux*, Lynne Rae Perkins's *As Easy as Falling off the Face of the Earth* (2010), and Adam Gidwitz's *A Tale Dark & Grimm* (2010). These narrators weave fascinating tales, infuse their stories with humor, and address the reader with interesting and often funny asides. After the mouse community banishes her hero, Despereaux, to the dungeon with the rats because of his unmouse-like behavior (he actually reads books instead of eating them!), DiCamillo's narrator asks, "Reader, do you believe that there is such a thing as happily ever after? Or, like Despereaux, have you, too, begun to question the possibility of happy endings?" (58). In Perkin's novel, Ry finds himself in a strange town when he leaves the train he was on to make a phone call and the train leaves without him. He is befriended by an adult, Del, a MacGyver-type, and the two of them travel by car, plane, and boat across country and even to Caribbean islands to locate the boy's grandfather and parents. With many miles behind them, they finally arrive at Ry's home and Ry heads for the shower. At this point, the narrator chimes in:

> While he is doing so (taking a shower), a tribute to showers: They are amazing. You could call them "transformers." Especially if its' been a couple/few days. You feel like a different person afterward, a person who is ready. A person who can take it on. Deal with it. Whatever it might be. This fades over time, but for at least half an hour, everything is within the realm of possibility. . . . If you decide to do something big right after a shower, maybe you should wait an hour. Count to 216,000, then decide. I don't know. I'm just saying. (171–72)

In Adam Gidwitz's book, Hansel and Gretel leave home because of their parents' cruelty and wander into eight Grimm-like tales, each more deliciously horrifying than

the previous one. Throughout these stories, the narrator constantly assures readers, in bold print, that what he is relating really happened; or warns them to gird their loins for the worst yet to come, and, especially, to make sure the young ones are safely out of earshot; or even warns his characters, as he does with Gretel when she is about to ignore voices that tell her not to venture into the home of a handsome stranger:

> GRETEL!
> What are you doing? Turn around! Go home! Go home!
> You would go home, wouldn't you, dear reader? You wouldn't be taken in by such a man as this. You would turn right around and leave.
> Tell me you would. Say you would. (95)

Several recent books feature characters with some form of autism. Listening to their unique voices and watching them in action can give readers a good idea of what life as an autistic person can be like. Marcelo, spelled with one "l" he insists (Stork, *Marcelo in the Real World*, 2009),  hears music no one else can hear as a consequence of the kind of autism he has. His father wants him to live in the "real world," go to a regular school, and to take a summer job at his law firm instead of working in the stables taking care of the ponies ridden by disabled children. Marcelo speaks with a naiveté that is touching, mentions himself in the third person, and tells us he is glad his desk in the mail room faces the wall with no one facing him. He takes statements literally so that when his mentor tells him that in the firm "Everything these people do is urgent and everything needs to be done yesterday," 17-year-old Marcelo answers, "Yesterday already happened" (52). Yet, when he discovers a terrible secret in the firm, Marcelo has the strength and compassion to do something about it. As an autistic 12-year-old, Jason (Baskin, *Anything but Typical*, 2009) experiences challenges every day. He has an extremely hard time gauging other people's feelings and reactions and interacting with them. He flaps his hands when he tries to say something or when he is thinking, and his unusual mannerisms ostracize him from his peers. He seeks refuge from his difficult life in writing, at which he excels. "When I write," Jason says, "I can be heard. And known. But nobody has to look at me. Nobody has to see me at all" (3). But Jason never stops trying to navigate as an "atypical" boy in a "neurotypical" world, and his loving family constantly gives him cues to ease his way: "My mother . . . had a little sign she'd make with her hands. I needed to say something, no matter how hard it was. If someone asks you a questions, you are supposed to say something" (24). Readers will love the story Jason tells in his own "atypical" voice. Caitlin (Erskine, *Mockingbird (mok'ing-bûrd)*, 2010),  a bright fifth grader and talented artist, has Asperger's

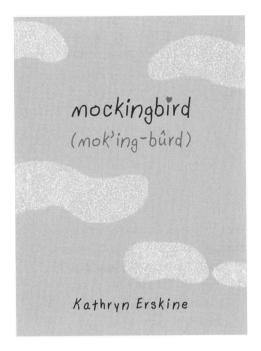

syndrome. Her older brother, Devon, always explained things to her and helped her navigate in a world which, to her black-and-white view of things, was just plain confusing. But her brother was killed in a school shooting and her grieving father simply cannot cope. Her school counselor is now her refuge, and Mrs. Brook works with Caitlin, helping her make eye contact, read people's feelings, and interact with other children. We get inside Caitlin's head as she tells us what she is thinking and how she is trying to GET IT. The dictionary explains words to her, but it is still hard. A simple exchange between Caitlin and Michael, a little boy whose mother was also killed in the school shooting, helps us understand just how difficult living in a literal world can be. Caitlin gives Michael some stickers and he thanks her.

She says,
*You're welcome. See? I'm good at Your Manners too.*
He giggles. *They're not MY manners.*
*I know. They're YOUR Manners.*
*What?*
*Everyone has to learn Your Manners*, I explain.
*You're silly!* He giggles some more.
*Why are you laughing?*
 *Because they're EVERYONE'S Manners! MY manners are when I say please and thank you. YOUR manners are when YOU say please and thank you.*
I Look At The Person. All this time I thought I was learning YOUR Manners when really I was learning My Manners? *But then everyone's manners are the same. Now you Get It!* (59–60)

Readers will cheer for Caitlin, understand why she "sucks on her sleeve" or "covers her head with her purple fleece" when things are too hard to bear, and, above all, applaud her efforts to find CLOSURE, which the dictionary tells her is "the state of experiencing an emotional conclusion to a difficult life event such as the death of a loved one" (67).

Tod Munn, the eighth-grade hero of Mark Shulman's *Scrawl* (2010), is a vandal, a thief, and, because of his size, someone who can bully weaker kids into giving him lunch money. But is he really all these things? When he and his friends get in trouble for something the reader only gradually discovers as the tale progresses, Tod is forced to stay in detention every day and write in a notebook under the watchful eye of his guidance counselor. Through the stories he writes in his own powerful voice, we and his counselor discover what Tod faces at home and what really makes him tick. We discover that he is an impressive, bright human being who deserves a chance.

Isabel, a young teenage slave, is a wonderfully developed character in Laurie Halse Anderson's *Chains* (2008), whose strong voice comes through repeatedly in the novel as she struggles for the freedom that is her due. She and her young sister, Ruth, were freed by her mistress before her death, but, to her dismay, Isabel discovers she has been sold once again:

> "Ruth and me are free, Pastor. Miss Finch freed us in her will. . . . It was done up legal, on paper with wax seals." "I saw the will, sir. After the lawyer wrote it, Miss Mary had me read it out loud on account of her eyes being bad." I spoke up again, "We're to be freed, sir. The Lawyer, Mr. Cornell, he'll tell you. Ruth and me, we're going to get work and a place of our own to sleep." (9, 10)

That thirst for her freedom never abates through this novel set during the American Revolution, and Isabel even works as a spy for the rebels to secure it. She must constantly call on her inner strength and resolve as she endures her captivity, all the while keeping her eye on her goal.

Matt, the son of a Vietnamese mother and American soldier, was air-lifted to the United States in 1975 and adopted by a loving American family in Ann E. Burg's *All the Broken Pieces*

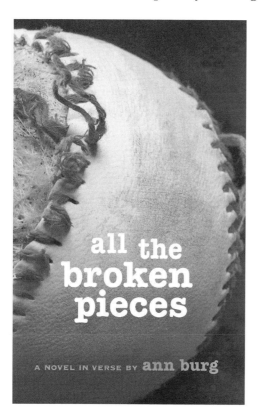

(2009). But despite their caring, he is haunted by memories of the war and the mother and maimed younger brother he left behind. Burg lets Matt speak of his agony and, later in the book, his gradual healing, in poignant verse that will surely move readers:

> I try to remember
> the colors,
> but I cannot.
> My Vietnam
> is drenched
> in smoke and fog.
> It has no parks
> or playgrounds,
> no classrooms
> or teachers.
> My Vietnam is
> only
> a pocketful
> of broken pieces
> I carry
> inside me. (22–23)

LaVaughn's (Wolff, *Make Lemonade*, 1993) dream, and her mother's constant refrain, is to get excellent grades and go to college. But the time she spends babysitting two small children for a young single mother might just sabotage that goal. In her inimitable voice, LaVaughn tells us what she faces at Jolly's (the single mother) house in contrast to her own hopes for the future:

> The mirror is smeared with toothpaste.
> The kitchen floor has the creamed spinach I spilled a month ago.
> I pull up a corner of the living room curtain and smell it:

you'd die.
You can't imagine the things that live
down the plugged drain.
If I get out of here to college, I'll get a good job . . .
I'll work in a office and wear those jackets like you see
and I'll have my own filing cabinet
and also a desk with a calendar on it,
where you put your appointments down in the squares, and everybody will
know
"Oh, that's LaVaughn's department,"
and I'll never see a place like this again. (23)

After listening to her and watching her take charge in difficult situations, readers become certain she will succeed.

Just about nothing is right in 13-year-old Milo's world (Silberberg, *Milo: Sticky Notes and Brain Freeze*, 2010) since his mother died. The girl of his dreams does not know he' is alive, his dad has just moved them for the fifth time, and he must get through another school year in a new place.

"The way I see it," Milo says, "surviving this year is all I have to do. Start to finish in one whole piece and then I win. Of course, being me, winning doesn't come easy, which is why I created an alias, a supercool guy who will step in when I mess up or can't talk or both—Dabney St. Claire." (2–3)

But Dabney can't save Milo from the constant ache in his heart:

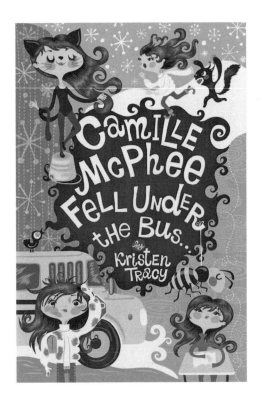

What do I miss?
I miss laughing.
I miss orange peels.
I miss staying home from school just because she (mom) says it's okay.
I miss a dinner table that doesn't feel lop-sided and a kitchen that's full of her. (13)

Milo's funny, and a klutz, and occasionally speaks his own secret language: SAPTOGEMIX-LIKS. Plus, his full name is Milo Cruikshank—not exactly the kind of guy who gets the lead in the school play. But readers will love his voice, his quirky notes and his drawings, and know he will win, in spite of himself.

Life just is not fair for Camille McPhee (Tracy, *Camille McPhee Fell under the Bus*, 2009). She falls under the school bus—not hurt, mind you, just a laughing stock in front of her classmates. Her best friend has moved to Japan, she has lost three cats, her parents fight over money constantly and finally separate, she has to sit under a papier-maché hornet and in front of a kid who constantly pokes her with his pencil in class, and she gets a crummy part in the school play. She even has to carry a cooler with extra food so her blood sugar will not get dangerously low.

> Up and down. Up and down. That's what life was like for me in fourth grade. And I never knew when the downs were going to show up. I couldn't look at the calendar and plan for them like I could the Fourth of July or Valentine's Day. They just arrived. And hit me. Like a spit wad, or a slaughterball. (113)

Camille has hope, though, and we do, too, as we watch her meet her challenges.

Ruth White's novels grow out of her childhood experience living in a coal camp in Jewell Valley, between the hills of southwestern Virginia. They ring with the speech and dialect of the region and reading any or all of them will give students the flavor of the voices of these hard-working people. Her most autobiographical work is *Little Audrey* (2008), set in 1948 and told in the voice of an 11-year-old girl, just recovering from scarlet fever. Her mother has zoned out because a baby has died, her father drinks away his meager paycheck, and young Audrey has to keep the family together. "Our living room has some shabby furniture in it that Mommy and Daddy got secondhanded before I was borned. I pass through there and find the three little pigs (her siblings) eating oatmeal at the table in the next room. Yvonne and Eleanor get out of school before me, and Ruth Carol don't go to school yet" (12).

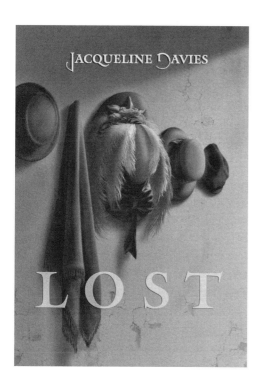

Two books about workers in the Triangle Shirtwaist Factory in New York who are caught in a horrific fire provide readers with an opportunity to hear the unique voices of Jewish immigrants at the turn of the twentieth century. *Lost* (Davies 2009) introduces readers to Essie, who must support her family by working in the factory. There she befriends a young heiress who is hiding from her family. The story of this friendship and Essie's love and longing for her beloved younger sister make riveting reading. Such Yiddish expressions as "nu" and "oy vey"; uncommon sentence structure; and peddler's calls as they ply their wares on the Lower East Side "Herring! Pickled! Herring! Chopped! Firm and fresh herring! / Livers and tongues. Livers and tongues!" (94) pepper the text. Friesner's *Threads and Flames* (2010) is set in 1910 New York where Raisa, a Polish girl, has just arrived to join her older sister. She finds work at the Triangle Shirtwaist Factory and manages to survive until that fateful day in 1911 when a spark sets the factory ablaze. The descriptions of crowded immigrant life and the sounds of the people's voices add to the enjoyment of this novel.

"I had not so good of a week," declares Clementine (Pennypacker, *Clementine*, 2006), one of the funniest and most unique voices in novels for young readers.

> Well, Monday was a pretty good day, if you don't count Hamburger Surprise at lunch and Margaret's mother coming to get her. Or the stuff that happened

in the principal's office when I got sent there to explain that Margaret's hair was not my fault and besides she looks okay without it, but I couldn't because principal Rice was gone, trying to calm down Margaret's mother. (1)

This long, rambling sentence is uttered by an energetic child who just never stops, and who constantly says "Okay, fine" when she's caught out in another escapade. But she always means well and her long-suffering parents and teachers love her with all her faults. Readers will, too. The good news is that there are two sequels for them to savor.

Another distinctive and funny voice in literature for older students is Liam's in Boyce's *Cosmic* (2008):

> Mom, Dad—if you're listening—you know I said I was going to the South Lakeland Outdoor Activity Center with the school?
> To be completely honest, I'm not exactly in the Lake District.
> To be completely honest, I'm more sort of in space.
> I'm on this rocket . . . two hundred thousand miles above the surface of the Earth. I'm all right . . . ish.
> I know I've got some explaining to do. This is me doing it. (1)

Liam got into this mess because he is so tall at age 13 that he passes for an adult, convinces a young schoolmate to pose as his daughter, and off they go on an experimental space journey. Readers will laugh out loud with this quirky character with a bent toward the dangerous side of life and thoroughly enjoy the cosmic ride.

Elise Primavera tells her heroine's story in the third person in her picture book, *Louise the Big Cheese and the La-Di-Da Shoes* (2010). "More than anything else in the world," Primavera tells readers, "Louise wanted to look like a big cheese." She considers her clothing boring. "Dopey skirt!" says Louise. But at least if she had some "la-di-da" shoes, things would improve, and she promptly chooses a pair when she and her mother go shopping. Her mother says they are not practical—too "la-di-da"—to which Louise replies, "You can never be too La-di-da." This little girl's voice and personality shine through in the narration and dialogue, and is a fine example of voice in picture books.

What about animal voices? Children's literature has many examples of animals that are unforgettable. Think of Charlotte, Baby Mouse (Holm 2005), and so many others. One of the most recent creatures to appear on the scene is Ebon, a pegasus who is bound to Sylvi in Robin McKinley's fantasy *Pegasus* (2010). Here is Ebon's assessment of Sylvi when they first meet:

> I know a lot about you. You ask too many questions and you can't sit still, and you're always showing up in your father's office at the wrong time, so you

know more than you should. I thought maybe it wouldn't be too bad to have a girl if she was another nosy fidget, like me. You're shorter than I was expecting though. (57)

Thus begins a fascinating relationship fantasy lovers will certainly enjoy reading.

### Summing It Up with Lilly

As we have said before, many of Kevin Henkes's picture books are treasures, not only for the marvelous language he uses, but also for the wonderful characters he develops, in spite of the brief space he has with which to work. It is important to note that in picture books, students can learn as much about a character's personality by studying the illustrations closely as they can by studying the text and dialogue. So many of the telling details that define a character's personality are in the pictures and therefore, do not need to be stated in words. Henkes's *Julius the Baby of the World* (1990) is a perfect book to use to help students of all ages see, in a relatively brief piece of literature, everything we have been emphasizing about developing memorable characters. We first meet Lilly, aside from the cover where she is wearing a disguise and looming ominously over her baby brother's bassinet, on the title page where she is pointing to her pregnant mother and saying, "You mean that bump is going to be a baby?! I thought you were just getting fat like Aunt Mona!" Precocious—yes. Outspoken—definitely! On that same title page, we see Lilly's attire: a crown on her head, a purple dress (the color of royalty), a red cape (superhero?), and red boots with stars on them. One foot is raised at a jaunty angle. Clearly, Lilly is a star in her own universe. Lilly goes from being delighted at the impending arrival of her sibling to being angered after he's born and she has to share the spotlight. She takes back the toys she had previously set aside for him and declares, "I am the queen. And I hate Julius." The illustrations depict her narrowed eyes, her "Royalty Only" sign when she is told she has to share her room with Julius, and her attempts to confuse him by mixing up alphabet letters and numbers. She even tries to frighten him with disguises and dreams terrible dreams about his demise (or hers at his hands). "Lilly's parents showered her with hugs and kisses . . . and even let her stay up fifteen minutes later every night. It didn't matter. Nothing worked." Lilly is stubborn. She is persistent. She is also full of ideas. An illustration shows her playing with a mouse doll, a replica of Julius, into which she has stuck pins. When asked to tell Julius a story, she entitles it "Julius, the Germ of the World" and likens him to "dust under your bed," "a raisin," which everyone knows "tastes like dirt," and, if he were a number, "zero." To all her parents' praises of Julius, Lilly says an emphatic "DISGUSTING!" But when her parents have a celebration for Julius and the relatives praise him, Cousin Garland retorts with "DISGUSTING!" At this, Lilly bristles and forces Garland to declare that "JULIUS IS THE BABY OF THE WORLD!" Fiercely loyal, Lilly steps up to defend her own when the chips are down. Students will enjoy discovering more and more aspects of Lilly's character as they study the words and pictures ever more closely. In these few short pages, Henkes gives us a character who grows and develops and who learns how to share her parents' affection. It is a masterful work.

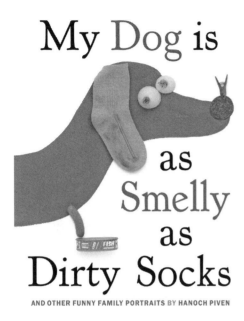

## A Project

I have undertaken this project with children as well as adults with great success. It always helps them understand better the many aspects that go into the creation of a character.

### Materials Needed

A box of "junk" such as buttons, feathers, empty spools of thread, toilet tissue and paper towel rolls, scraps of material, Styrofoam shapes—anything that can be stapled or glued to form a figure

glue

tape

staplers

different colored construction paper

colored tissue paper

large paper to use as a base

scissors

a copy of the Person reproducible (Chapter 4.2: Character Project) found in Appendix A

one appropriate picture book for EACH of the groups into which you divide the class

a copy of *My Dog Is as Smelly as Dirty Socks: And Other Funny Family Portraits* (Piven 2007) and/or *My Best Friend Is as Sharp as a Pencil: And Other Funny Classroom Portraits* (Piven 2010)

### Procedure

1. Read either or both of these books aloud. Discuss the similes used and how they capture the essence of the person being described. Talk about the illustrations and how the objects used suit the personality of each person depicted.

2. Divide the class into groups of three or four students and give each group a picture book to read together. Some books I have found work well are:

   *Mr. Williams* by Karen Barbour

   *Fancy Nancy* by Robin Preiss Glasser

*Don't Let the Pigeon Stay Up Late* by Mo Willems (also, any of the other Pigeon books)

*Ziba Came on a Boat* by Liz Lofthouse

*Louise the Big Cheese and the La-Di-Da Shoes* by Elise Primavera

*Back of the Bus* by Aaron Reynolds

*I Will Never Not Ever Eat a Tomato* by Lauren Child

*Lilly's Big Day* by Kevin Henkes

*Naked Mole Rat Gets Dressed* by Mo Willems

3. Distribute the reproducible of the person figure. Ask each group to discuss their main character in detail. Emphasize that they should spend a good deal of time TALKING. It is this exchange that will really help them see the character in detail. Do the illustrations shed any light on the character's traits? How? What about the character's words and actions? During this discussion, it is important for students to consider WHY a character says and does things. Two characters may act in exactly the same way: hit another child, for example. One may do it because she cannot read and is trying another way to get attention. The other may be abused at home and is acting according to what he has seen and experienced. Figuring out why a character does things gives us great insight into that character.

4. When they have finished talking, the group should write within the character figure all the internal qualities of the character—whether the person is kind, impatient, stingy, etc. Outside the figure, they should write the external characteristics—appearance, walks with head held high, etc. They should justify what they write from what they have read and seen in the book.

5. When they are ready, the groups should then use the "junk" to create a three-dimensional representation of their character. The materials they choose, the colors, etc. should be in keeping with the character's personality. Emphasize that this need not necessarily resemble the character physically—they do not have to create a pigeon, for example, if they are using Willem's book. This is a symbolic representation.

6. Have each group share its representation, giving reasons for the colors and other choices made.

7. Display the representations in the classroom.

## References

Alexander, Lloyd. 1999. *Gypsy Rizka*. New York: Penguin/Puffin. ISBN 978-014130980-4.
   A young girl who lives alone uses her considerable wits to trick and interfere in the lives of the townsfolk in this very funny novel.

Anderson, Laurie Halse. 2008. *Chains*. New York: Simon & Schuster. ISBN 978-1-4169-0585-1.
   After being sold to a cruel couple in New York City, a slave named Isabel spies for the rebels during the Revolutionary War.

Barbour, Karen. 2005. *Mr. Williams*. New York: Henry Holt. ISBN 978-080506773-6.
   Mr. Williams describes his life working the fields in Louisiana during the 30s and 40s.

Baskin, Nora Raleigh. 2009. *Anything but Typical*. New York: Simon & Schuster. ISBN 978-1-4169-8378-3.
    Jason, an autistic boy and an excellent writer, meets a writing partner online and is anxious to meet her at the Storyboard convention. But things do not turn out as he expects.

Bauer, Joan. 1998. *Rules of the Road*. New York: G. P. Putnam/Putnam & Grosset. ISBN 0-399-23140-4.
    Sixteen-year-old Jenna drives her boss, Mrs. Gladstone, from Chicago to Texas to confront Mrs. Gladstone's son who is trying to force her to retire.

Boyce, Frank Cottrell. 2008. *Cosmic*. New York: Walden Pond Press/HarperCollins. ISBN 978-0-06-183683-1.
    Because he is so tall, Liam passes as an adult and goes off on an experimental ride into space.

Burg, Ann E. 2009. *All the Broken Pieces: A Novel in Verse*. New York: Scholastic. ISBN 078-0-545-08092-7.
    A young Vietnamese American boy is adopted by an American family but still haunted by memories of the mother and maimed brother he left behind.

Card, Orson Scott. 1988. *Characters & Viewpoint*. Cincinnati, OH: Writer's Digest Books. ISBN 978-0-89879-927-9.
    The author offers writers tools for creating memorable characters.

Child, Lauren. 2000. *I Will Never Not Ever Eat a Tomato*. Cambridge, MA: Candlewick. ISBN 0-7636-1188-3.
    Lola is a fussy eater, but big brother, Charlie, knows how to convince her to eat her peas.

Davies, Jacqueline. 2009. *Lost*. Tarrytown, NY: Marshall Cavendish. ISBN 978-0-7614-5535-6.
    In 1911 New York, Essie Rosenfeld must stop taking care of her six-year-old sister when she goes to work at the Triangle Waist Company, where she befriends an heiress hiding from her family.

DiCamillo. Kate. 2000. *Because of Winn-Dixie*. Cambridge, MA: Candlewick. ISBN 978-076360776-0.
    Opal names her dog Winn-Dixie because she found him in a supermarket. He and friends she makes along the way help her come to terms with the disappearance of her mother.

DiCamillo, Kate. 2003. *The Tale of Despereaux: Being the Story of a Mouse, a Princess, Some Soup, and a Spool of Thread*. Cambridge, MA: Candlewick. ISBN 978-0763642839.
    Despereaux, a mouse, is banished to the dungeon with the rats because of his unmouse-like behavior and tries to save the princess with whom he is in love.

Erskine, Kathryn. 2010. *Mockingbird (mok'ing-bûrd)*. New York: Philomel/Penguin. ISBN 978-0-399-25264-8.
    Caitlin, who has Asperger's, tries to find CLOSURE after the death of her beloved older brother.

Fletcher, Ralph. 1993. *What a Writer Needs*. Portsmouth, NH: Heinemann. ISBN 0-435-08734-7.
    Fletcher discusses the writer's craft and those things the writer needs to learn to be successful.

Friesner, Esther. 2010. *Threads and Flames*. New York: Viking/Penguin. ISBN 978-0-670-01245-9.
    Essie, a Polish immigrant, finds work in the Triangle Shirtwaist Factory in New York where a factory fire changes her life.

Funke, Cornelia. 2009. *Inkheart*. New York: Scholastic Paperbacks. ISBN 0545046262.
  Meggie and her father possess the power to make book characters come alive. Now they must escape a villain, Capricorn, and find the author of *Inkheart* so he can write a better ending for the book.

Gidwitz, Adam. 2010. *A Tale Dark & Grimm*. New York: Dutton/Penguin. ISBN 078-0-525-42334-8.
  Hansel and Gretel leave home and find themselves in more trouble than they ever imagined as they wander into one horrible dilemma after another.

Graff, Lisa. 2007. *The Thing about Georgie*. New York: HarperCollins. ISBN 978-0-06-087589-3.
  As a dwarf, fourth-grader Georgie has many challenges, but he meets them all with humor and courage.

Grant, Karima. 2006. *Sophie and the City*. Illustrated by Janet Montecalvo. Honesdale, PA: Boyds Mills. ISBN 78-1590782736.
  Sophie, a newly arrived immigrant from Senegal, finds it difficult to adjust to her new country.

Henkes, Kevin. 1990. *Julius the Baby of the World*. New York: Greenwillow. ISBN 0-688-08943-7.
  Lilly has a difficult time adjusting to her new brother's arrival, but she comes through in the end.

Henkes, Kevin. 2006. *Lilly's Big Day*. New York: Greenwillow. ISBN 978-0060742362.
  Lilly wants to be a flower girl at her teacher's wedding, but he has other plans.

Holm, Jennifer. 2005. *Baby Mouse: Queen of the World*. Illustrated by Matthew Holm. New York: Random House. ISBN 978-0375-83229-1.
  In this graphic novel with many sequels, Baby Mouse schemes to get invited to Felicia Furryclaws's exclusive party.

Kerr, M. E. *Blood on the Forehead: What I Know about Writing*. New York: HarperCollins, 1998. o.p. ISBN 0-06-027996-6.
  Using her own writing as examples, Kerr offers readers advice about becoming successful writers.

Leaf, Munroe. 1936. *The Story of Ferdinand*. Illustrated by Robert Lawson. New York: Viking. ISBN 978-0670674244.
  Ferdinand prefers smelling flowers to fighting.

Lofthouse, Liz. 2007. *Ziba Came on a Boat*. Illustrated by Robert Ingpen. New York: Kane/Miller. ISBN 978-1933605524.
  Based on a true story, this recounts how Ziba, an Afghan, has to leave her country.

Mandell, Phyllis Levy. 2010. "Heard Any Good Books Lately? Must-Have Audiobooks for Tweens and Teens." *School Library Journal* 56(8): 32–38.
  Mandell discusses the best audio books available for middle and high school students.

Mazer, Anne, and Ellen Potter. 2010. *Spilling Ink*. Illustrated by Matt Phelan. New York: Roaring Brook. ISBN 978-1-59643-514-8.
  Two professional authors share their writing processes with young adult writers.

McKinley, Robin. 2010. *Pegasus*. New York: Putnam/Penguin. ISBN 978-0-399-24677-7.
  McKinley spins a tale of a princess and her pegasus and their exciting adventures.

Milne, A. A. 1996. *The Complete Tales of Winnie-the-Pooh*. Illustrated by Earnest H. Shepard. New York: Dutton. ISBN 978-0525457237.

This is an unabridged collection of all the Pooh stories along with biographies of the author and illustrator.

Morales, Melita. 2011. *Jam & Honey*. Illustrated by Laura J. Bryant. Berkeley, CA: Tricycle Press. ISBN 978-1-58246-299-8.
A little girl and a bee see a blueberry bush from their own point-of-view.

O'Connor, Jane. 2005. *Fancy Nancy*. Illustrated by Robin Preiss Glasser. New YorkHarper Collins. ISBN 978-0060542092.
Fancy Nancy loves fancy words, fancy clothes, and all other things fancy. See other books by O'Connor featuring this fancy lady.

Peck, Richard. 1998. *A Long Way from Chicago*. New York: Dial. ISBN 0-8037-2290-7.
A boy recounts his annual summer trips to rural Illinois with his sister to visit their grand-mother during the Great Depression.

Peck, Richard. 2000. *A Year Down Yonder*. New York: Dial. ISBN 0-8037-2518-3.
In 1937, 15-year-old Mary Alice is sent to live with her feisty, larger-than-life grandmother in rural Illinois and comes to a better understanding of this fearsome woman.

Peck, Richard. 2007. *On the Wings of Heroes*. New York: Dial. ISBN 978-0-8037-3081-6.
Davy Bowman remembers the home-front years of World War II in Illinois, especially his two heroes—his brother in the air force and his father, who fought in the previous war.

Pennypacker, Sara. 2006. *Clementine*. Illustrated by Marla Frazee. New York: Hyperion. ISBN 978-078683882-0.
Clementine, an overly energetic, lovable child, constantly gets in and out of trouble. See other books in this funny series.

Perkins, Lynne Rae. 2010. *As Easy as Falling off the Face of the Earth*. New York: Greenwillow/HarperCollins. ISBN 978-0-06-187090-3.
A teen encounters one comedic calamity after another when his train strands him in the middle of nowhere, and everything comes down to luck.

Polacco, Patricia. 2009 (reprint ed). *Mrs. Katz and Tush*. New York: Doubleday/Random House. ISBN 978-0-553-08122-0. (Orig. pub. 1994.)
A long-lasting friendship develops between Larnel, a young African American, and Mrs. Katz, a lonely Jewish widow, when Larnel presents her with a kitten.

Primavera, Elise. 2010. *Louise the Big Cheese and the La-Di-Da Shoes*. Illustrated by Diane Goode. New York: Paula Wiseman/Simon & Schuster. ISBN 978-1-41697181-8.
Louise wants a pair of "la-di-da" shoes and envies her friend who has such a pair—until . . .

Priven, Hanoch. 2007. *My Dog Is as Smelly as a Dirty Socks: And Other Funny Family Portraits*. New York: Schwartz & Wade/Random House. ISBN 978-0375840524.
Using similes, the narrator compares various family members to an object that best describes that person's personality. The collage illustrations are made up of objects that reinforce the simile.

Priven, Hanoch. 2010. *My Best Friend Is as Sharp as a Pencil: And Other Funny Classroom Portraits*. New York: Schwartz & Wade/Random House. ISBN 978-0375853388.
Using similes, the narrator compares various classmates to an object that best describes that child's personality. The collage illustrations are made up of objects that reinforce the simile.

Ray, Margaret, and H. A. 2001. *The Complete Adventures of Curious George, Anniversary Edition*. New York: Houghton Mifflin. ISBN 978-0618164417.
    Children's book historian Leonard Marcus introduces this anniversary collection of seven of the curious monkey's adventures.

Reynolds, Aaron. 2010. *Back of the Bus*. Illustrated by Floyd Cooper. New York: Philomel/ Penguin. ISBN 978-0399250910.
    A fictional boy who was on the bus describes Rosa Park's defiant action.

Rosenthal, Amy Krouse. 2009. *Duck! Rabbit!* Illustrated by Tom Lichtenheld. San Francisco: Chronicle. ISBN 978-0-8118-6865-5.
    Two unseen commentators debate about whether a creature is a duck or a rabbit.

Rylant, Cynthia. 1983. *Miss Maggie*. Illustrated by Thomas DiGrazia. New York: Dutton. o.p. ISBN 978-0525440482.
    Rylant writes about the special friendship between young Nat and Maggie, an old Appalachian woman.

Sachar, Louis. 2008. *Holes*. New York: Farrar, Straus and Giroux. ISBN 978-0374332662.
    Stanley is sent to a juvenile detention center in the desert for a crime he did not commit and is forced, along with the other inmates, to dig holes all day long.

Schmidt, Gary D. 2007. *The Wednesday Wars*. New York: Clarion/Houghton Mifflin. ISBN 978-0-618-72483-3.
    During 1967, Holling Hoodhood must stay in Mrs. Baker's classroom on Wednesday afternoons. They read Shakespeare's plays together and Holling learns much of value about the world in which he lives.

Seuss, Dr. 1957. *How the Grinch Stole Christmas*. New York: Random House. ISBN 978-0394800790.
    The Grinch tries to destroy Christmas for the citizens of Who-ville.

Shulman, Mark. 2010. *Scrawl*. New York: Neal Porter/Roaring Brook. ISBN 978-1-59643-417-2.
    When eighth-grade school bully, Tod, and his friends get caught committing a crime on school property, his penalty—staying after school and writing in a journal—reveals aspects of himself he prefers to keep hidden.

Silberberg, Alan. 2010. *Milo: Sticky Notes and Brain Freeze*. New York: Aladdin/Simon & Schuster. ISBN 978-1-4424-0988-0.
    Milo must get over the death of his mother and make his way in yet another new school.

Singer, Marilyn. 2010. *Mirror Mirror: A Book of Reversible Verse*. Illustrated by Josee Massee. New York: Dutton. ISBN 978-0525479017.
    This collection of poems based on fairy tales are mirror images of themselves, reading from top to bottom or bottom to top.

Stork, Francisco X. 2009. *Marcelo in the Real World*. New York: Arthur A. Levine/Scholastic. ISBN 978-0-545-05474-4.
    Marcelo, who is autistic, wants to work with ponies, but his father forces him to take a summer job in the "real world" at his law firm. While there, Marcelo discovers a terrible secret.

Tracy, Kristen. 2009. *Camille McPhee Fell under the Bus*. New York: Delacorte/Random House. ISBN 978-0-385-73687-9.

Camille's life is one big series of ups and downs, but she never loses hope that things will turn out okay.

Weeks, Sarah. 2010. *As Simple as It Seems*. New York: HarperCollins. ISBN 978-0-06-084663-3.
When she discovers she is adopted and her birth parents are an alcoholic and a criminal, Verbina's life changes as she comes to terms with who she really is and makes friends with a younger boy who initially believes she is a ghost.

White, Ruth. 2008. *Little Audrey*. New York: Farrar, Straus, and Giroux. ISBN 978-0-374-34580-8.
In 1948, 11-year-old Audrey holds the family together as they try to eke out a living in a coal camp in southwestern Virginia.

Wiles, Deborah. 2005. *Each Little Bird That Sings*. San Diego: Harcourt/Gulliver. ISBN 978-0152051136.
Comfort's family owns a funeral home, but death becomes even more personal when she suffers the loss of loved ones and even the apparent death of a friendship.

Willems, Mo. 2006. *Don't Let the Pigeon Stay Up Late*. New York: Hyperion. ISBN 978-0786837465.
Pigeon tries to convince an unseen person, the reader, to let him stay up late.

Willems, Mo. 2009. *Naked Mole Rat Gets Dressed*. New York: Hyperion. ISBN 978-1423114376.
Wilbur, to the dismay of the naked mole rats with whom he lives, insists on wearing clothes. But the Grand-pah, wisest of the mole rats, has a surprise for everyone.

Williams, Laura E. 2010. *The Can Man*. Illustrated by Craig Orback. New York: Lee & Low. ISBN 978-1600602665.
Following an unemployed man's example, Tim collects cans to buy a new skateboard, but when he sees the man's desperate need for a winter coat, Tim is faced with a difficult decision.

Wolff, Virginia Euer. 1993. *Make Lemonade*. New York: Henry Holt. ISBN 978-080-502228-5.
LaVaugh's dream is to escape poverty by going to college and getting a good job. But the time she spends babysitting for a young mother may hinder her plans. Readers can follow LaVaughn's life in two sequels, *True Believer* and *This Full House*, by the same author.

# 5

# Putting Passion and Voice into Non-fiction Writing

*You write to communicate to the hearts and minds of others what's burning inside you.*

—Arthur Polotnik

*What I like about non-fiction is that it covers such a huge territory. The best non-fiction is also creative.*

—Tracy Kidder

Our students will probably do more non-fiction writing than writing in any other genre throughout their school years. Reports, essays, biographies, letters, persuasive pieces—all these and more—are and will continue to be required of them. Think about the non-fiction writing your students have done over the years, or this term, or even this week. Did many of their efforts sound like reworked encyclopedia articles or textbook chapters? Would reading them in the evening be an excellent cure for insomnia? Were you able to hear your students' enthusiasm and unique voices in the writing? If not, perhaps we need to look at the sources our students used to gather their information. Online encyclopedia entries, articles, and/or textbooks are useful for providing an overview of a topic, an outline of the important aspects of that topic. But for heart, for sheer delight in the topic, for examples of writing that entices the reader to find out more and still more, it is hard to find better models than well-written non-fiction children's books. The authors of these books realize their audience will not tolerate boring texts, and they make every effort to present their material in a way that captures their readers' attention. Yet when asked about the books they read aloud, teachers most often mention works of fiction. Certainly, students of all ages love to listen to stories and read them on their own. The previous chapters of this book attest to the enjoyment, the ear-pleasing language, the wonderful characters, the fine examples of different writing techniques these kinds of books provide. We have stressed over and over again that offering our students these excellent models can ease the task of teaching them to write well. The same holds true for non-fiction writing. If we want their non-fiction pieces to ring with authenticity, voice, and passion, then we should surround our students with the works of non-fiction writers whose own passion for their subject, their cause, their idea, shines through on every page. Christopher Harris offers another cogent argument for exposing our students to fine non-fiction writing. In his article, "One-upping the Web" (*School Library Journal*, Nov. 2010, 14), he discusses the revised Blooms Taxonomy (see http://bit.ly/bloomsrevised) and concludes that the "only valid tasks" we should ask our students to perform are to evaluate what they learn and to create original work. They can handle all other tasks by accessing the Internet. "Don't just have students research a period in history, have them write a song about it or create a diary to tell the story," he says. An excellent and enjoyable way to bring students to these highest rungs on the Bloom's Taxonomy ladder is to enable them to experience how talented authors evaluate historical and scientific information and apply their knowledge by creating fine non-fiction work.

Providing excellent non-fiction books for our students is easier to do now than ever before, because there has been an explosion in the availability of fine non-fiction books for young people over the last few years—even very young people. (See a limited bibliography at the end of this chapter.) No longer do we have to wait for students to grow into these books when they reach the upper grades. Non-fiction now comes in board books, easy-to-read books, picture books, and longer books for older students. In research for her article "What Teachers Need to Know about the 'New' Nonfiction" (*The Reading Teacher*, December 2009/January 2010, 260–67), Sharon Ruth Gill reviewed recent award-winning books from three non-fiction awards: The Siebert Medal, the Orbis Pictus Award for Outstanding Nonfiction for Children, and Children's Choices for 2007. She found several outstanding features: "an emphasis on the visual, including illustrations and design layouts; and emphasis on accuracy, and engaging writing styles, including formats that invite interaction" (261). Clearly, today's non-fiction literature for children offers enticing topics, levers to pull, flaps to lift, gorgeous photography, snappy titles and chapter headings, and all manner of ways to lure students to explore a particular subject. Children's book publishers know only too well that they are competing for their readers' time and attention. It takes attractive, colorful, even interactive non-fiction books to win over children who are used to interactive websites, computer games, TV shows, and phones that bring the universe to the palms of their hands. My shelves abound with such inviting books. The titles that follow are just a taste of what is available.

## A Word about Narrative

Much non-fiction writing for children—especially young children—is in narrative form. This is fine, because story certainly captures young people's interest. Teachers and others who select books for children should just make certain these books are accurate and do not sacrifice fact in an attempt to be more appealing. Check the author's credentials and whether the book has been reviewed for accuracy by experts in the field. Many of these books are packed with information presented in a readable, interesting story and often contain additional facts in the back matter.

### Researching a Topic

Well-respected writers of non-fiction do extensive research for their books—more research, in most cases, than they will ever be able to use. Once they select what is most important and most interesting for their audience, they incorporate their research unobtrusively into the book so that readers are not distracted by it. In an interview with Carolyn Lehman, Russell Freedman, author of over 50 critically acclaimed non-fiction books for children and winner of the coveted Newbery Medal, stated, "That's the secret in writing history. You are telling a story, not telling research. The secret lies in telling the story in a way that the reader feels that the events are happening right there on the page" (Telling the Story in History: An Interview with Russell Freedman, 2007). It is informative for students to read carefully those parts of a non-fiction book

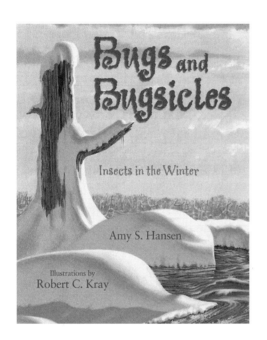

that provide information about an author's research. Often there are author's notes, bibliographies, sources for quotes, etc. Even the jacket flap that provides information about the author, and the acknowledgements that are often in the front or back of the book, can be eye-opening. Students may not realize that even writing what appear to be simple picture books requires a good deal of research. For example, Amy Hansen's *Bugs and Bugsicles* (2010), a picture book about what happens to insects in winter, tells readers, on the jacket flap, that the author was a science reporter and that most of her books "look at the science of everyday life." In addition, her Acknowledgements are two paragraphs long in which she thanks numerous professors and specialists for reviewing the book to make sure the text and the illustrations were accurate. She recognizes laboratories, the British Columbia Ministry of Agriculture, Food, and Fisheries, and others. The jacket flap of Suzanne Jurmain's *The Secret of the Yellow Death* (2009) lists all the primary sources the author used in her research and she lists an extensive bibliography. Albert Marrin lists 11 books he studied to gather information for his book *Oh, Rats!* (2006). (More about these rats later.)

Reading these and the research methods of other children's book authors will help students see that there are many, many ways to do research, and often enough, writers use more than one. They will learn about primary sources like newspaper articles, federal, state and local documents, artifacts, and period pictures. Ann Turner once told a group of fourth graders that artifacts like her great grandmother's tiny baby bonnet and her boot hook gave her information about the small stature and the attire of the people who lived in the time period in which her book, *Dakota Dugout* (1989), is set. The works of outstanding non-fiction writers such as Freedman, Jim Murphy, James Cross Giblin, and others demonstrate just how exciting and interesting historical writing can be when it is grounded in primary source material. They will learn that authors interview people if there are living subjects or witnesses, or read previously conducted interviews. They will even learn that writers travel to the actual locations where their story takes place, historical sites, the habitats of their animal subjects, etc.—all at their own expense. Russell Freedman says that when he was researching his Lincoln

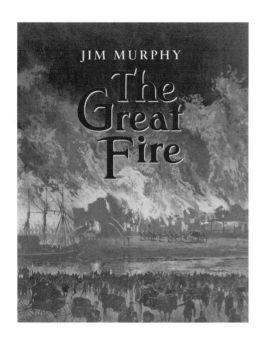

biography (1987), he went to Springfield, Illinois, and walked from Lincoln's home to his law office so he would get a feel for the route Lincoln traveled on foot several times a day. Jim Murphy, in the Acknowledgements for *The Great Fire* (1995), his masterful book about the Chicago fire of 1871, thanks "Charlie Hess for the many invaluable tours of his city." Students will see in these and other well-respected non-fiction books, that in addition to looking things up on the Internet, there are many other options for research open to them. When they are researching their own non-fiction pieces, older students might find it helpful to fill out the reproducible entitled Chapter 5.1: Researching Non-fiction, found in Appendix A. Younger students may wish to follow along on a research puzzle presented by James Cross Giblin in *Did Fleming Rescue Churchill?* (2008). Jason has to write a report about Sir Alexander Fleming and discovers via the Internet that his subject saved Winston Churchill's life. But did this really happen? As youngsters follow Jason while he tries to research the truth, they will learn a great deal about research methods. Especially helpful for students of all ages is the section at the end of the book: "Tips on Doing Research" (59–61), written by a master of the craft.

### Organizing a Topic

Children's book authors have found many interesting ways of presenting their information, and if your students always limit themselves to writing reports about the subject matter they are studying, you may wish to give them examples of different ways to share what they have learned. A variety of models are available, even for very young children. Geraldine Taylor's *What Are Clouds Made Of?* (2007) consists of one or more—usually three—questions on a two-page spread. Readers find the answer to each question by lifting a flap or pulling a lever. The questions are about many different aspects of the world around us, but young writers can imitate this format with a single topic as well. For example, if they are studying the life cycle of frogs, they can write one question on each page of a book and write the answer underneath a flap. They will need to know all about how frogs develop in order to do this, but they are showing what they know in a different way. You might divide the children into groups and have each group prepare a lift-the-flap book. The questions will probably be a bit different in each group, and the groups can switch books and answer each other's questions. The 13 books currently available in the Flip the Flaps series published by Kingfisher/Macmillan books follow a similar format. Each book covers a single topic, with information and an illustration on the left and three questions with their answers under a flap on the right. For example, a two-page spread in *Flip the Flaps: Animal Homes* (Allen and Mendez 2009) has the title "Trees." The brief text on the left describes the tree as an "apartment building" (4) housing animals of various kinds. The page on the right asks three questions about some tree-dwelling animals with answers under the flaps. Additional pictures show three animals that live on tree bark. Stephen Swinburne teaches youngsters about different kinds of shoes and their functions in his very simple *Whose Shoes? A Shoe for Every Job* (2010). A photograph depicting just the legs and shoes of a person in the location in which that person works appears above the question, "Whose shoes?" Readers decide and then turn the page to see the completed picture along with the answer. This is a very easy model for young children and children learning English as a second language to imitate. They can draw or find pictures of different kinds of an object—hats, for example—write the question underneath the picture and the answer on the next page. They can even extend the writing by using a complete

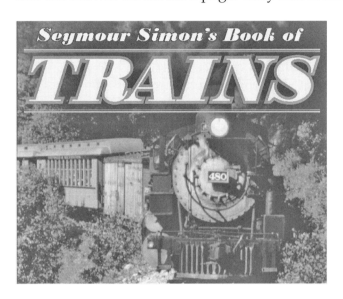

sentence for the answer. So, although Swinburne's answer is simply "A farmer," students can write, "A farmer wears this hat (or whatever the object is)." Youngsters can also follow the same format for any topic they happen to be studying—drawing different parts of an insect and writing a label for that part on the next page; drawing a community helper and providing the helper's title on the next page, etc. *Seymour Simon's Book of Trains* (2002) consists of beautiful full-page color photographs of all kinds of trains. A heading on the opposite page provides the train type, and a paragraph underneath it explains the train's characteristics and uses. Children can create books with a similar format about any topic they choose.

Alphabet books are a convenient way to organize material and there are many alphabet books for children on all kinds of topics. *Lights on Broadway: A Theatrical Tour from A to Z* by Harriet Ziefert (2009) is a dazzling book about all the aspects of putting on a Broadway play with words such as *audition* and *script* introduced with the different letters. Included are quotes from famous actors, side bars with additional information, and even an accompanying CD. Each letter is formed into the shape of an endangered animal in David McLimans's ground-breaking *Gone Wild: An Endangered Animal Alphabet* (2006). Information about each animal and how serious the threat is to its existence appears on each page, and there is additional material at the end of the book. Environmental studies will be enhanced with Mary McKenna Siddals's *Compost Stew: An A to Z Recipe for the Earth* (2010). For each letter of the alphabet, Siddals mentions something that can appropriately be added to make compost. Many of the ingredients, such as grass clippings, are well known, but readers might be surprised to learn that lint from clothes dryer traps works as well. Allen and Lindaman (*Written Anything Good Lately?*, 2010) provide writers with a plethora of different kinds of writing, one for each alphabet letter—kudos or congratulatory notes for classmates, fables, invitations, and much more. These books and many others readily available can serve as models for students who wish to create alphabet books of their own.

Written Anything Good Lately?

By Susan Allen and Jane Lindaman
Illustrated by Vicky Enright

Peter Sis found a novel way to write a book about the 50 states. He created a different circus train (*The Train of States*, 2007) for each of the states and a caboose for Washington, DC. Each page on which a train car appears is just packed with information about the state: the capitol, the symbol, flag, bird, and fun facts. The trains themselves are wonderfully designed, and each viewing uncovers something new. Students can create a book of trains or automobiles or just about anything they wish to display information on a topic.

The *Ask Dr. K. Fisher* series by Claire Llewellyn is a clever way to arrange information. Each book begins with a small envelope containing the doctor's letter to the reader about his counseling service. He provides advice on whatever topic the book is about, and the answer-seekers fall within that topic or are affected by the subject. For example in *Ask Dr. K. Fisher about Reptiles* (2008), different kinds of reptiles write to Dr. Fisher. A gecko writes about losing his tail when attacked by a snake. Dr. Fisher replies, "Your tail will regrow over the next few weeks. It might be a slightly different color and it will contain rubbery cartilage instead of hard bone." Readers learn a great deal about reptiles as the letters and answers mount up. Using this format will give students practice in letter writing while demonstrating what they know. They might work in pairs, one student writing the question letter and the other providing the answer.

## Capturing Readers' Interest

### Great Beginnings

As we mentioned in our discussion of fiction writing, it is important to capture a reader's attention right from the first sentence. Hearing excellent beginnings of nonfiction books read aloud can give young writers clues about starting their own pieces.

a) Questions—Many non-fiction writers tap into young people's natural curiosity by asking a question at the outset. In writing about *Aliens Are Coming! The True Account of the 1938 War of the Worlds Radio Broadcast* (McCarthy 2006) in her article for *The Reading Teacher* mentioned earlier, Sharon Ruth Gill says the author, with the very first sentence, "invites young readers into the book by using a reader-friendly tone, asking a question to make the reading interactive, and helping readers make connections between their experiences with television and the way people in the 1930s experienced radio: 'Hey, kids! Did you know that in the 1930s most Americans did not own TVs? But you know what they did have? The radio!' " (in Gill 260).

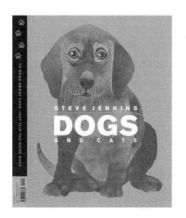

"Most people know about lions, zebras, monkeys, and bears, but what about bettongs and bilbies? Or potoroos and pademelons? Dibblers and dunnarts?" writes Nic

Bishop in *Marsupials* (2009). Surely readers will want to know more about these animals with the strange-sounding names. Steve Jenkins begins *Dogs and Cats* (2007):

> Why do dogs and people get along so well? Are dogs really our loyal, understanding friends? Dogs have lived with people for thousands of years and were the first animals to be domesticated, but they are also natural predators. Dogs have strong bodies, sharp teeth, and keen senses. How did we end up sharing our homes with animals that were once fierce wild hunters?

Perhaps readers have never thought about dogs in just this way. Such a question can make them begin to wonder and anxious to find some answers. Marion Dane Bauer's simple Ready-to-Read book, *Natural Disasters: Earthquake!* (2009), starts with this surprising question: "Did you know the ground we stand on is moving all the time?"

Kathleen Krull (2010) begins her well-researched and attractive picture book biography, *Kubla Khan: The Emperor of Everything*, with two questions:

> Who was Kubla Khan? He may be the least known, most mysterious of history's great leaders. He ruled over almost all of Asia and beyond. . . . For thirty-four years Kubla Khan held his extraordinary empire together. How did he do it?

b) Drama—Dramatic beginnings can arouse a reader's interest. Jurmain's riveting *The Secret of the Yellow Death*, mentioned previously, begins with the stark description of a young man's sickness and eventual death from yellow fever:

> he was . . . boiling hot. . . . His skin turned yellow. The whites of his eyes looked like lemons. Nauseated, he gagged and threw up again and again, spewing streams of vomit black with digested clots of blood across the pillow.

I could not put this 112-page book down. The stories of the men who risked their lives to understand this disease were gripping and inspiring. Fine writing, indeed!

In his book *Cicadas! Strange and Wonderful* (2010), Laurence Pringle confronts readers with a startling newspaper headline:

> Town Braces for Insect Invasion!
> Hordes of Insects Overrun Community!
> Attack of the 17-year Locusts! (3)

Pictured is a woman holding a newspaper bearing this frightening news. But a page-turn reveals the truth: "No! The insects are harmless cicadas, NOT locusts" (4). By this time, though, readers may be hooked, especially when they see the maps and the great illustrations of different kinds of cicadas and their parts, and just keep reading—even though the text is lengthy.

Students who love all things monstrous will want to know more after Caroline Arnold's dramatic description of a giant sea reptile in *Giant Sea Reptiles of the Dinosaur Age* (2007):

Two hundred and twenty million years ago . . . a huge marine reptile cruised the shallow seas. Propelling itself with flat, flipper-like limbs, the 70-foot animal hunted for shellfish and other small ocean animals, which it sucked into its long, toothless snout and swallowed. This fearsome creature was Shonisaurus sikanniensis. (5)

An awful sight, told in a young boy's own words, opens Russell Freedman's *Children of the Great Depression* (2005):

We had owned a small bakery that had failed a few months before. A little later we lost most of our savings at a local bank. . . . We were eating . . . But that was about all, and I guess the thought that he wouldn't be able to buy enough coal to get us through the winter was just too much for my father to take . . . for me the low point of the depression will always be the sight of my father that day, crying in the coal bin. (3–4)

A startling discovery introduces Shelley Rotner's and Anne Woodhull's *The Buzz on Bees* (2010):

One beautiful morning in 2006, professional beekeeper Dave Hackenberg went on a routine check of his hundreds of hives. But something was different. When he lifted the first cover, he discovered the hive was empty. As he continued lifting cover after cover, he was surprised to find that all of the hives were empty.

In Sy Montgomery's *Kakapo Rescue: Saving the World's Strangest Parrot* (2010), readers meet a parrot unlike any other they have seen—and it lives in a most unexpected place:

It's hours past midnight. You'd think any self-respecting parrot would be asleep. But not Lisa.
    No, despite the late hour, this huge, soft, moss-green bird, looking somewhat like a parakeet who has eaten one side of the mushroom in *Alice in*

*Wonderland* and grown into an eight-pound giant, decides this is a great time to waddle out of her nest—a nest that's not in a tree, like a normal parrot's, but *underground*. (1)

c) Humor—a humorous beginning is almost a sure hit. Non-fiction writers frequently spice their books with a funny start or with humorous titles and headings certain to catch the reader's eye. Here are a few examples:

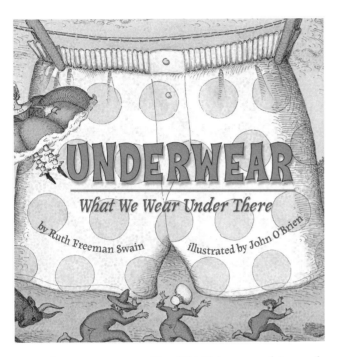

People have giggled about it, snickered about it, and whispered about it (shhh) for hundreds of years. They've made jokes; they've teased. They've been too embarrassed to talk about it out loud, even though they have a pretty good idea what's under there.

What is it? What is so funny about underwear? (Swain, *Underwear: What We Wear Under There*, 2008)

Nicola Davies begins *Just the Right Size* (2009) like this:

In comics and movies, superheroes zoom across the sky, run up walls, lift things as big as buses, and use their powers to fight giant monsters! It's all very exciting, but it's a complete load of nonsense. (7)

Readers will enjoy this readable and funny book and even learn that geometry has its uses.

In *How Fast Is It?* (2008) Ben Hillman discusses the speed, or lack thereof, of different animals and objects. A humorous illustration for each object or animal spreads across one page and onto the facing one where a lengthy side bar provides information. I had intended to peruse this book quickly, but the funny beginning of the entry on the sloth grabbed me and I was hooked:

The windup! The pitch! The crack of the bat! A hit! The batter sprints toward first base! Time for a nap.

If your team is winning a lot this season, it might be because one of your opposing teammates is a sloth—the slowest mammal on Earth.

If a sloth is ever lucky enough to hit a fair ball, it might move slothily toward first base at a ground speed of maybe 6 feet per minute. This gives you and your teammates plenty of time to relax—have a drink of lemonade, catch up on some reading or just take a catnap. (11)

The humorous title of Georgia Bragg's book about the deaths of some well-known people, *How They CROAKED: The Awful Ends of the Awfully Famous* (2011), along with the cover image of a smiling skeleton wearing a physician's head lamp and stethoscope, is certain to attract adolescent readers. Once they begin reading, they will not only learn about the lives of these famous individuals, but also about their illnesses, the horrendous medical treatments they endured, and other deliciously gory details. Funny chapter titles such as "Christopher Columbus: Death by Dirt" and cartoon illustrations will maintain their interest right to the end. In addition to information presented in this lively manner, Bragg also provides readers with her sources for each chapter.

James Sutherland discusses the important events in each of the 10 years of the twenty-first century and calls his book *The Ten-Year CENTURY* (2010) because "it seems like the world has been spinning a little faster. We live in a new era where historical events seem to be a weekly occurrence" (1). He peppers his entries with such amusing titles and headlines as: "The Election that Wouldn't End" (12); "Getting Swift-Boated" (66); "You Have Six Billion Friend Requests" (80); and "The Incredible Shrinking President" (90). Even the title is humorous in Steve Sheinkin's *Which Way to the Wild West? Everything Your Schoolbooks Didn't Tell You about America's Westward Expansion* (2010), and funny headings appear throughout the book as he describes the Louisiana Purchase, the journey of Lewis and Clark, and the pioneer movement west. Although this account is quite funny, it is well researched with pages of endnotes regarding sources for quotes and other research. If your students are studying the westward expansion, this is a book that will launch an enthusiastic beginning and serve as a model for how to tell history through story. Different students could write researched stories about various aspects of the westward movement, perhaps taking their cue from the different short sections into which Sheinkin's work is divided. They may wish to illustrate their entry with cartoon drawings like the illustrations in the book. Bind all the entries together into a book and share it with another class or place it in the library.

### Eye-Catching Graphics

Authors who write non-fiction for young people know they must appeal to an audience of readers used to learning things visually. One of the most dramatic changes in non-fiction writing in recent years has been the inclusion of great graphics. No longer do non-fiction books consist of pages and pages of text broken up by small black-and-white visuals and very little white space. Now, beautifully colored illustrations in a variety of media, graphs, fold-outs, photographs, even dramatic period photos in historical works, are the norm.

In his account of the Great Chicago Fire of 1871 (1995), Jim Murphy uses wonderful period photos to enrich his gripping story. Readers can see fire wagons pulled by horses, people jumping out of windows with their belongings, crowds filling the streets, and much more. He also includes a grid of the city showing the progress of the fire as it spreads. On pages 24 and 25, the map shows a tiny area as the fire starts. The grid on pages 56 and 57 shows a large area to which the fire spread. By the time they reach pages 98 and 99, readers see a large gray area spread over both pages of the grid. They can follow the fire visually as it spreads and engulfs the city. Visuals such as these make history alive and immediate.

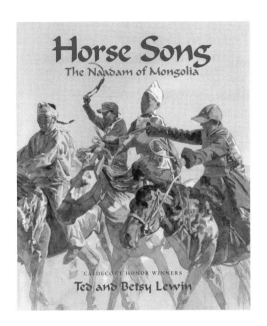

Seymour Simon is one of the most prolific and well-respected writers of non-fiction for children, and his works are noted, not only for the fine writing through which he makes sometimes dense subjects very understandable, but also for the wonderful and informative photographs that grace his books. Simon's books about body systems and different organs enable readers to see the inner workings of their bodies. His books about the planets and our solar system bring these heavenly bodies close-up. Readers can experience the devastation of storms in Simon's books about the weather. A search of his name will bring up any number of excellent books for students to explore. Fortunately, some of Simon's more recent work is accessible for very young children as well.

Non-fiction writers such as Ted Lewin, Jim Arnosky, and Steve Jenkins illustrate their own books. Lewin (*Horse Song*, 2008) and Arnosky (*Slither and Crawl: Eye to Eye with Reptiles*, 2009) and his gorgeous *Wild Tracks!* (2008) with its fold-outs of life-size illustrations of different animal prints, travel great distances and sketch on site to make their illustrations as authentic and beautiful as possible. Students can go to http://www.stevejenkinsbooks.com/makinganillustration_CD.mov to see how Jenkins created the illustrations for *Move!* (2006), a book he illustrated for Robin Page, about how different animals move. At this site they will see all the books Jenkins studies for reference to make sure he gets it right.

### Speaking Directly to the Reader

Addressing the reader with a direct or implied "you" immediately involves that reader in the writer's subject. This is not an encyclopedia article going out into space. The author cares about his or her subject and wants the reader to care as well. This conversational tone invites the reader into the dialogue. When I was writing a teacher guide for an encyclopedia article on the circulatory system, I had a difficult time understanding the research until I turned to Seymour Simon's *The Heart: Our Circulatory System* (2006).

> Make a fist. This is about the size of your heart. Sixty to one hundred times every minute your heart muscles squeeze together and push blood around your body. . . . In one year your heart beats more than thirty million times. In an average lifetime a heart will beat over two thousand million times. (1)

He was speaking to me. He was telling me how amazing my heart was. I began to care, to want to find out more. "I can do this. I can learn this," became my mantra, and I was able to write the guide. In his book on the respiratory system, Simon even addresses the reader in the title: *Lungs: Your Respiratory System* (2007), and again he begins by speaking directly to the reader:

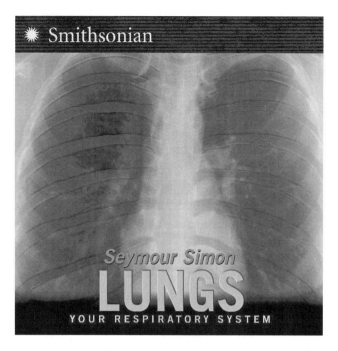

Take a deep breath and hold it for as long as you can... time yourself. You may be surprised to find that you have to take a breath before a minute or two has passed. Humans may be able to go for days without food or water, but we can live for only a few minutes without air. (5)

In *Organs! How They Work, Fall Apart, and Can Be Replaced (Gasp!)* (2009), Nancy Winslow Parker talks to the reader this way: "While some people might say music is vital to life, you could live without it. But unlike the pipe organ, vital organs are body parts that keep you breathing, digesting, thinking, and so much more" (7).

"Geology is the most down-to-earth of all the sciences. It's gritty and lets you get your hands dirty. You may not have realized it, but the rocks and minerals under our feet hold the secrets of our planet," (4) writes Dan Green in *Rocks and Minerals: A Gem of a Book!* (2009). Even students who may only be studying rocks and minerals because they have to, may become enthusiastic about the subject because they are addressed directly and because the writing is so interesting. Green gives each rock and mineral a personality, which is emphasized in Simon Basher's cartoon illustrations. Students might wish to create a PowerPoint presentation with their own drawings for each slide and information they have discovered about different rocks and minerals.

Loree Griffin Burns's *The Hive Detectives: Chronicle of a Honey Bee Catastrophe* (2010) is another recent book about the disaster facing beekeepers and all of us who depend upon bees for our food supply. Burns immediately invites readers to participate in the scientific investigation into why honey bees are dying in great numbers:

> Put on your veil, grab your hive tool, and light up your smoker ... we're going into a beehive.
> Before we begin, remember this: Honey bees are gentle insects.
> Gentle? you ask. But don't they have giant stingers on their rear ends?
> Well, yes, ... But they only use it in emergencies. (1)

### Beautiful Writing

Non-fiction writing does not have to be merely a collection of facts strung together with sentences and paragraphs. We should expect writers of non-fiction to craft their sentences and paragraphs as carefully as do the writers of fiction, to communicate what they know as engagingly as possible. These writers do just that.

Cynthia Rylant's *Appalachia: The Voices of Sleeping Birds* (1998) is a lyrical essay that pays homage to the people and the land where she grew up. Rylant describes the houses, inside and out; the people's hard lives mining coal; their worship; and community activities. "Morning in these houses in Appalachia is quiet and full of light and the mountains out the window look new. . . . Night in these houses is thick, the mountains wear heavy shawls of fog" (13). Students who are writing essays on a particular place would do well to read this author's work.

Stephen Swinburne (*Wings of Light: The Migration of the Yellow Butterfly*, 2006) writes about the incredible 2,000-mile journey the yellow butterfly makes each year from the Yucatan rain forest to the shores of North America. His text matches the beauty of the creatures he describes: "It is a summer morning on the rain forest floor in the Yucatan Peninsula. A yellow butterfly with a notch in its wing, sliced by a bird's beak, flutters across the sunbeams. The butterfly spirals upward and weaves around moss and orchid-covered branches."

"I give you truth—truth in history, truth in existence—presented as story, full of tension, detail, and momentum" (28). These words in her author's note aptly describe the story Selene Castrovilla (*Upon Secrecy*, 2009) tells about the Culper Spy Ring. Her book centers around George Washington's need to find out whether the British general knew a French fleet was coming to aid his beleaguered army during the Revolutionary War and hiring the Culper Spy Ring to find out. It is a breathless tale, full of danger and intrigue. Readers will be engrossed. Especially valuable is the author's discussion of her process, what she could and could not find out for sure, what is true and what may not be true in her account, and the primary and other sources she used in her research. This is an excellent lesson for students doing research on their own projects.

In short, rhyming poetic verses, April Pulley Sayre (*Vulture View*, 2007) describes the turkey vulture's daily soaring in search of food: "Vultures like a mess./They land and dine./Rotten is fine./They eat, then clean./Splash! Dry. Preen." She provides additional information about these birds, including the Turkey Vulture Society's website, and thanks her expert reviewers. This is an interesting model for students to imitate. Can they present their information in the form of a poem?

### Interesting Topics

The number and variety of topics in non-fiction literature for children and adolescents is endless. You can meet fascinating people (as we shall see in the "Biography" section); learn about scientific discoveries and historical events; and, of course, those gross and disgusting topics that are sure to appeal to young people. Some of the titles

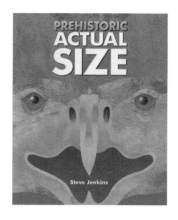

below may give students ideas for subjects they wish to explore further and write about. At the very least, these books can revive in them that curiosity they exhibited as toddlers when they wanted to know about everything around them and one of their favorite words was probably *why*.

*Never Smile at a Monkey* (Jenkins 2009) is about "creatures—both large and small—whose dangerous nature may not be so obvious. Their teeth, claws, spines, and venom can be deadly to an unsuspecting or careless human." Wonderful illustrations, interesting text, and snappy, alliterative headings such as "Never clutch a cane toad" and "Never jostle a jellyfish" provide some cautionary tales for youngsters to heed.

One look at the cover of Jenkins's *Prehistoric Actual Size* (2005) with its head-on view of a creature, red eyes staring, huge mouth open, will be enough to convince readers to look inside. The author/illustrator's collage renderings of these monsters bleed off the pages, often allowing room to show just animal parts—great teeth or claws, for example. Back matter contains more information. Students may wish to write a book featuring the "biggest" of different categories: biggest insects, mammal, birds, fish, people, etc. This is an opportunity to combine writing with some interesting artwork. How will the students depict their subjects to convey their actual size? Can they use math to figure out to scale how big to make their illustrations?

Two books that are very high in the "ew" and "really gross" category are Nicola Davies's *Poop: A Natural History of the Unmentionable* (2011) and *It's Disgusting and We Ate It! True Food Facts from Around the World and Throughout History* (Solheim 2001). Although the topics, headings, and cartoon illustrations in these books are very funny, both provide a great deal of information. Davies discusses the different kinds of animals, even prehistoric ones, and their excrement; what scientists learn from studying poop; and its various uses. (Goodman's *The Truth about Poop* (2004) would make a humorous and informative companion.) Students will be amazed at the variety of things humans eat when they read Solheim's book. Worms, insects, snakes—all these and more make up people's diets somewhere in the world. They will even find out about the surprising origins of some common foods they themselves eat.

Extreme sports have been getting some attention in recent years. How about extreme scientists? Donna M. Jackson (*Extreme Scientists: Exploring Nature's Mysteries from Perilous Places*, 2009) shows three daring scientists in action. They brave all kinds of dangers, go to any heights and depths, to save lives or uncover the information we need to preserve our planet. Paul Flaherty tracks dangerous storms, even flying into hurricanes. Hazel Barton explores caves and lowers herself miles beneath the earth's surface to study microbes. Stephen Sillett climbs giant redwoods to study the forest canopy. The author includes interviews with her subjects, provides glossaries of terms, and extensive sources. These courageous scientists will surely inspire students. Might they be interested in finding out about other scientists who do dangerous but necessary jobs?

Loreen Leedy has written several non-fiction books with catchy titles. A good deal of the information she shares about her different topics is done through cartoon

illustrations, good captions, and speech balloons—a fine way to attract students who love comics. Leedy's latest book as of this printing is *The Shocking Truth about Energy* (2010).

### Connect the Information to a Person, Especially a Child or Children

It is especially interesting if an author can show real people who are intimately involved in the subject about which they are writing. This gives readers someone with whom they can connect—someone who might share the same fears; someone whose body might ache or rebel at the physical challenges required in the pursuit of information, just as the reader's would under similar circumstances; someone whose discoveries can awaken the reader's interest in the topic. Author Sy Montgomery and photographer Nic Bishop accompany Tom McCarthy, director of the Snow Leopard Trust, on a difficult climb among the mountains of Mongolia to find and study snow leopards, elusive animals whose coloring makes them almost impossible to spot. Readers can follow them and other dedicated scientists engaged in the project in Montgomery's wonderful book, *Saving the Ghost of the Mountain* (2009). Tom says, "We start our climb at 9:45 a.m., at 5,747 feet. The mountain before us looks like a wall of rock, steep as a cliff. It looks impossible to climb, and nearly is!" (42). Great writing; maps; gorgeous photographs, including pictures of the Mongolian people (even a brief written conversation written in phonetic Mongolian); and close-ups of the magnificent leopard make this a journey older students will be eager to follow.

Older students studying the history of the Civil Rights Movement should surely include Susan Campbell Bartoletti's *They Called Themselves the K.K.K.* (2010). Bartoletti traces the history of the Klan and its inception shortly after the end of the Civil War up to the present day, including period photos and drawings. What is especially interesting about this wonderful book is that it contains the photographs and testimonies of several African Americans who suffered at the hands of the K.K.K. Seeing these people and hearing their stories transforms Bartoletti's book from a history lesson into an account of events that affected real people, changed real lives, and even violently ended lives for so many. William Luke's letter (99) to his wife shortly before he was hanged by a Klan mob is especially poignant. Students may wish to research some of the people in the book. They can also read slave narratives by going to: http://xroads.virginia.edu/~hyper/wpa/index.html.

"At an international conference in 1989, nearly every ... [amphibian scientist] was telling the same story. There seemed to be fewer amphibians. ... Each scientist thought it was happening just to the animals he or she studied. But when the scientists talked to one another, they realized it was happening everywhere" (Turner, 2009, 13). This alarming discovery galvanized Dr. Tyrone Hayes, a professor at Berkeley, to study the effects of pesticides on frogs, a species of amphibians rapidly decreasing in numbers. Pamela S. Turner follows the work Dr. Hayes and his students did to find out what was happening to these creatures in her fine book, *The Frog Scientist*. Students can see many young college students of different ethnicities out in the field and in the lab with their mentor working to uncover this mystery. Colored photos show many different kinds of frogs as well as, unfortunately, frogs with malformations due to exposure to pesticides and other environmental problems. The work has implications, not only for frogs, but also for human food and water supply. After reading this book, students may wish to hear Hayes speak about his work, his disturbing findings, and his suggestions for action. They can go to: http://www.youtube.com/watch?v=z4lijvIjpRw.

It is enlightening for students to learn about the important role children played in key historical events. They are probably all familiar with Rosa Parks and how she refused to give up her seat on a bus in Montgomery, Alabama. But they may not know that months before Parks's action, a 15-year-old girl, Claudette Colvin, refused to relinquish her seat on a bus, was dragged from the vehicle, and arrested. She never received credit for this heroic act because civil rights leaders did not feel she would be an appropriate spokesperson for their cause. And so they chose Rosa instead. Phillip Hoose's *Claudette Colvin: Twice Toward Justice* (2000), winner of a National Book Award, finally gives Colvin her due by telling her compelling story, often in her own words. Students will learn about the Jim Crow laws that mandated segregation in the South, the many injustices suffered by African Americans at that time, and the famous Montgomery bus boycott.

"The first time Joanne Blackmon was arrested, she was just ten years old." This appalling first sentence in *Marching for Freedom* (Partridge 2009) ushers readers into the dramatic story of how African Americans struggled for the right to register and vote—a struggle that led to a five-day march from Selma to Montgomery, Alabama, and, finally, the passage of the Voting Rights Act in 1965. The amazing part of this story is that children, some quite young, were instrumental in this fight and without their involvement, the effort might have failed. Before they received a guarantee of protection, marchers, even the children, were water hosed, beaten, and attacked with dogs and tear gas, but none of them gave up. Students can view pictures of the children who endured these outrages, read Partridge's fast-moving text, and see quotes from the participants themselves.

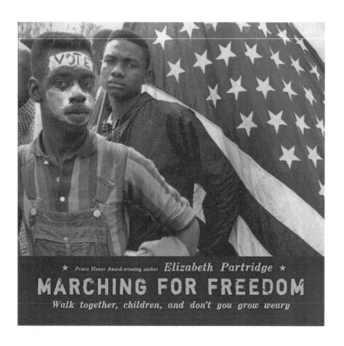

The children who are the subjects of Susan Campbell Bartoletti's *Hitler Youth* (2005) did not all work for good. She features 13 children who were growing up in Germany just as Hitler was coming on the scene. Some of these children were among the millions of boys and girls who joined an organization called Hitler Youth and worked energetically to help bring Hitler to power. Others joined the organization but later realized their freedoms were being curtailed and left. Still others, like Helmuth Hubener discussed in a previous chapter, gave their lives to sabbotage Hitler propaganda from spreading and to protest against the war. The book begins with a nutshell overview of each of these children, and the role they played in a terrible time in the history of the world unfolds in detail as the book begins.

To put a human face on the story of child labor in the United States at the turn of the century, Barbara Greenwood (*Factory Girl*, 2007) invented Emily Watson, a bright young girl who has to leave school to work in a garment factory to help support her destitute family. Alternating between Emily's fictional story and a non-fiction account enriched with period photographs, Greenwood tells readers about the terrible conditions factory workers endured at that time. They worked long hours for little pay and suffered life-threatening disease because of the air they had to breathe. This is a brilliant blend of fact and fiction to tell a heartbreaking story about child labor and the fight for humane working conditions. The photographs in this book as well as those in Russell Freedman's *Kids at Work: Lewis Hine and the Crusade against Child Labor* (1998) are very moving. Pair these books with the story of Iqbal Masih, a boy who was sold at age four to work in a carpet factory in Pakistan, escaped after several years, spoke out against child labor practices, and was murdered by those who wished to silence him. *Iqbal* (2003) is Francesco D'Adamo's fictional account of this boy's heroic life.

After reading about Iqbal's murder, Craig Kielburger, then a 12-year-old, decided to take action. He founded Free the Children, an organization run, amazingly, by children who research the issue, write letters to world leaders, and even run conferences on the topic. Kielburger, along with a chaperone, visited countries in South Asia to see for himself the plight of the children he was trying to help. [Students can read his story in *Free the Children: A Young Man Fights Against Child Labor and Proves that Children Can Change the World* (1999).] At the age of six, Zachary L. Bonner started the Little Red Wagon Foundation, a charity that raises money for homeless children. The *New York Times* reported on July 28, 2010 (A14), that Zachary was on a 2,478-mile walk from Tampa, Florida, to the Pacific Ocean, the third of such walks to obtain contributions for his foundation. (Go to http://www.nytimes.com/2010/07/28/us/28walking boy.html?_r=1&scp=1&sq=founding%20a%20charity%20at%206&st=cse to read the full NYT article about this very caring boy.) Students may be inspired by the books discussed in this section, or by learning about young people like Zachary, to take action on a particular issue that is important to them. They may wish to work as a class on one issue or in different interest groups. The opportunities for research and writing on such a project are enormous, and because the cause comes from the students themselves, motivation and effort will be high. After gathering information through research, the students can work on different ways to present it and offer solutions. They might make a video if the issue involves something in their neighborhood— cleaning up a vacant lot or working to clean up a pond or beach area, for example. They could prepare a PowerPoint presentation or write a class book about the problem. Many possibilities exist. The students can identify the person or group they wish to inform about the project; decide whether they need permission and/or funding and how they will get it; how they will make their issue widely known, etc. This is a chance for them to work on persuasive writing, letter writing, cause and effect, and more. They may wish to use the reproducible entitled Chapter 5.2: Writing and Working for a Cause, available in Appendix A. Once they have completed their project, students can write about the results, prepare an article for the newspaper, etc.

### Involve Readers through Interactive Text and Media

Recognizing students' love of, and affinity for, technology of all kinds, many authors and publishers provide opportunities for readers to learn even more about a

particular topic by accessing technology tie-ins or becoming involved in the text in some way. Sharing these books with students, especially the more reluctant writers, can motivate them to learn as much as they can about a topic and then write about it in a way that encompasses their technological expertise. Candlewick Press has a whole series of books about animals. They range from caterpillars to ice bears, to sharks, to tigers, and many more. You can find all the titles by searching the *Read Listen & Wonder* series from this publisher. These books are well written with text that is brief but informative and enhanced by fine illustrations. Many of the books have additional back matter, and also an index. A CD on which the text is read through once and then read again with musical signals that tell young children reading along when it is time to turn the page is included with each book. Students could write a book on a topic of interest, record the text, and give the book and recording to a younger class.

Students can learn about the Civil War from many different points of view in Patricia Bauer's *B Is for Battle Cry: A Civil War Alphabet* (2009). In addition to the short verses for each letter, which students can hear sung to the tune of Stephen Foster's song of that era, "Hard Times Come Again No More" by going to http://www.davidgeister.com/music/B%20is%20for%20Battle%20Cry-%20A%20Civil%20War%20Alphabet.mp3; sidebars provide additional information on medical practices, food, and much more.

Robert Levine's *Story of the Orchestra: Listen While You Learn About the Instruments, the Music and the Composers Who Wrote the Music!* (2000) is a delightful trip through musical history led by "Orchestra Bob." In the first part of the book, Levine presents different musical periods and features famous composers of those periods. The second part introduces readers to instruments of the orchestra by section. The text is enlivened by cartoon illustrations and quotes and, best of all, a CD that enables readers to listen to different instruments as they are presented in the text.

Capstone Press has published a series of books about U.S. history in which readers are invited to participate in the events and decisions made during each historical period. For example, in Allison Lassieur's *The Dust Bowl: An Interactive History Adventure* (2009), students can choose to stay on a farm that is not yielding crops, move to California, or become a government photographer. Some of the other books in the series provide interactive experiences for such subjects as the attack on Pearl Harbor, the westward expansion, the journey on the Mayflower, and the Underground Railroad.

Peter Crisp's *Atlas of Ancient Worlds* (2009) provides information about the cultures of many ancient civilizations and maps of their locations. Plastic overlays give readers cut-away views of ancient structures and a CD includes images of maps and different artifacts included in the book.

In an exciting blend of science and art, Mary Ann Hoberman and Linda Winston have selected poems that celebrate all life on earth, from the birth of the universe to the present day (*The Tree That Time Built*, 2009). Students can enjoy the poems of many different poets while at the same time learning scientific facts and appreciating the connections the selections make to all forms of life. For example, this note appears beneath the poem, "Butterfly," by D. H. Lawrence:

> The butterfly described here is probably *Pieris brassicae*, the Large Cabbage White, which is the largest white butterfly in England and on the Continent. It does not inhabit the Americas. Its poisonous larvae, brightly colored to warn off predators, feed on members of the cabbage family. It is a strong flyer and often migrates throughout Europe and the British Isles. (105)

In addition, the book comes with an audio CD featuring readings of 44 poems, 18 of which are read by the poets themselves. Pair it with Joyce Sidman's *Ubiquitous: Celebrating Nature's Survivors* (2010), a gorgeous book of poems about species still living on Earth. The poems are arranged in order of the species' appearance from the beginning of life to the present day. Information about that particular species accompanies each poem, and all poems and the additional text have been vetted by scientists. The linocut illustrations are outstanding, and an interesting illustrator's note describes how the fascinating timeline on the endpapers was created. Sidman encourages readers to check out two websites that enable them to see the work being done to find out about different species, hear podcasts, and more. These websites are: http://www.eol .org/and http://tolweb.org/tree/. Both books are wonderful additions to any science unit and fine models for writing about science.

Kids Can Press has a series of eight books in their *Citizen Kid: Change Can Happen One Kid at a Time* series. All of the books discuss ways in which children have and continue to make a difference for those less fortunate around the world: digging wells, protecting the environment, engaging in sustainable farming, and more. For example, *One Hen: How One Small Loan Made a Big Difference* (2008) by Katie Smith Milway tells the story of a young Ashanti boy who used a few coins to buy a hen and was then able to start a successful business and make a difference in his community. The book encourages readers to raise money for such loans and to start their own businesses. In *Ryan and Jimmy and the Well in Africa that Brought Them Together* (2006) by Herbb Shoveller, six-year-old Ryan Hreljac raised enough money to build a well for Jimmy's family in Uganda and later, when rebels kidnapped Jimmy for their army, Ryan's family was able to get him out of the country and adopt him. These books and the others in the series (a new book will be added in 2011) have a web connection that provides activities for children, suggestions for ways to become involved, and extended curriculum ideas for teachers. Many of the activities involve all kinds of writing: letters, plans for setting up a business, lists, essays, etc.

### Express Passion for the Subject

All of the books discussed in this chapter demonstrate the author's love of his or her subject or they would not have been included in our discussion. But the authors that follow just flat out tell us how they became interested in their subject, and how their enthusiasm spilled over into a book so they could share what they love with others.

I never thought I could love a book about rats. Just thinking about them gives me the shivers, even now. But Albert Marrin's *Oh, Rats! The Story of Rats and People* (2006) certainly gave me a new respect for these creatures that live successfully in every part of the planet in all kinds of habitats. Marrin begins by relating a childhood fright when he was surprised by a rat at a construction site. "Take it easy, kid," his father replied when Albert came running for help. "Learn about them; you'll feel better." "And I did," (5) says the author. A few pages into the book, he tells us, "Everything about the rat makes it a champion at survival. . . . Just think about what a rat can do" (10). We can hear the excitement in his voice. Marrin even tells us how useful rats are. We know that they are often the subjects of lab experiments that help us learn more about diseases and drugs. But students will be amazed to learn that rats have even been used to detect land mines!

Just the name of Hoose's *The Race to Save the Lord God Bird* (2004) tells us we are in the company of something very special—a bird so rare that it has captured human imagination for over two centuries and has prompted cries of "Lord God!" from the few people privileged enough to actually see it. Is it extinct? Yes, or maybe not. Hoose's account of those, including James Audubon, who have tried to sight the bird reads like a mystery story, a high adventure, and a burning love story of our planet and efforts to stem the tide of extinction.

> To become extinct is the greatest tragedy in nature. Extinction means that all the members of an entire species are dead; that an entire genetic family is gone, forever. . . . For the first time a single species, Homo sapiens—human-kind—is wiping out thousands of life forms by consuming and altering the earth's resources. (3–4)

It is little wonder that this passionate plea for the environment and one of its most majestic creatures has won numerous awards.

Even as a child, Charles Mann (*Before Columbus: The Americas of 1491*, 2009) wondered how the Pilgrims had survived a New England winter with meager shelter and supplies. When they fought the Wampanoag Indians, why did they win? Was America really "lightly settled" "as if Indians had lived there for thousands of years and hadn't built anything?" (vii). Was half the world "basically a wilderness: an empty landscape, nature in the raw?" (viii) as he had been told? "When I was in school in the 1970s," Mann writes, "my history books told me the answers to those questions. Now, however, many researchers think that almost everything I was taught about early American history was wrong, especially the parts about Native Americans" (viii). A burning desire to learn the truth led this author to do research and write a book himself—a well-documented, truthful, interesting account, complete with bibliographies and websites for further information.

Andrea Warren's *Escape from Saigon: How a Vietnam War Orphan Became an American Boy* (2004) begins,

> I will never forget the fear. In the first days of April 1975, the baby daughter we had never seen was trapped in Saigon, South Vietnam, half a world away from us. . . . We began to wonder if we would ever hold our baby girl. In a very short time, Saigon was surrounded by Communist troops. The only safe way out of the city was by air, and commercial airliners were no longer flying into Saigon. (xiii)

Warren and her husband were thrilled when the government agreed to airlift Vietnamese orphans to the United States, but that joy turned to horror when the first plane crashed, killing many of the children on board. Eventually, their adopted daughter did arrive safely, but, the author states, "I have long felt that the story of the plight of the war orphans, and of the Babylift itself, needed to be told" (xiv). Out of this need, out of love for her own daughter, out of a desire to learn more about the project that saved her daughter's life, out of compassion for child victims of war everywhere, Andrea Warren wrote *Escape from Saigon*, the true story of a young Amerasian boy who was airlifted and adopted by American parents. This is an engrossing story told by a writer who actually visited Vietnam, "experiencing for [her]self the landscape, the culture, the warmth of the people, and the ghosts of war" (103).

We could discuss his books in the "Biography" section, but it is fitting to talk about Sid Fleischman's biographies here because, above all, they resound with his love of his subjects and the sheer pleasure he had in writing about them. It is no surprise that Fleischman was drawn to Charlie Chaplin (*Sir Charlie: Chaplin, the Funniest Man in the World*, 2010) because he was a very funny man himself and his books are a hoot to read. In stating why he chose to write about Chaplin, Fleischman says, "His rags-to-riches story was, in two words, tragic and wonderful. And it was fun to write. I grew up laughing at his absurd walk, the amiable tipping of his bowler hat, and the comic skids on one foot as he turned corners" (v). Fleischman was a magician himself as a youth and traveled with a magic show. In speaking about his fascination with Houdini, probably the most famous magician of all time, Fleischman says, "He had set my fancies and ambitions aflame. . . . The red-backed book, written by a newspaper man named Harold Kellock, launched a thousand young magicians like me. Its pages set down scripture on the life of the great conjuror. I virtually knew the text by heart" (12). Out of such awe grew Fleischman's own book on the great con artist who could "walk through a red-brick wall . . . and [make] a five-ton Asian elephant disappear into thin air" (*Escape! The Story of the Great Houdini*, 2).

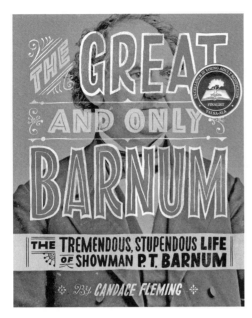

Candace Fleming's *The Great and Only Barnum: The Tremendous, Stupendous Life of Showman P.T. Barnum* (2009) is a tour de force that will draw students to this larger-than-life character. Candace tells readers she

> spent two years researching this book—from spending time in archives and libraries to learning how to play a steam calliope, riding an elephant, winning (and wearing) a red rubber nose at the Ringling Brothers and Barnum & Bailey circus when it came to Chicago, and even walking the tightrope (two feet off the ground) at Ringling Brothers' former winter quarters in Baraboo, Wisconsin. (Jacket Flap)

It is difficult to find more passion and enthusiasm than that! Everything about this book is wonderful. The acknowledgements read like the call of a Ringmaster announcing acts. She thanks "That dynamic duo"; "The Stupendously Generous"; "The Fearless"; and so on. Chapter dividers resemble old circus posters. Ticket stubs, playbills, period photos, and extensive sources and bibliography enrich the text. . Fleming also quotes from the great man himself, including a final message delivered in 1883 on Thomas Edison's new invention, the phonograph:

> I thus address the world through the medium of the latest wonderful invention, so that my voice, like my great show, will reach future generations, and be heard centuries after I have joined the great, and as I believe, happy majority. (138)

Certainly, Fleming's wonderful work will reach and delight her audience.

After reading one or more of these books together, discuss with the students those sections they feel are evidence of the writer's passion for his or her subject. What is it about these passages/sections that reveals the author's enthusiasm and voice?

## Biography

More and more biographies are being written for young people—even picture book biographies that can be enjoyed by younger children. In addition to the inclusion of wonderful graphics and period photos discussed previously, these books are quite different from those written years ago.

### Honesty

Probably the most important characteristic of recent biographies is their honesty. Rather than giving children white-washed versions of heroes and heroines who could do no wrong as biographers of an earlier time did, today's writers, because of their great respect for children, do not hesitate to deal with their subjects' faults and failings

as well as their many accomplishments. Tonya Bolden's well written and beautifully designed biography of George Washington Carver, (*George Washington Carver*, 2008) looking much like a big scrapbook of his life, mentions his fears and his refusal to assume an activist role. Filled with quotes, photos, and even some of Carver's own paintings, this is a great addition to many areas of curriculum studies. In his excellent biography of Charles Lindbergh (1997), superb non-fiction writer, James Cross Giblin, calls him "a human hero." Lindberg was the first person to be made a celebrity by the media, which hounded him even to sneaking into the funeral home and taking pictures of the aviator's son, who had been kidnapped and murdered. While acknowledging Lindberg's amazing feats as an aviator, Giblin writes, "Looking back over his life, one has to acknowledge that Charles Lindbergh's record was a mixed one. His acceptance of a medal from Adolph Hitler … and his prewar speeches on behalf of isolationism sound at best ill-advised, at worst downright destructive" (195). Great writing, period pictures, including several of the enormous crowds who greeted Lindbergh everywhere, make this an enjoyable read.

### A Plentiful Collection of Books about Little-Known Figures

Biographies of presidents and sports figures proliferate in children's literature, but a new development in the field is the appearance of many books about lesser-known people, especially women. You can choose many excellent examples, and we can only mention a few here. Students may be well aware of Amelia Earhart's achievements, but three recent picture book biographies bring other female aviators to light. Marissa Moss's *Sky High: The True Story of Maggie Gee* (2009) is the story of a Chinese American who overcame prejudice and joined WASP, a group of female pilots who ran missions during World War II. Her story is told in the first person, based on interviews the author had with her subject. The contributions of the women of WASP went unrecognized until they were awarded The Congressional Gold Medal for World War II Service in March 2010. Students who enjoy the book can learn more by watching a video at: http://www.youtube.com/watch?v=iCXu7Gx_MnI. This is a story of discrimination, service, and eventual triumph! Sherri Smith's novel, *Fly Girl* (2009), is the fictional story of Ida Mae, an African American who passes for White to join WASP during World War II. It would make an excellent pairing with Gee's biography as would *Almost Astronauts* (2009), Tanya Lee Stone's non-fiction account of the 13 women who entered NASA's training program in the 1960s, outshone the men on every test, and yet were never allowed to fly a mission. Harriet Quimby (Whitaker 2009) was a person of "firsts." She was the first woman to earn a pilot's license in the United States and the first woman to fly over the English Channel. She may have gone on to blaze other aviation trails, but she died when she lost control of her plane during an air show, only 11 months after beginning to fly. A timeline, photo of Quimby, author's note, websites, and bibliography complete this interesting biography. Elinor Smith (Brown, *Soar, Elinor!*, 2010) fell in love with flying when she was just 6 years old and earned her pilot's license at 16, "the youngest flier in the United States—boy or girl." And to silence the skeptics, she successfully flew under all four bridges spanning New York's East River—a dangerous flight requiring great skill. In addition to studying countless books and articles about Elinor Smith, the author received technical advice from Dr. John Kinney of the Aeronautics Division of the Smithsonian Institution's National Air and Space Museum and actually flew with John Corradi in his antique Waco ZPF-7—the same plane Elinor flew.

Who was the first woman elected to Congress? Who worked 10 ten years to achieve suffrage for women in the United States? Who labored for the rights of workers, for health care for women and children, and, most especially, for world peace? In Gretchen Woelfe's *Jeannette Rankin: Political Pioneer* (2007), a riveting and wonderfully written biography filled with anecdotes, informative sidebars, and period photographs and newspaper articles, readers first meet Jeannette Rankin almost at the end of her life when, still championing peace at age 87, she led five thousand women in Washington, DC, on a march against the Vietnam War. It is the culmination of a life begun in 1880 in Montana, a life during which she earned two college degrees and represented Montana in Congress twice. Both times she faced a vote on a declaration of war. Her vote against the World War I cost her reelection. When she voted years later against entering World War II, she stood alone—388 votes to 1—and was reviled throughout the country. But Rankin never betrayed her conscience for personal gain. Students should definitely get to know this inspiring woman.

Hellen Keller's accomplishments were incredible considering the many physical challenges she had to overcome. But what about Laura Bridgman who, in addition to being deaf and blind like Keller, lost her sense of smell and most of her sense of taste as a result of scarlet fever. Her one remaining sense was touch, yet she learned to read, write, communicate, and even became a teacher thanks to her enormous efforts and Dr. Samuel Gridley Howe, who spent years working with her. Sally Hobart Alexander, also blind, and Robert Alexander tell Laura's story in *She Touched the World* (2009). Students can see actual pictures of Laura and the materials she used to learn. All the quotes are sourced and there is an extensive bibliography for further information about this courageous woman.

Anita Silvey (*I'll Pass for Your Comrade: Women Soldiers in the Civil War*, 2008) writes about women who actually disguised themselves as men and fought in the battlefield on both sides in the Civil War. Students will be intrigued by these stories of women far ahead of their time and the ways in which they managed to keep their true identities secret. Although some women of the time served as nurses or even as spies, these women wanted to do more. Why they desired to risk their lives in a war that was exceptionally bloody along with the men and yet receive no pay or benefits as the men did, is a question students will likely ask themselves. Silvey lets the women speak for themselves in this collective biography that includes their pictures.

Henry Ford and Thomas Edison may be household names to today's students, but there are inventors of things they use frequently, even daily, who might not be known to them. Two picture book biographies among the many that feature inventors are Meghan McCarthy's *Pop! The Invention of Bubble Gum* (2010) and Kathleen Krull's *The Boy Who Invented TV: The Story of Philo Farnsworth* (2009). Both are inventions that are very popular with young people, and they are sure to be captivated by the stories of how these things came to be. Walter Diemer was actually an accountant in his company, but he became interested in what scientists were doing in the lab, and started mixing ingredients himself. After months of experimenting, what he finally came up with was a sensation—bubble gum! Philo Farnsworth, even as a young child, was drawing plans for new inventions. He held the great inventors in awe and had a passion for tinkering that finally led him to the invention that has become part of our landscape—TV. Students reading these books will see the power of perseverance and imagination. Can they, working in groups, come up with an invention no one has thought of yet? Is there something that would make their lives or the lives of people around them easier if only it existed? "What if" such a thing could be built and produced? That "what if" question we discussed in Chapter 2 can come into play here. I have asked students to grapple with this idea after reading biographies of inventors

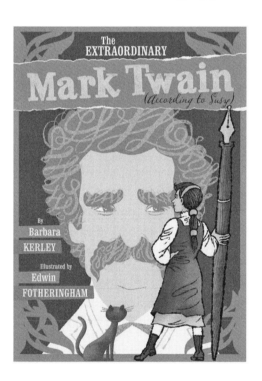

with them, and they have come up with amazing ideas, having fun all the while. Depending upon their ages, students can draw their inventions, write directions for making them, write about their uses, create a user manual, etc.

An obvious outgrowth of reading wonderful biographies is for the students to write a biography themselves. They can write about people involved in a particular historical period or aspect of science the class is studying. A search through books, documents available in the public library, or on the Internet might even uncover the names of little-known individuals no one has written much about. Or they might write a biography of someone in their family or community. Barbara Kerley's biography of Mark Twain (2010) was inspired by the writings of Susy, Twain's daughter. At age 13 she wrote a biography of her father and worked on it from 1885 to 1886. Students can use Kerley's book as a model. Also of great help in that same book is an entire page of instruc-

tions by the author for "Writing an Extraordinary Biography." Teachers can go to www.Barbarakerley.com/teachers.html to print out this page and use it with students. As discussed at the beginning of this chapter, students have different options for organizing their work, depending upon the personality and profession of their subject. We have seen how Candace Fleming included biographical information on graphics resembling circus posters and ticket stubs because she was writing about a man who founded a circus. J. Patrick Lewis has written a book of poems about famous and little-known people called *Heroes and She-roes: Poems of Amazing and Everyday Heroes* (2005) that might also serve as a model for students wishing to write a poem after researching their

subject. This book has a very moving poem about the student who stood in front of a moving tank in Tiananmen Square, in Beijing, China, on June 5, 1989. Laban Carrick Hill's lovely *Dave the Potter: Artist, Poet, Slave* (2010) is another example of using poetry to write about a person. Although he was a slave, Dave worked as a potter, making huge pots that he often signed and on which he sometimes inscribed a brief rhyme. We know him only through his pots and the rhymes he wrote. Bryan Collier, the illustrator, traveled to South Carolina to see the earth from which Dave fashioned his pots. The poems in this book describe Dave's process, from gathering the soil to making the finished glaze, and Collier's gorgeous illustrations, including a large fold-out, depict the potter at work.

## Persuasive Writing and Supporting Details

Students are sometimes required to write persuasive pieces or to back up a statement with supporting details. The title of Martin Jenkins's book, *Chameleons Are Cool* (2001), leaves no doubt about the way the enthusiastic narrator feels about these creatures. Even though there are some things chameleons cannot do, he says, "of all the different kinds of lizards, I still think chameleons are the best. Chameleons are cool" (7). For the remainder of the book, he tells readers some fascinating things about his favorite lizard, hoping, by the end, to persuade them to his side. In *Insects: Biggest! Littlest!* (2009), Sandra Markle persuades readers that there are good things about being a small insect as well as good things

about being a big one. In her book, *A Seed Is Sleepy* (2007), Dianna Aston makes a statement about seeds on each page and then provides details supporting that statement. For example, she says, "A seed is adventurous," and follows this with information that reveals why she makes this surprising observation: "It must strike out on its own in search of a less crowded place to put down roots." Aston goes on to mention that dandelion hairs travel 100 miles and that several other kinds of seeds float long distances on the water to find a place to lay down roots. *An Egg Is Quiet* (2006), also by Aston, follows the same pattern. Both books have stunning illustrations, even to the end papers, filled with different seeds in one book and with many different kinds of eggs in the other.

### Creative Drama and Pantomime: Two Ways to Foster Writing Non-fiction with Passion and Voice

Some of the most effective ways I know of to help students write non-fiction pieces with voice and passion is to do creative drama and/or pantomime projects with them. In creative drama, the students do not simply act out a scene. They BECOME the people living that event. They are totally in role, so that the person's difficulties are their difficulties; the person's hurts or triumphs are theirs as well. It is important to establish this at the outset, and if a child or group gets silly or out of role, stop the action, settle them, and begin again. Why do this? Because when students actually EXPERIENCE an event,

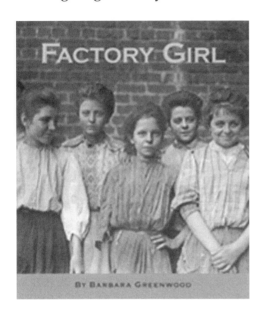

when they know what it feels like, for example, for a family to leave relatives and comfort behind and travel west to the unknown, then they can write with voice about westward expansion. When they know, in their bodies and minds, what it was like to arrive at Ellis Island not speaking a word of English, to be poked and prodded and treated like a cog in a wheel, they can write with added passion about the immigrant experience. I have done creative drama and pantomime with both children and adults on a variety of topics with spectacular results.

During a workshop, a group of teachers used Barbara Greenwood's *Factory Girl* to understand the lifestyle and extreme poverty experienced by newly arrived immigrants and the dreadful working conditions they and their children experienced. They decided how they would become Emily, her family, factory workers, and bosses, etc. The result was that Emily's "mother" approached her daughter in tears as she told her she would have to leave school. "Emily" and the girls in her factory felt what it was like to work under terrible conditions, and the factory "boss" felt what it was like to have such power over people and to want to protect his profits from the demands of the union. The writing that followed was full of heart.

Although I have not used it for creative drama, Ann Bausum's *Denied Detained Deported: Stories from the Dark Side of American Immigration* (2009) would be an excellent choice to use with older students. Bausum examines five immigrant stories, presenting the history and the voices of actual people within those groups—all instances of unfair immigration policy. Some of the groups featured are Japanese Americans who were interred during World War II, Mexicans deported as illegals, Jews whose ship was turned away when they were fleeing Nazi Germany, and more. With all the discussion about immigration reform and what to do about illegal immigration, this book provides a way for students to get inside the hearts and minds of those most deeply affected by the issue. Although it is a work of fiction, Youme Landowne's picture book, *Mali Under the Night Sky: A Lao Story of Home* (2010), is based on the author's real-life trauma, at age five, when she walked with her family from Laos to Thailand to escape the ravages of war. The book is laced with Lao words and recounts the peaceful life

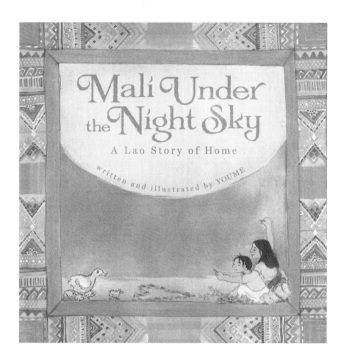

and environment the family was forced to leave behind and their detention in Thailand as undocumented refugees. Younger students would certainly be able to engage in a creative drama experience that would help them understand and write about the plight of people in Mali's circumstances.

Two great pantomime experiences took place when teachers used Shaun Tan's surreal wordless book, *The Arrival* (2007), as inspiration for becoming a newly arrived immigrant at Ellis Island. The confusion and the chaos in the immigrant's mind all played out in their bodies. In another pantomime experience, the teachers used Claire Nivola's *Planting the Trees of Kenya* (2008) to understand the importance of trees in the environment and Wangari Maathai's efforts to reclaim destroyed land in Kenya. In a surprise ending that touched us all, those who were curled in a ball on the floor miming barren land then sprouted and rose up as trees when women touched them in the act of planting seeds, then moved into the audience touching each person so that each one of us in turn stood waving our arms as glorious trees swaying in the wind. It was an awesome moment and a tangible demonstration of how care for the planet can spread.

If you have never tried creative dramatics, you may wish to experiment. Two selective bibliographies of books on child labor and the environment follow at the end of this chapter. You may also wish to go to http://www.yale.edu/macmillan/pier/resources/lessons/MSaccardi.htm to see a lengthy creative drama unit on Chinese Ughurs.

## References

Alexander, Sally Hobart, and Robert Alexander. 2009. *She Touched the World: Laura Bridgman, Deaf-Blind Pioneer*. New York: Clarion. ISBN 078-0-618-85299-4.
  Although she was blind, deaf, and had only the sense of touch, Laura Bridgman accomplished a great deal during her 59 years.

Allen, Judy, and Simon Mendez. 2009. *Flip the Flaps: Animal Homes*. New York: Kingfisher/Macmillan. ISBN 978-0-7534-6258-4.
  The authors provide information on different animal homes in a life-the-flap format. See the other 12 books in this series.

Allen, Susan, and Jane Lindaman. 2010. *Written Anything Good Lately?* Illustrated by Vicky Enright. Minneapolis: Millbrook/Lerner. ISBN 978-0-7613-5477-2.
  The authors mention a different kind of writing for each alphabet letter.

Arnold, Caroline. 2007. *Giant Sea Reptiles of the Dinosaur Age.* Illustrated by Laurie Caple. New York: Clarion. ISBN 978-0-618-50449-7.

Arnold writes about several massive reptiles that swam the seas during the time of the dinosaurs.

Arnosky, Jim. 2008. *Wild Tracks! A Guide to Nature's Footprints.* New York: Sterling. ISBN 978-1-4027-3985-9.

Arnosky reveals what different animal tracks tell us about how the animal lives. The book includes wonderful fold-out illustrations of life-size prints.

Arnosky, Jim. 2009. *Slither and Crawl: Eye to Eye with Reptiles.* New York: Sterling. ISBN 978-1402739866.

Arnosky provides life-size portraits and information about mostly North American reptiles.

Aston, Dianna. 2006. *An Egg Is Quiet.* Illustrated by Sylvia Long. San Francisco: Chronicle. ISBN 978-0-8118-4428-4.

Aston makes several statements about eggs and backs each statement with details.

Aston, Dianna Hutts. 2007. *A Seed Is Sleepy.* Illustrated by Sylvia Long. San Francisco: Chronicle. ISBN 978-0-8118-5520-4.

Aston supports several surprising statements about seeds with details.

Bartoletti, Susan Campbell. 2005. *Hitler Youth: Growing up in Hitler's Shadow.* New York: Scholastic. ISBN 0-439-35379-3.

Bartoletti tells the story of 13 children, some of whom joined the Hitler Organization and some of whom worked to defeat its efforts.

Bartoletti, Susan Campbell. 2010. *They Called Themselves the K.K.K.: The Birth of an American Terrorist Group.* Boston/New York: Houghton Mifflin Harcourt. ISBN 978-0-618-44033-7.

Bartoletti traces the history of the Klan from its beginnings to the present day.

Bauer, Marion Dane. 2009. *Natural Disasters: Earthquake!* Illustrated by John Wallace. New York: Aladdin/Simon & Schuster. ISBN 978-1-4169-2551-4.

Bauer explains in simple terms why earthquakes occur.

Bauer, Patricia. 2009. *B Is for Battle Cry: A Civil War Alphabet.* Illustrated by David Geister. Ann Arbor, MI: Sleeping Bear Press. ISBN 978-1-585363568.

Each letter of the alphabet stands for a different aspect of the Civil War.

Bausum, Ann. 2009. *Denied Detained Deported: Stories from the Dark Side of American Immigration.* Washington, DC: National Geographic. ISBN 978-1-4263-0332-6.

Baum presents the stories of five groups treated unjustly under U.S. immigration policy.

Bishop, Nic. 2009. *Marsupials.* New York: Scholastic. ISBN 978-0-439-87758-9.

Gorgeous photos and even a giant fold-out accompany interesting text about Australian animals.

Bolden, Tonya. 2008. *George Washington Carver.* New York: Abrams Books for Young Readers. ISBN 978-0810993662.

Bolden recounts the life and many accomplishments of Carver, a former slave, especially the many uses he found for the peanut.

Bragg, Georgia. 2011. *How They CROAKED: The Awful Ends of the Awfully Famous.* Illustrated by Kevin O'Malley. New York: Walker Books. ISBN 978-0-8027-9817-6.

With great humor and accompanying cartoon illustrations, Bragg describes the illnesses and horrendous medical treatments endured by many famous individuals.

Brown, Tami Lewis. 2010. *Soar, Elinor!* Illustrated by François Roca. New York: Farrar Straus Giroux. ISBN 978-0-374-37115-9.
   This picture book biography recounts Elinor Smith's amazing feats as an aviator at a time when very few women obtained a pilot's license.

Burns, Loree Griffin. 2010. *The Hive Detectives: Chronicle of a Honey Bee Catastrophe.* Photographs by Ellen Harasimowicz. Boston/New York: Houghton Mifflin Harcourt. ISBN 978-0-547-15231-8.
   Griffin describes the alarming disappearance of honey bees and the efforts being made to protect these valuable insects.

Castrovilla, Selene. 2009. *Upon Secrecy.* Illustrated by Jeff Rosby and Shelley Ann Jackson. Honesdale, PA: Calkins Creek/Boyds Mills. ISBN 978-1-59078-573-7.
   Using primary resources and other materials, Castrovilla recounts the exciting story of the Culper Spy Ring that aided George Washington during the Revolutionary War.

Crisp, Peter. 2009. *Atlas of Ancient Worlds.* Illustrated by Plumer. New York: DK Publishing. ISBN 978-0756645120.
   The author discusses several ancient civilizations. This book has maps, plastic overlays, and a CD that provides images of maps and artifacts.

D'Adamo, Francesco. 2003. *Iqbal.* Transl. by Ann Leonori. New York: Atheneum. ISBN 978-0689854453.
   After escaping a Pakistani carpet factory where he has worked since age four, Iqbal speaks out against child labor and is murdered.

Davies, Nicola. 2008. *Just the Right Size: Why Big Animals Are Big and Little Animals Are Little.* Somerville, MA: Candlewick. ISBN 978-0-7636-3924-2.
   Davies uses geometry to explain how size and strength work in different creatures.

Davies, Nicola. 2011. *Poop: A Natural History of the Unmentionable.* Illustrated by Neal Layton. Cambridge: Candlewick. ISBN 978-0763641283. (pb)
   Davies discusses different kinds of animal excrement.

Dowson, Nick. 2008. *Tigress with Audio: Read, Listen and Wonder.* Illustrated by Jane Chapman. Somerville, MA: Candlewick, . ISBN 978-0763638726.
   A tigress cares for her cubs until they are old enough to leave her. Includes CD. (See others in this series.)

Fleischman, Syd. 2006. *Escape! The Story of the Great Houdini.* New York: Greenwillow/HarperCollins. ISBN 978-0-06-085094-4.
   Fleischman presents the childhood and career of the great magician.

Fleischman, Syd. 2010. *Sir Charlie: Chaplin, the Funniest Man in the World.* New York: Greenwillow/HarperCollins. ISBN 978-0-06-189648-8.
   Fleischman tells Chaplin's story from his poor youth to his rise to fame.

Fleming, Candace. 2009. *The Great and Only Barnum: The Tremendous, Stupendous Life of Showman P.T. Barnum.* Illustrated by Ray Fenwick. New York: Schwartz & Wade/Random House. ISBN 978-0-375-84197-2.
   This is an entertaining look at the life of the founder of the Barnum & Bailey Circus.

Freedman, Russell. 1987. *Lincoln: A Photobiography.* New York: Clarion/Houghton Mifflin. ISBN 978-0899193809.
   Freedman's Newbery award-winning biography presents Lincoln in period photos as well as text.

Freedman, Russell. 1998. *Kids at Work: Lewis Hine and the Crusade against Child Labor.* Photographs by Lewis Hine. CA: Sandpiper. ISBN 978-0395797266. (pb)
Freedman describes how Hine risked his life to enter factories to photograph children working with dangerous machinery. His photos were instrumental in changing child labor laws.

Freedman, Russell. 2005. *Children of the Great Depression.* New York: Clarion. ISBN 0-618-44630-3.
Freedman tells the story of the Depression through period photographs and the stories of the children who suffered through it.

Giblin, James Cross. 1997. *Charles A. Lindbergh: A Human Hero.* New York: Clarion. ISBN 0-395-63389-3.
Giblin writes a biography that reveals a life full of controversy and tragedy, but also great achievements.

Giblin, James Cross. 2008. *Did Fleming Rescue Churchill? A Research Puzzle.* Illustrated by Erik Brooks. New York: Henry Holt. ISBN 978-0-8050-8183-1.
Jason does research to find out if the information in an Internet article is true and readers follow his process.

Gill, Sharon Ruth. 2009/2010. "What Teachers Need to Know about the 'New' Nonfiction." *The Reading Teacher* 63(4): 260–67.
Gill discusses recent developments in the field of non-fiction literature for children and what makes an excellent non-fiction book.

Goodman, Susan E. 2004. *The Truth about Poop.* Illustrated by Elwood Smith. New York: Viking/Penguin. ISBN 978-0670036745.
Funny illustrations and text provide information about different animals' poop.

Green, Dan. 2009. *Rocks and Minerals: A Gem of a Book!* Illustrated by Simon Basher. New York: Kingfisher. ISBN 978-0-7534-6314-7.
The author provides information about many different rocks and minerals. A glossary and index accompany the text as well.

Greenwood, Barbara. 2007. *Factory Girl.* Tonawanda, New York: Kids Can Press. ISBN 978-1-55337-648-4.
Greenwood tells the story of child labor and those who fought against it by combining a non-fiction account with the fictional life of Emily Watson.

Hansen, Amy S. 2010. *Bugs and Bugsicles: Insects in the Winter.* Illustrated by Robert C. Kray. Honesdale, PA: Boyds Mills Press. ISBN 978-1-59078-269-9.
The author describes the changes different insects undergo to survive the winter.

Harris, Christopher. 2010. "One-upping the Web: Finding Our Place in Bloom's Revised Taxonomy." *School Library Journal* 56(11): 14.
Harris contends that the information explosion enables students to find almost all the information they need on the web and that we should concentrate on requiring that they evaluate what they learn and create original work.

Hill, Laban Carrick. 2010. *Dave the Potter: Artist, Poet, Slave.* Illustrated by Bryan Collier. Boston: Little Brown. ISBN 978-0-316-10731-0.
Carrick describes Dave's pottery making process in poems accompanied by Collier's beautiful illustrations.

Hillman, Ben. 2008. *How Fast Is It? A Zippy Book All about Speed.* New York: Scholastic. ISBN 978-0-439-91867-1.

Hillman discusses how fast or slow many different animals and objects are. (See also *How Weird Is It? How Big Is It? How Strong Is It?*)

Hoberman, Mary Ann, and Linda Winston (sel.). 2009. *The Tree That Time Built: A Celebration of Nature, Science, and Imagination*. Naperville, IL: Sourcebooks Jabberwocky/Sourcebooks. ISBN 978-1-4022-2517-8.
Hoberman and Winston have selected poems that celebrate life on earth. Scientific information accompanies many of the poems and a CD is included.

Hoose, Phillip. 2004. *The Race to Save the Lord God Bird*. New York: Dutton/Penguin. ISBN 0-374-36173-8.
Hoose follows biologists who have tried to track the Ivory-billed Woodpecker.

Hoose, Phillip. 2009. *Claudette Colvin: Twice toward Justice*. New York: Melanie Kroupa/Farrar Straus Giroux. ISBN 978—0-374-31322-7.
Hoose recounts Colvin's role in the Montgomery bus boycott and the injustices suffered by African Americans in the South during the 40s and 50s.

Jackson, Donna M. 2009. *Extreme Scientists: Exploring Nature's Mysteries from Perilous Places*. New York: Houghton Mifflin Harcourt. ISBN 978-0-618-77706-8.
Jackson recounts the work of three scientists who engage in dangerous work.

Jenkins, Martin. 2001. *Chameleons Are Cool*. Illustrated by Sue Shields. Somerville, MA: Candlewick. ISBN 978-0763611392. (pb)
A young boy convinces readers that chameleons are amazing.

Jenkins, Steve. 2005. *Prehistoric Actual Size*. Boston: Houghton Mifflin. ISBN 0-618-53578-0.
To show prehistoric animals in their actual size, Jenkins often shows only parts of the creatures to accompany text about how they lived.

Jenkins, Steve. 2007. *Dogs and Cats*. Boston: Houghton Mifflin. ISBN 978-0-618-50767-2.
Half the book talks about dogs and their characteristics. Turn the book the other way and find out about cats.

Jenkins, Steve. 2009. *Never Smile at a Monkey*. Boston: Houghton Mifflin Harcourt. ISBN 978-0-618-96620-2.
Jenkins discusses animals that are dangerous to humans because of their teeth, claws, or venom.

Jurmain, Suzanne. 2009. *The Secret of the Yellow Death: A True Story of Medical Sleuthing*. Boston: Houghton Mifflin Harcourt. ISBN 978-0-618-96581-6.
Jurmain tells the story of four American army doctors who go to Cuba and risk their lives to combat yellow fever.

Kerley, Barbara. 2010. *The Extraordinary Mark Twain (According to Susy)*. Illustrated by Edwin Fotheringham. New York: Scholastic. ISBN 978-0-545-12508-4.
Kerley includes information written by Twain's daughter in this biography and also includes a useful page on how to write an interesting biography.

Kielburger, Craig, and Kevin Major. 1999. *Free the Children: A Young Man Fights against Child Labor and Proves That Children Can Change the World*. New York: Harper Perennial. ISBN 978-0060930653.
This is the story of Craig's work fighting child labor and a call to young people to join the cause.

Krull, Kathleen. 2009. *The Boy Who Invented TV: The Story of Philo Farnsworth*. Illustrated by Greg Couch. New York: Knopf/Random House. ISBN 978-0375845611.
  Krull shows how a boy who grew up investigating how things work invented TV at a very young age.

Krull, Kathleen. 2010. *Kubla Khan: The Emperor of Everything*. Illustrated by Robert Byrd. New York: Viking/Penguin. ISBN 978-0-670-01114-8.
  Krull's biography tells readers how Kubla Khan was able to conquer almost all of Asia and maintain control over 34 years.

Landowne, Youme. 2010. *Mali Under the Night Sky: A Lao Story of Home*. El Paso, TX: Cinco Puntos Press. ISBN 978-1-[933693-68-2.
  Mali and her family walk from Laos to Thailand to escape the ravages of war.

Lassieur, Allison. 2009. *The Dust Bowl: An Interactive History Adventure*. Mankato, MN: Capstone Press. ISBN 9781429623438.
  Readers have a chance to participate in the story of the Dust Bowl by making decisions about what they would do if they were living at that time.

Leedy, Loreen. 2010. *The Shocking Truth about Energy*. New York: Holiday House. ISBN 978-0-8234-2220-3.
  Leedy explores different forms and sources of energy.

Lehman, Carolyn. 2007. "Telling the Story in History: An Interview with Russell Freedman." http://dadtalk.typepad.com/cybils/2007/03/telling_the_sto.html, accessed March 17, 2011.
  Lehman conducts an interview with non-fiction writer, Russell Freedman.

Levine, Robert. 2000. *Story of the Orchestra: Listen While You Learn about the Instruments, the Music and the Composers Who Wrote the Music!* Illustrated by Meredith Hamilton. New York: Black Dog and Leventhal. ISBN 978-1579121488.
  The author introduces children to different musical periods and composers, and to the instruments of the orchestra. CD included.

Lewin, Ted, and Betsy. 2008. *Horse Song: The Naadam of Mongolia*. New York: Lee & Low. ISBN 978-1584302773.
  The Lewins write about the annual horse race they witnessed on a trip to Mongolia and about a young boy who trained for and participated in this race.

Lewis, J. Patrick. 2005. *Heroes and She-roes: Poems of Amazing and Everyday Heroes*. Illustrated by Jim Cooke. New York: Dial. ISBN 978-0-803-72925-4.
  Lewis writes moving poems about people students will recognize and unknown persons as well.

Llewellyn, Claire. 2008. *Ask Dr. K. Fisher about Reptiles*. Illustrated by Kate Sheppard. New York: Kingfisher/Macmillan. ISBN 978-0-7534-6272-0.
  Letters provide questions and answers about reptiles. See several other books in the series.

Mann, Charles C. 2009. *Before Columbus: The Americas of 1491*. New York: Atheneum/Simon & Schuster. ISBN 978-1-4169-4900-8.
  Mann writes about the Americas before Columbus landed.

Marrin, Albert. 2006. *Oh, Rats! The Story of Rats and People*. Illustrated by C. B. Mordan. New York: Dutton/Penguin. ISBN 0-525-47762-4.
  Marrin presents the fascinating history of rats through science and folklore and their amazing survival skills.

Markle, Sandra. 2009. *Insects: Biggest! Littlest!* Photographs by Dr. Simon Pollard. Honesdale, PA: Boyds Mills. ISBN 978-1-59078-512-6.

Markle's text, augmented by incredible photographs, provides information about the smallest and the largest insects.

McCarthy, Meghan. 2006. *Aliens Are Coming! The True Account of the 1938 War of the Worlds Radio Broadcast.* New York: Knopf/Random House. ISBN 978-0375835186.

McCarthy transports readers back to radio days in this picture book story of the Orson Wells broadcast of a fictitious invasion of aliens.

McCarthy, Meghan. 2010. *Pop! The Invention of Bubble Gum.* New York: Paula Weisman/Simon & Schuster. ISBN 978-1416979708.

Walter Diemer invents bubble gum quite by accident.

McLimans, David. 2006. *Gone Wild: An Endangered Animal Alphabet.* New York: Walker/Bloomsbury. ISBN 9780802795632.

Each letter of the alphabet is shaped like an endangered animal.

Milway, Katie Smith. 2008. *One Hen.* Illustrated by Eugene Fernandes. Tonawanda, NY: Kids Can Press. ISBN 978-1-55453-028-1.

A young African boy buys one hen and from there develops a successful business.

Montgomery, Sy. 2009. *Saving the Ghost of the Mountain: An Expedition among Snow Leopards in Mongolia.* Photographs by Nic Bishop. Boston/New York: Houghton Mifflin Harcourt. ISBN 978-0-618-91645-0.

Readers follow an exhausting journey among the mountains of Mongolia where scientists search for the elusive snow leopard.

Montgomery, Sy. 2010. *Kakapo Rescue: Saving the World's Strangest Parrot.* Photographs by Nic Bishop. Boston/New York: Houghton Mifflin Harcourt. ISBN 978-0-618-49417-0.

Montgomery introduces readers to the few kakapo parrots remaining on Codfish Island off New Zealand, and the efforts being made to save them.

Moss, Marissa. 2009. *Sky High: The True Story of Maggie Gee.* Illustrated by Carl Angel. Berkeley, CA: Tricycle Press. ISBN 978-1582462806.

Moss tells how Maggie Gee, a Chinese American, became a member of WASP, female pilots during World War II.

Murphy, Jim. 1995. *The Great Fire.* New York: Scholastic. ISBN 0-590-47267-4.

In breathtaking text and period maps and pictures, Murphy follows the progress of the great Chicago fire of 1871.

Nivola, Claire A. 2008. *Planting the Trees of Kenya: The Story of Wangari Maathai.* New York: Farrar Straus and Giroux. ISBN 978-0374399184.

Wangari Maathai founds the Green Belt Movement to replant millions of trees in Kenya.

Page, Robin. 2006. *Move!* Illustrated by Steve Jenkins. Boston: Houghton Mifflin. ISBN 978-0-618-64637-1.

The author and illustrator show how different animals move.

Parker, Nancy Winslow. 2009. *Organs! How They Work, Fall Apart, and Can Be Replaced (Gasp!).* New York: Greenwillow. ISBN 978-0-688-15105-8.

Parker describes, with a good deal of humor, how the organs of our bodies work.

Partridge, Elizabeth. 2009. *Marching for Freedom: Walk Together, Children, and Don't You Grow Weary.* New York: Viking/Penguin. ISBN 978-0-670-01189-6.

Partridge recounts the role children played in the march from Selma to Montgomery to secure voting rights for African Americans.

Pringle, Laurence. 2010. *Cicadas! Strange and Wonderful*. Illustrated by Meryl Henderson. Honesdale, PA: Boyds Mills. ISBN 978-1-59078-673-4.
Pringle describes the amazing life cycle of cicadas, the different kinds of cicadas, and his own efforts to relocate them.

Rotner, Shelley, and Anne Woodhull. 2010. *The Buzz on Bees: Why Are They Disappearing?* Photographs by Shelley Rotner. New York: Holiday House. ISBN 978-0-8234-2247-0.
The authors discuss the disturbing disappearance of the bee population, its implications for humans, and the work of those trying to solve the mystery.

Rylant, Cynthia. 1998. *Appalachia: The Voices of Sleeping Birds*. Illustrated by Barry Moser. San Diego: Voyager/Harcourt Brace. ISBN 0-15-201893-X. (pb)
Rylant writes about the lives of the people of Appalachia and the area in which they live.

Sayre, April Pulley. 2007. *Vulture View*. Illustrated by Steve Jenkins. New York: Henry Holt. ISBN 978-0—8050-7557-1.
Pulley poetically describes the turkey vulture's hunt for food. The book is beautifully illustrated by Jenkins.

Sheinkin, Steve. 2010. *Which Way to the Wild West? Everything Your Schoolbooks Didn't Tell You about America's Westward Expansion*. Illustrated by Tim Robinson. New York: Flash Point/Macmillan. ISBN 978-1-59643-626-8,
This is an amusing account of the events of the westward expansion.

Shoveller, Herb. 2006. *Ryan and Jimmy and the Well in Africa That Brought Them Together*. Tonawanda, NY: Kids Can Press. ISBN 978-1-55337-967-6.
The author tells the story of six-year-old Ryan who raised money for a well for Jimmy's family in Uganda.

Siddals, Mary McKenna. 2010. *Compost Stew: An A to Z Recipe for the Earth*. Illustrated by Ashley Wolff. Berkeley, CA: Tricycle Press. ISBN 978-1-58246-316-2.
A different compost ingredient is given for each alphabet letter.

Sidman, Joyce. 2010. *Ubiquitous: Celebrating Nature's Survivors*. Illustrations by Beckie Prange. Boston/New York: Houghton Mifflin Harcourt. ISBN 978-0-618-71719-4.
Poems arranged in order of their appearance on Earth celebrate species that have survived since the beginning of life on the planet.

Silvey, Anita. 2008. *I'll Pass for Your Comrade: Women Soldiers in the Civil War*. New York: Clarion. ISBN 978-0-618-57491-0.
Defying conventions of the time, the women in this collective biography dressed as men and fought on the Civil War battlefields.

Simon, Seymour. 2002. *Seymour Simon's Book of Trains*. New York: HarperCollins. ISBN 0-06-028475-7.
Simon provides information about many different kinds of trains.

Simon, Seymour. 2006. *The Heart: Our Circulatory System*. New York: Collins/HarperCollins. ISBN 978-0-06-087721-7. (pb)
Incredible photographs accompany Simon's readable discussion of the circulatory system.

Simon, Seymour. 2007. *Lungs: Your Respiratory System*. New York: Collins/HarperCollins. ISBN 978-0-06-054754-0.
Simon explores the movement of oxygen throughout our bodies.

Sis, Peter. 2007. *The Train of States*. New York: Greenwillow. ISBN 978-0060578404. (pb)
    A circus train for each state of the Union carries information about that particular state.

Smith, Sherri. 2009. *Fly Girl*. New York: Putnam/Penguin. ISBN 978-0-399-24709-5.
    Ida Mae, an African American, passes for White so she can join the WASP during World War II.

Solheim, James. 2001. *It's Disgusting and We Ate It! Food Facts from Around the World and Throughout History*. Illustrated by Eric Brace. New York: Aladdin. ISBN 978-068-984393-8. (pb)
    Solheim discusses all the seemingly disgusting foods people around the world eat. The illustrations are very humorous.

Stone, Tanya Lee. 2009. *Almost Astronauts: 13 Women Who Dared to Dream*. Somerville, MA: Candlewick. ISBN 978-0763636111.
    Thirteen women entered NASA's training program in the 1960s, outscored the men on tests, but were never allowed to fly on a mission.

Sutherland, James. 2010. *The Ten-Year CENTURY*. New York: Viking/Penguin. ISBN 978-0-670-01223-7.
    Sutherland provides information about the key events that happened in each of the 10 years of the twenty-first century.

Swain, Ruth Freeman. 2008. *Underwear: What We Wear Under There*. Illustrated by John O'Brien. New York: Holiday House. ISBN 978-0-8234-1920-3.
    Swain discusses the different kinds of underwear worn by people throughout the ages. The illustrations are very funny.

Swinburne, Stephen R. 2006. *Wings of Light: The Migration of the Yellow Butterfly*. Illustrated by Bruce Hiscock. Honesdale, PA: Boyds Mills. ISBN 1-59078-082-5.
    Swinburne describes the yellow butterfly's migration from the Yucatan Peninsula to North America.

Swinburne, Stephen R. 2010. *Whose Shoes? A Shoe for Every Job*. Honesdale, PA: Boyds Mills. ISBN 978-1-59078-0.
    Readers must decide who uses each pair of shoes after viewing pictures of different shoes on a person's feet.

Tan, Shaun. 2007. *The Arrival*. New York: Arthur A. Levine/Scholastic. ISBN 978-0439 895293.
    Tan's wordless book illustrates the confusion experienced by a newly arrived immigrant who does not understand the language.

Taylor, Geraldine. 2007. *What Are Clouds Made of? And other Questions about the World around Us*. New York: Scholastic. ISBN 978-0-545-08861-9.
    The author provides answers under flaps to different questions about the natural world.

Turner, Ann. 1989. *Dakota Dugout*. Illustrated by Ronald Himmler. New York: Aladdin/Simon & Schuster. ISBN 978-0689712968. (pb)
    In a lyrical poem, Turner writes about a family whose first home on the prairie was a dugout.

Turner, Pamela S. 2009. *The Frog Scientist*. Photographs by Andy Comins. New York: Houghton Mifflin Harcourt. ISBN 978-0-618-71716-3.
    Turner follows the work of scientist Tyrone Hayes and his students as they study frogs to determine why their populations are diminishing.

Warren, Andrea. 2004. *Escape from Saigon: How a Vietnam War Orphan Became an American Boy.* New York: Melanie Kroupa/Farrar, Straus and Giroux. ISBN 0-374-32224-4.
Warren tells the true story of Operation Babylift and of Long, an Amerasian orphan, who was airlifted from Vietnam and adopted by a family in the United States.

Whitaker, Suzanne George. 2009. *The Daring Miss Quimby.* Illustrated by Catherine Stock. New York: Holiday House. ISBN 978-0-8234-1996-8.
Harriet Quimby was the first woman in the United States to earn her pilot's license.

Woelfe, Gretchen. 2007. *Jeannette Rankin: Political Pioneer.* Honesdale, PA: Calkins Creek/Boyds Mills. ISBN 978-1590784372.
Woelfe tells the amazing story of a woman who represented Montana in Congress before the rest of the states gave women the right to vote and who worked tirelessly for peace throughout her life.

Zieffert, Harriet. 2009. *Lights on Broadway: A Theatrical Tour from A to Z .* Illustrated by Elliot Kreloff. Tarrytown, NY: Blue Apple Books. ISBN 978-1934706688.
This alphabet book and accompanying CD celebrate the different components of the Broadway theater.

## A Few Non-fiction Children's Books about Child Labor

Atkin, S. Beth. 2000. *Voices from the Fields: Children of Migrant Farm Workers Tell Their Stories.* Boston: Little Brown. ISBN 978-0316056205. (pb)

Bartoletti, Susan. 1996. *Growing Up in Coal Country.* Boston, MA: Houghton Mifflin. ISBN 978-0395778470.

Bartoletti, Susan. 1999. *Kids on Strike.* Boston, MA: Houghton Mifflin. ISBN 978-0618369232. (pb)

Chambers, Catherine. 2005. *Living as a Child Laborer: Mehboob's Story.* New York: Gareth Stevens. ISBN 978-0836859584.

Currie, Stephen. 1996. *We Have Marched Together: The Working Children's Crusade.* Minneapolis, MN: Lerner. ISBN 978-0822517337.

Freedman, Russell. 1998. *Kids at Work: Lewis Hine and the Crusade against Child Labor.* New York: Sandpiper. ISBN 978-0780780200.

Houle, Michelle M. 2002. *Triangle Shirtwaist Factory Fire: Flames of Labor Reform* (American Disasters). New York: Enslow. ISBN 978-0766017856.

Kielburger, Craig. 1998. *Free the Children: A Young Man's Personal Crusade against Child Labor.* New York: HarperCollins. ISBN 978-0060930653.

Kuklin, Susan. 1998. *Iqbal Masih and the Crusaders against Child Slavery.* New York: Henry Holt. o.p. ISBN 978-0805054590.

## A Few Non-fiction Children's Books about the Environment

Alter, Anna. 2009. *What Can You Do with an Old Red Shoe?: A Green Activity Book about Reuse.* New York: Christy Ottaviaro/Henry Holt. ISBN 978-0-8050-8290-6.

Arnold, Caroline. 2009. *Global Warming and the Dinosaurs.* Illustrated by Laurie Caple. Boston: Houghton Mifflin Harcourt. ISBN 978-0-618-80338-5.

Bang, Molly, and Penny Chisholm. 2009. *Living Sunlight: How Plants Bring the Earth to Life*. New York: Blue Sky/Scholastic. ISBN 978-0-545-04422-6.

Brenner, Barbara. 2004. *One Small Place in a Tree*. Illustrated by Tom Leonard. New York: HarperCollins. ISBN 978-0688171803.

Dellanoy, Isabelle. 2008. *Our Living Earth: A Story of People, Ecology and Preservation*. Photographs by Yann Arthus-Bertrand. New York: Abrams Books for Young Readers. ISBN 978-0810971325.

Glaser, Linda. 2010. *Garbage Helps Our Garden Grow*. Photographs by Shelley Rotner. MN: Millbrook Press. ISBN 978-0-7613-4911-2.

Guiberson, Brenda Z. 2010. *Earth: Feeling the Heat*. Illustrated by Chad Wallace. New York: Henry Holt. ISBN 978-0805077193.

Magner, Tim. 2009. *An Environmental Guide from A to Z*. DesPlaines, IL: Green Sage Press. ISBN 978-0982041765.

Reynolds, Jan. 2009. *Cycle of Rice, Cycle of Life: A Story of Sustainable Farming*. New York: Lee & Low. ISBN 978-1600602542.

Ride, Sally, and Tim O'Shaughnessy. 2009. *Mission Save the Planet: Things You Can Do to Help Fight Global Warming*. Illustrations by Andrew Arnold. New York: Flash Point/Roaring Brook. ISBN 978-1-59643-3.

Rohmer, Harriet. 2009. *Heroes of the Environment: True Stories of People Who Are Helping to Protect Our Planet*. Illustrated by Julie McLaughlin. San Francisco: Chronicle. ISBN 978-0-8118-6779-5.

Ross, Kathy. 2009. *Earth-Friendly Crafts: Clever Ways to Reuse Everyday Items*. Illustrated by Céline Malépart. MN: Millbrook. ISBN 978-0-8225-9099-6.

Simon, Seymour. 2010. *Global Warming*. New York: Collins/HarperCollins. ISBN 978-0-06-114250-5.

Wechsler, Doug. 2006. *Frog Heaven: Ecology of a Vernal Pond*. Honesdale, PA: Boyds Mills. ISBN 978-1590782538.

## A Few Non-fiction Children's Books Suitable for Very Young Children (in Addition to the Flap Books Discussed Earlier)

Arnosky, Jim. 2007. *Babies in the Bayou*. New York: Putnam, Penguin. ISBN 978-0-399-22653-3.

Bill, Tannis. 2010. *Pika: Life in the Rocks*. Photographs by Jim Jacobson. Honesdale, PA: Boyds Mills. ISBN 978-1—59078-803-5.

Campbell, Sarah C. 2008. *Wolfsnail: A Backyard Predator*. Photographs by Sarah C. Campbell and Richard P. Campbell. Honesdale, PA: Boyds Mills. ISBN 978-1-59078-554-6.

Cowley, Joy. 1999. *Red-Eyed Tree Frog*. Photographs by Nic Bishop. New York: Scholastic. ISBN 0-590-87175-7.

Macken, JoAnn Early. 2008. *Flip, Float, Fly: Seeds on the Move*. Illustrated by Pam Paparone. New York: Holiday House. ISBN 978-0-9234-2043-8.

Peterson, Cris. 2010. *Seed Soil Sun: Earth's Recipe for Food*. Photographs by David R. Lundquist. Honesdale, PA: Boyds Mills. ISBN 978-1-59078-713-7.

Pfeffer, Wendy. 1997. *A Log's Life*. Illustrated by Robin Brickman. New York: Simon & Schuster. ISBN 0-689-80636-1.

Simon, Seymour. 2002. *Baby Animals*. New York: SeaStar. ISBN 1-58717-170-8

Thomson, Sarah L. 2005. *Amazing Gorillas!* New York: HarperCollins. ISBN 0-06-054460-0.

# Appendix A: Reproducibles

## Chapter 1.1: Alliteration (p. 17)

Create a book for younger children like Doreen Cronin's books, *Wiggle* and *Bounce*. Each page of your book will have a question that contains at least two words that begin with the same consonant sound just the way the lively dog in *Wiggle* asks, "Can you **w**iggle in the **w**ater?" Write your question on one side of the page and draw a funny illustration on the other side to go with it. To begin, look at the two examples below. Then fill in the rest of the chart with words you choose and turn your questions into a book. Give your book to a younger class in your school.

Examples:

| VERB OR ACTION WORD | WITH WHOM OR WHAT? WHERE? | QUESTION |
|---|---|---|
| ride | on a roller coaster | Can you ride on a roller coaster? |
| swim | with the seals | Can you swim with the seals? |

| VERB OR ACTION WORD | WITH WHOM OR WHAT? WHERE? | QUESTION |
|---|---|---|
| | | |
| | | |
| | | |
| | | |
| | | |
| | | |
| | | |
| | | |
| | | |
| | | |
| | | |
| | | |
| | | |
| | | |
| | | |

From *Books That Teach Kids to Write* by Marianne Saccardi. Santa Barbara, CA: Libraries Unlimited. Copyright © 2011.

# Chapter 1.2: Nonsense Words in *Once Upon a Twice* (p. 22)

| INVENTED WORD | WORDS WITHIN INVENTED WORD | HOW THE INVENTED WORD ENRICHES MEANING |
|---|---|---|
| scoutaprowl | scout and prowl | The one word contains the idea the mice were hunting and trying to lay low, be unnoticed |
| | | |
| | | |
| | | |
| | | |
| | | |
| | | |
| | | |
| | | |
| | | |
| | | |
| | | |
| | | |
| | | |
| | | |
| | | |
| | | |
| | | |
| | | |
| | | |
| | | |
| | | |
| | | |
| | | |
| | | |
| | | |
| | | |

**Chapter 2.1: Favorite Day/Activity (p. 37)**

My favorite day or activity is _____

_____

    It is my favorite because _____

_____

    Now write about this day or activity. Make your piece interesting by telling what you do, how you do it, the people you see, etc. Make your activity sound so special that your readers will want to do it, too. Continue on the other side of this paper if you wish, and include a drawing of yourself doing that activity.

_____

_____

_____

_____

_____

_____

_____

_____

_____

_____

_____

_____

_____

_____

_____

_____

_____

_____

_____

_____

_____

_____

_____

_____

_____

_____

_____

_____

_____

_____

## Chapter 2.2: Story Featuring a Nonsense Creature (Modeled after Tasha Pym's *Have You Ever Seen a Sneep?*) (p. 40)

Fill in the blanks below. Then use the ideas you have come up with to write a humorous story about a nonsense creature and how that creature comes into your life.

Nonsense creature's name _____

Main character or characters (if creature is discovered by more than one person) _____

Where the main character(s) first discover(s) the creature _____
_____

Some ways the nonsense creature affects the life or lives of whoever finds it:

1. _____
_____

2. _____
_____

3. _____
_____

4. _____
_____

5. _____

6. _____

How is the problem solved? Does the character learn to live with the creature, give it away, scare it away, etc.?_____
_____
_____
_____
_____
_____
_____
_____
_____
_____
_____

## Chapter 2.3: Story Featuring a Nonsense Object (Modeled after Il Sung Na's *The Thingamabob*) (p. 40)

Fill in the blanks below. Then use the ideas you have come up with to write a humorous story about a character who finds an unknown object and tries to use it for different purposes until he or she discovers its real use.

Real object's name _____

Object's nonsense name _____

Creature or person who finds the object _____

Other characters (not strictly necessary) _____

Some ways the main character tries to use the object:

1. _____

_____

_____

2. _____

_____

_____

3. _____

_____

_____

4. _____

_____

_____

What his friends/ family suggest (if using other characters):

1. _____

_____

_____

2. _____

_____

3. _____

_____

What happens to help the main character discover the real use of the object? Or perhaps he or she never discovers the real use but comes up with a great way to use it.

_____

_____

_____

_____

_____

_____

_____

## Chapter 2.4: Great Beginnings (p. 45)

To help you get started with your piece of fiction writing, answer the questions below. Then use the remaining space to write a beginning you think will get the attention of readers and make them want to keep reading.

1. What kind of piece are you planning to write? (a funny story, an adventure story, a personal narrative, etc.)

_____

2. What story beginnings have you read as good models for beginning the kind of piece you plan to write? List the titles here:

_____
_____
_____
_____
_____

3. Now that you have thought about your piece and studied the work of other authors, try writing your beginning sentences here. Then, test them on your teacher and classmates. Did you grab their attention? Did they offer suggestions for ways you can make your opening even better? Do you agree with what they said? Why or why not?

_____
_____
_____
_____
_____
_____
_____
_____
_____
_____
_____
_____
_____
_____
_____
_____
_____
_____
_____
_____
_____
_____

**Chapter 2.5: Pattern for Fischer's *Jump!* (p. 53–54)**

Well, I'm a _____.

I'm a _____.

I'm a _____.

I'm a _____

and I'm sleeping _____ .

Until I see a _____ and I _____ .

Well, I'm a _____.

I'm a _____.

I'm a _____.

I'm a _____

and I'm sleeping _____ .

Until I see a _____ and I _____ .

Well, I'm a _____.

I'm a _____.

I'm a _____.

I'm a _____

and I'm sleeping _____ .

Until I see a _____ and I _____ .

**Chapter 2.6: Poems of Praise for Creatures (p. 55) (Modeled after David Elliott's** *And Here's to You!)*

Here's to _____!

The _____ people!

_____!

Here's to the _____ones,

The _____ ones.

The _____ ones.

The _____ ones.

Oh, I love the _____!

**Draw and color a picture below of the creatures you have written about.**

**Chapter 3.1: Reading the World (p. 66)**

Where were you when you "read the world" around you? (at home, on the way to school, on a walk with the class, in the school yard, etc.) _____

What are some things you saw in this setting? _____

_____

_____

_____

What are some things you heard? _____

Was there a special person in the setting? What did the person say, wear? Do?

_____

_____

_____

What other things did you observe that made this scene unique or different? (smells, tastes, weather, objects) _____

_____

_____

What story or description could you—and only you—write based on your careful reading of this scene?

_____

Begin writing that story or description here or in your writer's notebook. Be as specific as you can. Use as many of your senses as you can so that your reader can experience the scene or event with you. Use the other side and/or another sheet if you need to.

_____

_____

_____

_____

_____

_____

_____

_____

_____

_____

_____

_____

_____

_____

_____

_____

_____

_____

_____

**Chapter 3.2: Colors in the Seasons/Classroom (p. 72)**

The purpose of this exercise is to help you notice the "small" unusual things in your world. Bringing such details to your reader is what will make your piece of writing stand out. If you are writing about spring or summer, for example, it is not enough to say the grass is green. Everyone knows that. But notice what Sidman does with this color in her book *Red Sings from Treetops*. She says "Green is new/ in spring. Shy." Calling green shy is a way of saying spring green is just coming out, not yet at the full brilliance of summer. It is an unusual way of looking at that color. After enjoying *Red Sings from Treetops*, try finding some "small" unnoticed ways of talking about colors in different seasons. Or you may choose to write about colors in your classroom, the school yard, or other areas with which you are familiar. Use all your senses and as many sheets as you wish.

Example: In our classroom, RED is

a shiny rectangle in Lilly's hair

floating hearts on a sock

the smell of a new marker

the taste of jam on crackers


SEASON/ CLASSROOM/OTHER SPACE _____

COLOR _____

In _____

_____ is

_____

_____

_____

_____

_____

_____

_____

_____

_____

_____

_____

_____

_____

_____

_____

_____

_____

## Chapter 4.1: Distinctive Character Names (p. 82)

**Based on some books you have read yourself or in class, fill in the chart below. Then fill in the blanks on the bottom half of this sheet in preparation for creating and naming your own character.**

| NAME OF BOOK | MAIN CHARACTER'S NAME | REASON THIS NAME FITS THE CHARACTER |
|---|---|---|
| | | |
| | | |
| | | |
| | | |

\*\*\*\*\*\*\*\*\*\*\*\*\*\*\*\*\*\*\*\*\*\*\*\*\*\*\*\*\*\*\*\*\*\*\*\*\*\*\*\*\*\*\*\*\*\*\*\*\*\*\*\*\*\*\*\*\*\*\*\*\*\*\*\*\*\*\*\*\*\*\*\*\*\*\*\*\*\*\*\*\*\*\*\*\*\*\*\*\*\*\*\*\*\*\*\*\*\*\*\*

The story I am preparing to write is about _____
_____
_____

Some things I have discovered about my character by writing a short biography about him or her before my story begins are: _____
_____
_____
_____
_____

An appropriate name for this character is _____

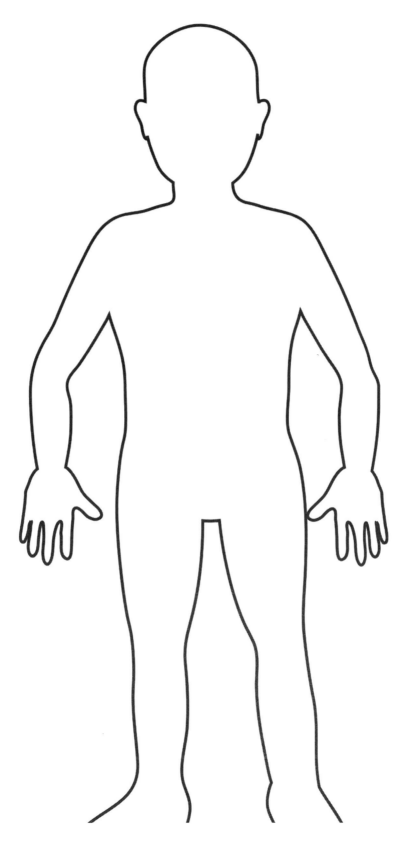

## Chapter 5.1: Researching Non-fiction (p. 104)

What is the topic of your non-fiction piece? _____

What subject does your topic come under? (history, science, etc.) _____

In what time period does your subject or topic take place? (contemporary, what year(s) )
_____

Based on the time period, fill out the table below with all the possible ways you can think of to research your topic. For example, if the time period is recent, you might wish to find people to interview. State where you might obtain each kind of research material and whether you will need the help of an adult. If you are going to consult a book or the Internet, for example, you can do that alone. If you need to find pictures in a library, visit a subject for an interview, obtain a DVD, etc. you will likely need transportation. Be sure to list more than one research method.

| RESEARCH METHOD/MATERIAL | LOCATION/HOW IT WILL BE OBTAINED |
|---|---|
|  |  |
|  |  |
|  |  |
|  |  |
|  |  |
|  |  |
|  |  |
|  |  |
|  |  |
|  |  |
|  |  |
|  |  |
|  |  |
|  |  |
|  |  |
|  |  |
|  |  |

## Chapter 5.2: Writing and Working for a Cause (p. 118)

What issue/problem does your class or group wish to work on or solve? Be specific in describing the issue or problem. _____

_____

Why is this an issue or problem? _____

_____

How will you find out more information about the issue/problem? _____

_____

_____

What can you do to solve this problem or work on this issue? _____

_____

_____

_____

_____

Will you need permission? funding? If so, what can you do to obtain it? _____

_____

Will you need adult help? If so, whom will you ask and how will you go about it? __

_____

_____

What kinds of writing can you do or what kind of presentation can you prepare, and for whom, to relate what you have learned about the issue and what you plan to do about it? Can you involve the local newspaper, for example? Should you partner with any local organizations? _____

_____

_____

_____

_____

_____

_____

_____

_____

_____

_____

_____

_____

_____

_____

_____

_____

From *Books That Teach Kids to Write* by Marianne Saccardi. Santa Barbara, CA: Libraries Unlimited. Copyright © 2011.

# Appendix B:
# A Bibliography of Books Featuring Characters Who Write

Alexie, Sherman. 2007. *The Absolutely True Diary of a Part-Time Indian*. Boston: Little Brown. ISBN 978-031601368-0.

Arnold Spirit writes in his diary about the trials of growing up on the res, leaving and being the only Indian in his high school.

Aliki. 2005. *A Play's the Thing*. New York: HarperCollins. ISBN 0060743557.

Miss Brilliant's class turns the nursery rhyme "Mary Had a Little Lamb" into a play.

Auch, Mary Jane, and Herm Auch. 2009. *The Plot Chickens*. New York: Holiday House. ISBN 978-0-8234-2087-2.

When Henrietta the chicken writes a book, no one will publish it, so she does so herself. It gets a terrible review, but the children at the library love it.

Birdsall, Jeanne. 2005. *The Penderwicks: A Summer Tale of Four Sisters, Two Rabbits, and a Very Interesting Boy*. New York: Knopf/Random House. ISBN 978-0375831430.

Four sisters, ages 12 to 4, spend a vacation in a Berkshire cottage with their professor father where they meet Jeffrey and his domineering mother. Jane is the writer in the group and she never misses an opportunity to narrate what is going on around her.

Byars, Betsy, et al. 2010. *Cat Diaries: Secret Writings of the MEOW Society*. Illustrated by Erik Brooks. New York: Henry Holt. ISBN 978-0-8050-8717-8.

One night every year, cats in the Memories Expressed in Our Writing society gather to read from their diaries, hearing a variety of stories.

Choldenko, Gennifer. 2003. *Notes from a Liar and Her Dog*. New York: Puffin. ISBN 978-0142500682. (pb)

Ant, who has perfect siblings, feels unloved and gains attention by lying. But a sympathetic art teacher helps her find her place in her family constellation.

Christelow, Eileen. 2008. *Letters from a Desperate Dog*. New York: Clarion. ISBN 978-0-618-51003-0.

Feeling misunderstood and unappreciated by her owner, Emma the dog writes to the local canine advice columnist for advice.

Clements, Andrew. 1999. *The Landry News*. Illustrated by Salvatore Murdocca. New York: Simon & Schuster. ISBN 978-0689818172.
When Cara Landry writes an editorial about her ineffectual teacher, the teacher starts the class on a project to create a newspaper.

Codell, Esme Raji. 2004. *Sahara Special*. New York: Hyperion. ISBN 978-0786816118.
When a school counselor finds letters Sahara has written to her dad, who disappeared long ago, she puts Sahara in a special class—hence her nickname. Sahara wants to write more than anything, and she finally overcomes her difficult school situation and her guilt over her father's disappearance.

Cofer, Judith Ortiz. 2006. *Call Me Maria*. New York: Scholastic. ISBN 978-0439385787.
Maria chooses to leave Puerto Rico and live with her father in a basement apartment in New York. She dreams of becoming a writer and becomes more and more aware of the power of language to help her achieve her goals.

Creech, Sharon. 2001. *Love That Dog*. New York: Joanna Cotler. ISBN 978-0060292874.
Written in free verse, this is the wonderful story of a boy who hates writing poetry—it's girls' stuff—until his teacher introduces him to the poetry of Walter Dean Myers.

Cronin, Doreen. 2000. *Click, Clack, Moo: Cows That Type*. Illustrated by Betsy Lewin. New York: Simon & Schuster. ISBN 0689832133.
Farmer Brown's cows type requests for such items as electric blankets.

Cronin, Doreen. 2003. *Diary of a Worm*. Illustrated by Harry Bliss. New York: HarperCollins. ISBN 978-006000150-6.
A young son in the worm family writes a diary about the ups and downs of being a worm. See other books in this wonderful series.

Cronin, Doreen. 2002. *Giggle, Giggle, Quack*. Illustrated by Betsy Lewin. New York: Simon & Schuster. ISBN 978-1416903499.
Duck finds a pencil and writes notes for extraordinary privileges for the barnyard animals while Farmer Brown is away.

Dotlich, Rebecca Kai. 2009. *Bella & Bean*. Illustrated by Aileen Leijten. New York: Atheneum/ Simon & Schuster. ISBN 978-0-689-85616-7.
When Bean constantly distracts her while she tries to write, Bella finds her poems taking unexpected and silly twists, till she realizes she has written a wonderful poem about her best friend.

Durant, Alan. 2004. *Dear Tooth Fairy*. Illustrated by Vanessa Cabban. Somerville, MA: Candlewick. ISBN 978-0763621759.
Holly and the Tooth Fairy exchange letters.

Giff, Patricia Reilly. 2008. *Water Street*. New York: Yearling. ISBN 978-0440419211.
Bird, child of Irish immigrants, lives on Water Street in Brooklyn in 1875. Thomas Neary, who writes about everything, moves in upstairs and the two become friends. A wonderful novel.

Gifford, Peggy. 2008. *Moxy Maxwell Does Not Love Writing Thank-you Notes*. New York: Schwartz & Wade/Random House. ISBN 978-0-375-84270-2.
Ten-year-old Moxy Maxwell has promised to write 12 thank-you notes by the day after Christmas so that she and her two brothers can go to Hollywood to visit their father, but her ideas to get the job done cause chaos.

Green, Jessica. 2007. *Diary of a Would-be Princess*. Cambridge, MA: Charlesbridge. ISBN 978-158089167-7 (pb).
   Fifth-grader Jillian, an unpopular girl, is looked down upon by the "princesses" in her class. In fact, there is so much back-biting and bullying going on that she invites everyone to her birthday party to try to bring the class together. She writes of her many adventures in a diary that is sure to keep students laughing.

Grindley, Sally. 2007. *Dear Max*. New York: Aladdin/Simon & Schuster. ISBN 978-1416934431.
   Max's letter to his favorite author, D. J. Lucas, begins a wave of correspondence between the two. Max learns a good deal about writing from this famous author, but the two share much more as they talk about their lives and what means most to them.

Haber, Melissa Glenn. 2010. *Dear Anjali*. New York: Aladdin/Simon & Schuster. ISBN 978-1-4424-0434-2.
   In an attempt to come to grips with her best friend's sudden death, Meredith writes her a series of letters about their friendship and her current activities.

Haddix, Margaret Peterson. 2008. *Dexter the Tough*. Illustrated by Mark Elliott. New York: Aladdin/Simon & Schuster. ISBN 978-1-4169-1170-8.
   A sympathetic teacher and her writing assignment help fourth-grader Dexter deal with being the new kid in school after he punches a student on the first day.

Henkes, Kevin. 2005. *Olive's Ocean*. New York: Greenwillow. ISBN 978-0060535452.
   Olive dies in a car crash and her mother gives Martha a page of the dead girl's journal in which she talks about Martha as "the nicest girl in our class." Martha learns more from Olive's writing than she ever did from the girl herself. This is a beautiful coming-of-age novel.

Hoestlandt, Jo. 2008. *Gran, You've Got Mail!* Translated by Y. Maudet. New York: Delacorte/Random House. ISBN 978-0-38590553-4.
   Through the letters they write back and forth, Annabelle and her great-grandmother develop a deep relationship.

Holm, Jennifer L. 2007. *Middle School Is Worse Than Meatloaf: A Year Told through Stuff*. New York: Atheneum. ISBN 978-0689852817.
   Seventh grade is definitely a year of ups and downs for Ginny. She is trying to get her mother married, and win the role of the Sugar Plum Fairy in the Nutcracker. But lots of things can go wrong when you are in middle school. Told through notes, letters, to-do lists, announcements, etc., this is a funny romp through a young girls seventh-grade year.

Joseph, Lynn. 2001. *The Color of My Words*. New York: HarperCollins. ISBN 978-0-06-447204-3 (pb).
   Anna Rosa loves to write, but in the Dominican Republic, only the president is allowed to write books. Still, readers experience island life through the writings of this young girl and share a tragic event with her as well.

Kelley, True. 2005. *School Lunch*. New York: Holiday House. ISBN 978-0-8234-1894-7.
   When Harriet, the cook at Lincoln School, goes on a vacation, the staff and students send her letters complaining about her replacements and trying to persuade her to return.

Kinney, Jeff. 2007. *Diary of a Wimpy Kid*. New York: Amulet/Abrams. ISBN 978-0810993136.
   Greg writes in a diary throughout a year of middle school and accompanies his writing with funny illustrations. This wildly popular series has other books, too.

Kuijer, Guus. 2006. *The Book of Everything*. Arthur A. Levine/Scholastic. ISBN 0439749182.
   Thomas lives in a family where his father beats his wife and children. Only his writing in the *Book of Everything* and the kindness of a neighbor helps him and his family survive.

Leedy, Loreen. 2004. *Look at My Book: How Kids Can Write & Illustrate Terrific Books*. New York: Holiday House. ISBN 0-8234-1590-2.
  The kids in this book talk about different genres, and different stages of the writing process.

Lloyd, Saci. 2009. *The Carbon Diaries 2015*. New York: Holiday House. ISBN 978-0823421909.
  Laura Brown, a teen living in London, chronicles in her diary life during the first year of the government's carbon rationing. She includes newspaper clippings and other items in her account. See also *The Carbon Diaries 2017*.

Morgan, Michaela. 2007. *Dear Bunny: A Bunny Love Story*. Illustrated by Caroline Jayne Church. New York: Scholastic. ISBN 978-0439748346.
  Two very shy bunnies simultaneously decide to express their feelings for each other in a note.

Morris, Jennifer E. 2010. *Please Write Back!* New York: Scholastic. ISBN 978-0-545-11506-3.
  In this Easy Reader, Alfie writes a letter to Grandma and waits patiently for an answer.

Moss, Marissa. 2006. *Amelia Writes Again*. New York: Simon and Schuster/Paula Wiseman. ISBN 978-1416909040.
  Amelia writes all her thoughts and ideas and even a story in her notebook. This series includes many *Amelia* books in which the young author discusses everything from how-to projects to drawing.

Nelson, Theresa. 2004. *Ruby Electric*. New York: Aladdin. ISBN 978-0689871467.
  Ruby, 12, has a difficult life, including a dad who does not show up. But in the screen play she is writing, all turns out well.

O'Connor, Barbara. 2007. *How to Steal a Dog*. New York: Frances Foster/Farrar, Straus and Giroux. ISBN 978-0-374-33497-0.
  To get enough money to move her family out of the car in which they live and into an apartment, Georgina persuades her younger brother to help her steal a dog and then claim the reward. She writes down her plans in her spiral notebook.

O'Connor, Jane. 2010. *Fancy Nancy: Poet Extraordinaire!* New York: Harper/HarperCollins. ISBN 978-0-06-189643-9.
  Fancy Nancy tells her many fans how much she loves poetry, talks about the poetry club she and her friends have started, and shares some favorite poems as well as tips for writing poetry.

Oppenheim, Joanne. 2006. *Dear Miss Breed*. New York: Scholastic. ISBN 978-0439569927.
  This book is a must for those who teach older students. It is the story of how Clara Breed, a librarian, kept up the spirits of her middle and high school Japanese American students by sending them letters and books while they were imprisoned during World War II.

Palmer, Robin. 2010. *Yours Truly, Lucy B. Parker Girl vs. Superstar*. New York: Puffin/Penguin.
  When her life suddenly turns upside down, 12-year-old Lucy Parker writes to Dr. Maude for advice.

Park, Linda Sue. 2004. *When My Name Was Keoko*. New York: Yearling. ISBN 978-0440419440.
  Living in South Korea during the Japanese occupation, Sun-hee tries to maintain her Korean identity by writing in a journal even though it is against the Japanese rules.

Pattison, Darcy. 2003. *The Journey of Oliver K. Woodman*. Illustrated by Joe Cepeda, San Diego, CA: Harcourt. ISBN 978-0152023294.
  Oliver K. Woodman, a man made of wood, takes a remarkable journey across America, as told through the postcards and letters of those who meet him along the way.

Ray, Deborah Kogan. 2006. *To Go Singing through the World*. New York: Farrar, Straus and Giroux. o.p. ISBN 978-0374376277.
This picture book biography of Pablo Neruda illustrates how the people in his childhood, especially his school principal, influenced him to become a poet.

Ryan, Pam Muños. 2010. *The Dreamer*. Illustrated by Peter Sis. New York: Scholastic. ISBN 978-0-439-24970-4.
A perfect marriage of words and illustration tells the story of poet Pablo Neruda's difficult childhood in Chile. In spite of his father's wishes to the contrary, the boy always desired to be a writer, and some of the adult poet's poems appear at the end of the book.

Rylant, Cynthia. 2004. *Mr. Putter and Tabby Write the Book*. San Diego: Harcourt. ISBN 978-0152002411.
Mr. Putter wants to write a mystery novel but he gets distracted along the way.

Schotter, Roni. 1999. *Nothing Ever Happens on 90th Street*. Illustrated by Krysten Brooker. New York: Scholastic. ISBN 978-0531071366.
While Eva sits on her porch trying to write, neighbors give her wonderful advice. This book is a treasure for teachers of students of all ages.

Sheinmel, Courtney. 2010. *Sincerely: Sincerely, Sophie, Sincerely, Katie*. New York: Simon & Schuster. ISBN 978-1-4169-4010-4.
Sheinmel writes this as two books in one volume. Brought together as pen pals by a school assignment, Sophie and Katie, 11-year-olds living on opposite sides of the country, find comfort in their growing relationship when problems at home and at school disrupt their lives.

Shulman, Mark. 2010. *Scrawl*. New York: Neal Porter/Roaring Brook. ISBN 978-1-59643-417-2.
When eighth-grade bully, Tod, and his friends get caught committing a crime on school property, his penalty—staying after school and writing in a journal under the eye of the school guidance counselor—reveals aspects of himself that he prefers to keep hidden.

Silberberg, Alan. 2010. *Milo: Sticky Notes and Brain Freeze*. New York: Aladdin/Simon & Schuster. ISBN 978-1-4424-0988-0.
Milo must get over the death of his mother and make his way in yet another new school. He writes humorous illustrated notes about his thoughts and daily ups and downs.

Smith, Yeardley. 2009. *I, Lorelei*. New York: Laura Geringer/HarperCollins. ISBN 978-0-06-149344-7.
In letters to her recently deceased cat, Mud, 11-year-old Lorelei chronicles the ups and downs of her sixth-grade year.

Teague, Mark. 2008. *Letters from the Campaign Trail: LaRue for Mayor*. Blue Sky/Scholastic. ISBN 978-0439783156.
When Ike, the writing dog, dislikes the campaign platform of the mayoral candidate, he decides to run for mayor himself. (See other LaRue books by Teague.)

White, Ruth. 2006. *Buttermilk Hill*. New York: Farrar, Straus and Giroux. ISBN 978-0374410032.
Piper's parents are divorced and her mother doesn not have much time for her since she has returned to school and must also work. Piper, an avid word collector, finds solace in writing poetry.

Wiles, Deborah. 2001. *Love, Ruby Lavender*. San Diego: Harcourt. ISBN 978-0152023140.
When her quirky grandmother goes to Hawaii for the summer, nine-year-old Ruby learns to survive on her own in Mississippi by writing letters, befriending chickens and the new girl in town, and finally coping with her grandfather's death.

Wiles, Deborah. 2005. *Each Little Bird That Sings*. San Diego: Harcourt/Gulliver. ISBN 978-0152051136.
Comfort's family runs a funeral home and Comfort writes death notices for the local newspaper. She is also planning a cookbook of great funeral food.

Williams, Marcia. 2007. *Archie's War*. Cambridge, MA: Candlewick. ISBN 978-0-76363532-9.
Ten-year-old Archie keeps a scrapbook/diary during World War I revealing how the war affects his life.

Williams, Marcia. 2008. *My Secret War Diary: My History of the Second World War 1939–1945*. Cambridge, MA: Candlewick. ISBN 978-0-76364111-5.
Flossie, a nine-year-old English girl, writes a detailed, illustrated diary while her father is serving in the war.

Winter, Jonah. 2009. *Gertrude Is Gertrude Is Gertrude*. Illustrated by Calef Brown. New York: Atheneum/Simon & Schuster. ISBN 978-1-4169-4088-3.
Following the style of Gertrude Stein, Winter writes about this author and the circle of artists and writers she entertained regularly.

Winthrop, Elizabeth. 2007. *Counting on Grace*. New York: Yearling. ISBN 978-0553487831 (pb).
Elizabeth and her friend are forced to leave school to work in a mill. Their teacher encourages them to write a letter to the National Child Labor Committee about the dangers young children face working at the mill.

Woodson, Jacqueline. 2003. *Locomotion*. New York: Putnam/Penguin. ISBN 978-0399231155.
Lonnie's fifth-grade teacher gets him started writing poems about his life in foster care and his little sister, Lili.

Zucker, Naomi. 2010. *Write On, Callie Jones*. New York: Egmont USA. ISBN 978-1-60684-027-6.
The articles Callie writes in her online newspaper create turmoil in her school and an impromptu town meeting.

# Cover Credits

## Chapter 1

*The Word Snoop* by Ursula Dubosarsky, illustrated by Tohby Riddle. Copyright © 2009. Used with permission of Dial Books for Young Readers, a division of Penguin Young Readers Group.

Jacket image copyright © 2010 by Debra Frasier from *A Fabulous Fair Alphabet* written & illustrated by Debra Frasier. Used with permission of Beach Lane Books, an imprint of Simon & Schuster Children's Publishing.

Jacket image copyright © 2004 by Karen Barbour from *Wonderful Words: Poems About Reading, Writing, Speaking, and Listening* selected by Lee Bennett Hopkins. Used with permission of Simon & Schuster Books for Young Readers, an imprint of Simon & Schuster Children's Publishing.

*Busy Chickens* by John Schindel; Photographed by Steven Holt. Published by Tricycle Press, an imprint of Random House Children's Books.

*HOORAY FOR FISH!* Copyright © 2005 Lucy Cousins. Reproduced by permission of the publisher, Candlewick Press, Somerville, MA on behalf of Walker Books, London.

*Have You Ever Tickled a Tiger?* by Betsy E. Snyder. Published by Random House Books for Young Readers, an imprint of Random House Children's Books.

Cover image from *BARNYARD BANTER*. Written and illustrated by Denise Fleming. Copyright © 2004 by Denise Fleming.

*The Real Mother Goose* © 2000 by Blanche Fisher Wright, published by Cartwheel Books, an imprint of Scholastic.

From Noah Webster, *Weaver of Words* by Pegi Deitz Shea, illustrated by Monica Vachula. Copyright © 2009 by Pegi Deitz Shea and Monica Vachula. Published by Calkins Creek Books, an imprint of Boyds Mills Press. Used by permission.

*Fancy Nancy's Favorite Fancy Words* by Jane O'Connor : Text Copyright 2008 by Jane O'Connor. Illustration copyright 2008 by Robin Preiss Glasser.

*I Don't Want a Cool Cat* © by Emma Dodd, published by Little Brown and Company a division of Hachette Book Group.

Cover from *Please Don't Tease Tootsie* by Margaret Chamberlain. Copyright © 2008. Used with permission of Dutton Children's Books, a division of Penguin Young Readers Group.

Cover from *Ooh La La Polka-Dot Boots* by Ellen Olson-Brown and Christiane Engel. Published by Tricycle Press, an imprint of Random House Children's Books.

Cover reprinted from *The Rain Stomper* by Addie Boswell, illustrations by Eric Velasquez, with permission of Marshall Cavendish.

Cover from *Ballerina* by Peter Sis: Copyright 2001 by Peter Sis.

Cover from *A Crossing of Zebras: Animal Packs in Poetry* by Marjorie Maddox, illustrated by Philip Huber. Copyright © 2008 by Marjorie Maddox and Philip Huber. Published by Wordsong, an imprint of Boyds Mills Press. Used by permission.

Jacket image copyright © 2007 by Scott Menchin from *Bounce* written by Doreen Cronin. Used with permission of Atheneum Books for Young Readers, an imprint of Simon & Schuster Children's Publishing.

Cover from *Princess Pigtoria and the Pea* © 2010 by Pamela Duncan Edwards, illustrated by Henry Cole, published by Orchard Books, an imprint of Scholastic.

The cover of *ROAR!* appears with the permission of Carolrhoda Books, a division of Lerner Publishing Group, Minneapolis, MN. Copyright © 2006 by Alex Ayliffe.

Cover from *ONE DUCK STUCK*. Text copyright © 1998 by Phyllis Root. Illustrations copyright © 1998 by Jane Chapman. Reproduced by permission of the publisher, Candlewick Press, Somerville, MA.

Cover from *Dancing Feet!* by Lindsey Craig; illustrated by Marc Brown. Published by Alfred A. Knopf, an imprint of Random House Children's Books.

Cover from *Mom and Dad Are Palindromes* by Mark Shulman, illustrated by Adam McCauley, published by Chronicle Books 2006.

Cover from *HOW DO YOU WOKKA-WOKKA?* Text copyright © 2009 by Elizabeth Bluemle. Illustrations Copyright © 2009 by Randy Cecil. Reproduced by permission of the publisher, Candlewick Press, Somerville, MA.

Cover from *Grandpappy Snippy Snappies* by Lynn Plourde: Text Copyright 2009 by Lynn Plourde. Illustration Copyright 2009 by Christopher Santoro.

Cover from *There's a Frog in My Throat* by Loreen Leedy Copyright © 2003 by Loreen Leedy.

Cover from *The Wonder Book* by Amy Krouse Rosenthal: Text Copyright 2010 by Amy Krouse Rosenthal. Illustration copyright 2010 by Paul Schmid.

Cover from *Mirror, Mirror: A Book of Reversible Verse* by Marilyn Singer, illustrated by Josee Massee. Copyright © 2010. Used with permission of Dutton Children's Books, a division of Penguin Young Readers Group.

## Chapter 2

Jacket image copyright © 2002 by Teresa Flavin from *You Have to Write* written by Janet S. Wong. Used with permission of Margaret K. McElderry Books, an imprint of Simon & Schuster Children's Publishing.

Cover image from *EVERY FRIDAY*. Written and illustrated by Dan Yaccarino. Copyright © 2007 by Dan Yaccarino.

Cover from *I Am a Backhoe* by Anna Grossnickle Hines; Illustrated by Anna Grossnickle Hines. Published by Tricycle Press, an imprint of Random House Children's Books.

Cover from *Muddy as a Duck Puddle and other American Similes* by Laurie Lawlor Illustration copyright © 2010 by Ethan Long.

Cover from *With a Little Luck: 11 Serendipitous Discoveries*, Written and illustrated by Dennis Fradin. Copyright © 2006. Used with permission of Dutton Children's Books, a division of Penguin Young Readers Group.

Cover from *Yes Day!* by Amy Krouse Rosenthal: Text Copyright 2009 by Amy Krouse Rosenthal. Illustration copyright 2009 by Tom Lichtenheld.

Cover from *Shark vs Train* © 2010 by Chris Barton, illustrated by Tom Lichtenheld, published by Little Brown and Company a division of Hachette Book Group.

Cover from *How to Clean Your Room in 10 Easy Steps* by Jennifer LaRue Huget; illustrated by Edward Koren. Published by Schwartz & Wade, an imprint of Random House Children's Books.

Cover from *The Fabled Fifth Graders of Aesop Elementary School* by Candace Fleming. Published by Schwartz & Wade, an imprint of Random House Children's Books.

Cover from *Al Capone Shines My Shoes* by Gennifer Choldenko. Copyright © 2009. Used with permission of Dial Books for Young Readers, a division of Penguin Young Readers Group.

Cover from *The Gardener* by S.A. Bodeen: Cover art copyright 2010 © Matt Mahurin. Cover design by Rich Deas and Kathleen Breitenfeld. Used with permission from Feiwel and Friends, an imprint of the Macmillan Children's Publishing Group.

Cover from *Rules of the Road* by Joan Bauer. Copyright © 2005. Used with permission of Speak, a division of Penguin Young Readers Group.

Cover image from *CAT DIARIES: Secret Writings of the Meow Society*, Written by Betsy Byars, Betsy Duffey and Laurie Myers. Illustrated by Erik Brooks. Image copyright © 2010 by Erik Brooks.

Jacket image copyright © 2010 by Yan Nascimbene from *Shooting Kabul* written by N.H. Senzai. Used with permission of Paula Wiseman Books, an imprint of Simon & Schuster Children's Publishing.

Cover image from *THE ACCIDENTAL ADVENTURES OF INDIA McALLISTER* Written and illustrated by Charlotte Agell. Copyright © 2010 by Charlotte Agell.

Jacket image copyright © 2007 by Michael Frost from *Phineas L. MacGuire . . . Gets Slimed!* written by Frances O'Roark Dowell. Used with permission of Atheneum Books for Young Readers, an imprint of Simon & Schuster Children's Publishing.

Cover from *Imaginalis* by J.M. DeMatteis: Copyright 2010 by J.M. DeMatteis.

Cover from *The End* © 2007 by David LaRochelle, illustrated by Richard Egielski, published by Arthur A. Levine Books, an imprint of Scholastic.

Jacket image copyright © 2010 from *The Last Great Getaway of the Water Balloon Boys* written by Scott William Carter. Used with permission of Simon & Schuster Books for Young Readers, an imprint of Simon & Schuster Children's Publishing.

## Chapter 3

Cover from *MY HAVANA*. Text copyright © 2010 by Rosemary Wells. Illustrations copyright © 2010 by Peter Ferguson. Reproduced by permission of the publisher, Candlewick Press, Somerville, MA.

## Chapter 4

Cover from *The Can Man*, text copyright © 2010 by Laura E. Williams. Illustrations copyright © 2010 by Craig Orback. Permission arranged with LEE & LOW BOOKS Inc.

Cover from *Spilling Ink*, text © 2010 by Anne Mazer and Ellen Potter. Illustrations copyright © 2010 by Matt Phelan. Reprinted with permission.

Cover from *THE WEDNESDAY WARS* by Gary D. Schmidt. Jacket art copyright © by Jonathan Gray. Reprinted by permission of Clarion Books, an imprint of Houghton Mifflin Harcourt Publishing Company. All rights reserved.

Cover from *BECAUSE OF WINN-DIXIE*. Text copyright © 2000 by Kate DiCamillo. Jacket copyright © 2000 by Chris Sheban. Reproduced by permission of the publisher, Candlewick Press, Somerville, MA.

Cover from *On the Wings of Heroes* by Richard Peck. Copyright © 2007. Used with permission of Dial Books for Young Readers, a division of Penguin Young Readers Group.

Cover from *As Simple as It Seems* by Sarah Weeks: Copyright 2010 by Sarah Weeks.

Cover from *Duck! Rabbit!* by Amy Krouse Rosenthal, illustrated by Tom Lichtenheld, published by Chronicle Books 2009.

Cover from *Marcelo in the Real World* © 2009 by Francisco X. Stork, published by Arthur A. Levine Books, an imprint of Scholastic.

Cover from *Mockingbird* by Kathryn Erskine. Copyright © 2010. Used with permission of Philomel Books, a division of Penguin Young Readers Group.

Cover from *All the Broken Pieces* © by Ann Burg, published by Scholastic Press, an imprint of Scholastic.

Cover from *Camille McPhee Fell Under the Bus . . .* by Kristen Tracy. Published by Delacorte Press, an imprint of Random House Children's Books.

Cover reprinted from *Lost* by Jacqueline Davies, with permission of Marshall Cavendish.

Jacket image copyright © 2010 by Diane Goode from *Louise the Big Cheese and the La-Di-Da Shoes* written by Elise Primavera. Used with permission of Paula Wiseman Books, an imprint of Simon & Schuster Children's Publishing.

Cover from *My Dog is as Smelly as Dirty Socks* by Hanoch Piven. Published by Schwartz & Wade, an imprint of Random House Children's Books.

Cover from *My Best Friend Is as Sharp as a Pencil: And Other Funny Classroom Portraits* by Hanoch Piven. Published by Schwartz & Wade, an imprint of Random House Children's Books.

## Chapter 5

Cover from *Bugs and Bugsicles: Insects in the Winte*r by Amy Hansen, illustrated by Robert Clement Kray. Copyright © 2010 by Amy Hansen and Robert Clement Kray. Published by Boyds Mills Press. Used by permission.

Cover from *The Great Fire* © 1995 by Jim Murphy, published by Scholastic Press, an imprint of Scholastic.

Cover from *Seymour Simon's Book of Trains* by Seymour Simon. Copyright 2002 by Seymour Simon.

The cover of *Written Anything Good Lately?* appears with the permission of Millbrook Press, a division of Lerner Publishing Group, Minneapolis, MN. Copyright © 2006 by Vicky Enright.

Cover from *DOGS AND CATS* by Steve Jenkins. Jacket art copyright © 2007 by Steve Jenkins. Reprinted by permission of Houghton Mifflin Harcourt Publishing Company. All rights reserved.

Cover from *Cicadas! Strange and Wonderful* by Laurence Pringle, illustrated by Meryl Henderson. Copyright © 2010 by Laurence Pringle and Meryl Henderson. Published by Boyds Mills Press. Used by permission.

Cover from *CHILDREN OF THE GREAT DEPRESSION* by Russell Freedman. Copyright © 2005 by Russell Freedman. Reprinted by permission of Clarion Books, an imprint of Houghton Mifflin Harcourt Publishing Company. All rights reserved.

Cover from *Underwear: What We Wear Under There* by Ruth Freeman Swain Illustrations copyright © 2008 by John O'Brien.

Cover from *Horse Song The Naadam of Mongolia*. Copyright © 2008 by Ted and Betsy Lewin. Permission arranged with LEE & LOW BOOKS Inc.

Cover from *Lungs* by Seymour Simon. Copyright 2007 by Seymour Simon.

Cover from *APPALACHIA VOICES: The Voices of Sleeping Birds* by Cynthia Rylant and Barry Moser. Cover illustrations copyright © 1991 by Pennyroyal Press, Inc. Reprinted by permission of Harcourt Books, an imprint of Houghton Mifflin Harcourt Publishing Company. All rights reserved.

Cover from *PREHISTORIC ACTUAL SIZE* by Steve Jenkins. Jacket art © 2005 by Steve Jenkins. Reprinted by permission of Houghton Mifflin Harcourt Publishing Company. All rights reserved.

Cover from *The Shocking Truth about Energy* by Loreen Leedy Copyright © 2010 by Loreen Leedy.

Cover from *Marching for Freedom* by Elizabeth Partridge. Copyright © 2009. Used with permission of Viking Children's Books, a division of Penguin Young Readers Group.

Cover from *TIGRESS*. Text copyright © 2004 by Nick Dowson. Illustrations copyright © 2004 by Jane Chapman. Reproduced by permission of the publisher, Candlewick Press, Somerville, MA, on behalf of Walker Books, London.

Cover from *T. Barnum* by Candace Fleming; illustrated by Ray Fenwick. Published by Schwartz & Wade, an imprint of Random House Children's Books.

Cover from *CHARLES A. LINDBERG: A Human Hero* by James Cross Giblin. Jacket illustration copyright © 1997 by Barry Moser. Reprinted by permission of Clarion Books, an imprint of Houghton Mifflin Harcourt Publishing Company. All rights reserved.

Cover from *The Extraordinary Mark Twain According to Susy* © 2010 by Barbara Kerley, illustrated by Edwin Fotheringham, published by Scholastic Press, an imprint of Scholastic.

# Index

# About the Author

MARIANNE SACCARDI, M.S., is a children's book reviewer and, as a children's literature and early literacy consultant, works with teachers in professional development sessions. She has written *Art in Story* (Libraries Unlimited, 2006) and co-authored *Using Computers to Teach Literature*.